CONTEMPORARY

CATHOLIC THEOLOGY

CONTEMPORARY CATHOLIC THEOLOGY

Second, Revised Edition

❖

John Tully Carmody
Denise Lardner Carmody

1817

HARPER & ROW, PUBLISHERS, SAN FRANCISCO

Cambridge, Hagerstown, New York, Philadelphia,
London, Mexico City, São Paulo, Singapore, Sydney

CONTEMPORARY CATHOLIC THEOLOGY: *Second, Revised Edition.* Copyright © 1980, 1985 by John Tully Carmody and Denise Lardner Carmody. All rights reserved. Printed in the United States of America. No part of this book may be used or reproduced in any manner whatsoever without written permission except in the case of brief quotations embodied in critical articles and reviews. For information address Harper & Row, Publishers, Inc., 10 East 53rd Street, New York, NY 10022. Published simultaneously in Canada by Fitzhenry & Whiteside, Limited, Toronto.

Published 1980. Second Edition 1985

Library of Congress Cataloging in Publication Data

Carmody, John.
  CONTEMPORARY CATHOLIC THEOLOGY.

  Bibliography: p.
  Includes index.
  1. Catholic Church—Doctrines—History—20th century.
2.Theology, Doctrinal—History—20th century.
I. Carmody, Denise Lardner. II. Title.
BX1747.C35 1985   230'.2   84-48213
ISBN 0-06-061316-5

85 86 87 88 89 10 9 8 7 6 5 4 3 2 1

For Jim and Sheila Lardner, Nancy and Rich Thesing,
who have given us a taste of having six kids

Contents

Preface

In making this revision of the 1980 edition, we have first striven to simplify the general language, so as to facilitate the use of the book in college courses. To this end we have also added a Glossary, in which readers can find technical terms that appear in the main text in boldface. Each chapter now begins with an outline, concludes with a summary, and offers a list of study questions. The references for each chapter now appear at the end of each chapter.

Our second goal in this revision has been to bring the discussion abreast of recent happenings in the Catholic world. Thus we have changed some examples, introduced considerably more materials that have a spiritual dimension, increased the treatment of the sacraments, and added new discussions of peacemaking, business ethics, ecology, feminist Christology, parish life, and more. We have also (marvelous to say) deleted some portions of the first edition: the chapter on recasting Catholic theology (methodology) and the appendix on the theology of Pope John Paul II. The former seemed too technical for the book's sharpened focus toward undergraduates, and the latter has been supplanted by a section in the Conclusion entitled "The Pope and the People."

Our thanks to the many people who gave us advice (even when we did not always initially welcome it), especially John Loudon of Harper & Row, Michael P. Walsh, S.J. (1912–1982), Helen Connolly, Joann Wolski Conn, Richard Keady, and many more. Thanks as well to Karla Kraft, who retyped the whole manuscript.

CHAPTER 1

Introduction

THE CATHOLIC CHURCH EN ROUTE TO 1990

Every book begins from a definite place on the map of space and time, and often it is good for authors of a book that has concretely personal implications to acknowledge where they begin. We begin in the United States of the last fifth of the twentieth century. While many of the topics we treat have guided Christians since the beginning, they resonate differently today than they did in biblical or medieval times. For instance, the pope, who today has visited Mexico, Poland, Ireland, the United States, Turkey, and Africa, was in early centuries of the Church a local bishop. In medieval times he resembled a prince, but again his world was quite limited: he knew nothing of the Western Hemisphere, East Asia, or Africa. Thus, even if a pope such as John Paul II claims today to be teaching what the apostle Peter or Pope Gregory the Great taught, his words ring with different overtones. A book such as ours misfires from the beginning if it ignores this basic fact.

The overtones that mark the tunes of the contemporary American Catholic church are complex. The liberal press is filled with news of theologians such as Hans Küng and Edward Schillebeeckx, who have been trying to update traditional doctrines. In the liberal press's view, the **Vatican*** does not understand the value of such theologians' work. If, in rethinking the doctrine that the Holy Spirit secures the Church in Christ's truth, Küng comes up with a rejection of **papal infallibility**, he should be

*Terms in boldface appear in the glossary.

allowed to publish the fruits of his research. Other scholars may disagree with him, and when they publish the fruits of their research the resulting conflict will sharpen the issues involved in both "securement by the Holy Spirit" and "papal infallibility." This process is how scholars, serious students of serious issues, collectively advance our understanding. It is how scientists advance their understanding of nature, historians advance their understanding of the past, sociologists advance their understanding of group interactions. If theology is to be a respectable intellectual enterprise, it too must proceed with a fair exchange of new, and opposing views. Forbidding theologians to publish their scholarly opinions runs counter to the process by which humanity has, in the last four hundred years or so, greatly extended its knowledge. It revives the ghost of the Spanish **Inquisition** that persecuted "deviants" in the sixteenth century, for example, the ghost of Galileo who suffered in the seventeenth century because he saw the earth move around the sun. Thus the stress of the liberal press on free speech.

The conservative press sees things differently. In its view, the Catholic church has, since **Vatican II** (1962–1965) muddled things badly. Prior to Pope John XXIII's unfortunate brainstorm in thinking up Vatican II, the Catholic church had for centuries known exactly what it was, what it believed. But the Second Vatican Council "Protestantized" the Catholic church. It placed new emphasis on scripture, individual rights, and the laity that echoed themes of the sixteenth-century Protestant reformers. By moving in their direction, the Catholic church changed its agelong character. No longer could one go into a Catholic church anyplace in the world and hear Mass in Latin. No longer were the clergy clearly the leaders and the laity clearly the followers. Especially in sexual matters, all sorts of confusion broke loose. Divorce, homosexuality, contraception, priestly celibacy, even abortion were discussed as though traditional morality could change.

Even worse, theologians overly responsive to Protestant colleagues or overly concerned to make sense of Catholic faith to the "world" deemphasized the church's privileges, deemphasized even Christ's divinity. Confused, they made theology another academic discipline subject to the common rules of intellectual research and debate. In so doing, they forgot that theology is **sacred** science, knowledge whose control God has entrusted only to the Church's teaching authority, only to the **magisterium** of the pope and the bishops. Thus the stress of the conservative press on obedience.

In simple sketch, or even caricature, the two presses, liberal and conservative, go at one another in such terms. But what about the vast middle range of Catholic believers? On the whole, they seem largely unmoved by this sort of war. Neither what the liberal intellectuals say nor what the conservative church leaders say is likely to direct their thinking. The bread-and-butter issues of ordinary Catholics' faith are things that make a difference in their own households and neighborhoods: the quality of the local school, the sort of counseling available in the local parish, the human warmth shown or not shown by their local fellow believers. Above all, sociologists have found that household peace, and accord with one's spouse, most influence the ordinary American Catholic's religious affiliation and life.[1]

In that context, the Catholic church's teachings on sexual morality, which its ordinary faithful largely reject (three-fifths of the most pious—those who receive Communion every week and pray every day—approve of divorce and three-quarters approve of birth control), loom very large. Indeed, since Pope Paul VI's **encyclical** *Humanae Vitae* (1968), which reaffirmed the traditional ban on artificial contraception, Catholic church authority has come into genuine crisis. Presently, eighty-five percent of American Catholics reject the Church's right to teach (to bind consciences) on either racial integration or birth control. Even the bread-and-butter issues, then, have made it a new ball game. In the foreseeable future, the Catholic tradition will likely be a lively battleground.

To illustrate this further, let us refer to the issue of women's rights in the Catholic church. The issue came to special prominence during John Paul II's visit to the United States in 1979, when a representative of female religious ("nuns") petitioned him to give women who feel they are called to the priesthood a fair hearing. The pope's stony silence made it clear that the tradition that says only males may be ordained Roman Catholic priests will continue during his pontificate.

It is not clear how the middle range of American Catholics feel about the possibility of women priests, but it appears that the tide is running toward greater acceptance of it. What is clear is that enough theologians now see the Catholic church as significantly sexist to ensure that in the future it will find its scripture and faith quoted against itself. Few such theologians are more sensitive to the roots that Christianity has in the biblical prophets' concern for justice—especially for justice toward society's marginalized peoples—than Rosemary Radford Ruether. In a recent article, she put pungently the sort of thinking feminists presently share about Catholic Christianity:

> Although it may not be true, in terms of strict theological tradition, that maleness can be literally ascribed to God or regarded as *essential* to the incarnation of God in Christ, operationally the psychic identification between these figures and male identity is very deep. So much so that when the very idea of severing the connection between the two is suggested, we witness, again and again, what amounts to a public "freak-out" by church leaders and teachers. After a couple of encounters with this kind of behavior, it is not surprising when some women conclude that they ought to clear out of the church (or the synagogue) and find a women's religion.[2]

To be sure, there are alternate views of women's possibilities within the Church, and following Ruether's piece is an interview with Giglia Tedesco, an Italian woman who is a mother, a Communist, a senator, and a

Catholic.[3] No stereotypes, then, do justice in this presently volatile area. Nonetheless, the issue of women's rights in the Church represents the sort of challenge that Catholicism is sure to face in the decades ahead. Politically, ecologically, economically, it is sure to be challenged to show how Christ fulfills our best human intuitions of the ways to build a better world. It will be legitimate to answer this challenge rather paradoxically. That is, it will be legitimate to draw on the obvious New Testament fact that Jesus of Nazareth did not conceive human "fulfillment" as worldly people of his time, or of any other time, conceived it. On the other hand, it will not be legitimate to avoid the challenge of relating Jesus of Nazareth—his person, teaching, death, and resurrection—to the task of co-existing with nature and other human beings justly and lovingly.

To women of any gumption, certainly, it will not be legitimate for the Church to ignore what feminists consider a long neglect, a present injustice, or even a call from God. To citizens of ecological sensitivity, it will not be legitimate for the Church to ignore lethal contamination such as that perpetrated by the Hooker Chemical Company on the people of Niagara Falls and its Love Canal. Many of the most dedicated political activists of Latin America will not put up with the Church's neglect of massive social injustice there. Many of the most sensitive readers of the New Testament will ask how the Church can seek fellowship with Wall Street and Capitol Hill when Jesus rejected worldly wealth and power.

In the future that stretches before the Catholic theological tradition, acute challenges such as these may force a return to old, core insights. The Church will either rethink its charter from Jesus, retrieve its saints' best understandings of the Spirit's liberating love, or it will totter to the sidelines. That means that theologians like ourselves, who want to communicate the Catholic tradition popularly because they find it rich and deep, have to try to repenetrate its heart. Fortunately, the movements of the last thirty years, in the midst of which stands Vatican II, give us considerable help. A great many other Catholic theologians have been struggling to reinvigorate their faith and church, and a good deal of our work here will be simply to present their findings. In that way, we may be able to suggest the full future the Catholic church could have.

A CENTRAL VISION: KARL RAHNER

Just about a century ago (August 4, 1879), Pope Leo XIII's encyclical *Aeterni Patris* inaugurated a renewal of Thomistic studies. From that time until Vatican II, the philosophy and theology of St. Thomas Aquinas (1225–1274) had a privileged place in Roman Catholic priests' education. Other theological movements of the late nineteenth and early twentieth century paved the way for the biblical, liturgical, historical, and **ecumenical** studies that finally gained official recognition at Vatican II, but the core reconception of Catholic theology that the Council popularized came from what a number of gifted philosophical theologians did with Leo XII's motto, "to augment and perfect the old by the new."

For instance, in the theory of knowledge, the Canadian Jesuit Bernard Lonergan correlated Aquinas's basic insights with modern physics and statistics. In the area of political science, the American Jesuit John Courtney Murray reread medieval theories of Church and state to shed light on the function of religious liberty in a **pluralistic** society. The European Dominican theologians Yves Congar and Edward Schillebeeckx updated Aquinas's theories of the Church and the sacraments. The Swiss theologian Hans Küng launched a career in ecumenical theology by comparing Protestant theologian Karl Barth's theories of **grace** and **justification** with those of the Catholic tradition and Aquinas.

All these theologians, and many more, extended, amplified, and enriched the **scholastic** heritage they had regained by studying Aquinas. But one other **neo-Thomist**, by the extent and depth of his redoing of Aquinas, furnished the whole skeleton of a new Catholic theology. He was a German Jesuit named Karl Rahner.

The extent of Rahner's output is overwhelming: more than three thousand books and articles. Its depth is daunting: he goes to the bedrock of both Christian faith and human experience. Nonetheless, we plan to make special use of Rahner here, because his theology, more than that of any other recent Catholic theologian, has the prime qualities we hope to convey. It is traditional, in the sense that it has studied the past carefully and builds on it. It is contemporary, in the sense that it listens for new questions and does not assume that old answers are adequate. Because Rahner is passionately (not fanatically) **religious**, his theology usually has personal or affective undertones—usually reflects his prayer. Because he has a **systematic** mind, his treatment of a given topic usually leads into ideas that are immediately implied. For instance, when Rahner treats **baptism** he shows how it depends on the basic **sacramentality** of the Church and Jesus. When he treats grace he shows how faith is a share in the trinitarian God's own love life. To read Karl Rahner, then, is to journey through the whole kingdom of Christian wisdom. That is exciting, and we write in good measure to help you share such excitement.

Karl Rahner was born in Bavaria in 1904 and died in Munich in 1984. His parents and family were sturdy, traditional Catholics (his mother lived to be more than 100), and he went off to a Jesuit seminary, following an older brother, when he was seventeen. The course of studies that the Jesuits set for young men in those days included two years of **novitiate**, where they learned the traditions of the Society of Jesus and the rudiments of the spiritual life; two years of classical studies and literature; three years of philosophy; three years or so for practical experience, such as teaching in a Jesuit high school; four years of theology; another year of spiritual exercises like those of the novitiate; and finally, for certain gifted members, doctoral studies at a secular university. Out of that lengthy preparation came, at least for the hardy, an unusual breadth of intellectual background and an unusual self-discipline.

Physically, Rahner was small and round, and possessed a serious nature. Those who attended his courses at Innsbruck, Munich, or Münster used to describe how he would pace back and forth, hands behind his back, spinning out staggeringly complex reasonings in Latin or German. His written style in German tends to very long sentences, full of subordinate clauses, on occasion taking up an entire page. (Rahner folklore tells the story that his older brother Hugo, who also became a well-known Jesuit theologian, would not read Karl's books until they had been translated into French.) More historically, we saw him approach an American lectern, read, in halting English, a few sentences of his prepared text, and then retire to the back of the stage to say his rosary (and fall asleep) while a stand-in read the rest of his text.

For all the efforts of Rahner's followers to simplify his work, though, he remained a serious, sober man. Perhaps that was a legacy from his years under Hitler and war. Perhaps it resulted from long meditation on human waywardness. Whatever the reason, under the human traits of a simple piety and a fascination with toys, one found a complete absorption with God's holy mystery. More and more through the years, Rahner came to center precisely in divine mystery. One glimpses this early on in his *Foundations of Christian Faith:*

> For a Christian, his Christian existence is ultimately the totality of his existence. This totality opens out into the dark abysses of the wilderness which we call God. When one undertakes something like this, he stands before the great thinkers, the saints, and finally Jesus Christ. The abyss of existence opens up in front of him. He knows that he has not thought enough, has not loved enough, and has not suffered enough.[4]

Rudolf Otto, a pioneer in comparative religious studies, once defined the holy as "the mystery that is both tremendous and fascinating." In its Latin roots, "tremendous" does not mean huge or gigantic, as popular American usage now has it. Rather it means "fear-inducing" or "awe-inspiring." Throughout human history, to meet the holy, the sacred, the divine has been a matter of chills down the spine, hair standing on end. It has also been a matter of ardent, we might even say erotic, response to splendor and beauty. Today, in industrialized societies such as ours, it is hard to accredit this raw religious core experience. We have so tamed the natural world, so laid things out in concrete and neon, that the primitive *be-*ing of things hardly shocks us. Unlike prehistoric or ancient peoples, we do not find sun and storm nearly incredible marvels. Unlike medieval or Fourth-World peoples, we do not expect death as a near certainty by age thirty-five. Rahner's "mystery," then, is for most of us a wilderness first glimpsed from within. It is the fathomless depth, the foundation out of sight that we start to suspect whenever we begin to ponder the way things are.

Mystery links God and human beings, because our natural, inbuilt sense of "God" makes him (or her*) the origin and goal of the totality of things (which is too immense for us to grasp). It also links them because having this sense, wondering about the origin and goal of the totality of things, is essential to what we mean by "humanity." We human beings are the species that raises questions. There is no science, no art, no philosophy or theology in a pride of lions or a gaggle of geese. By focusing so resolutely on mystery, Rahner therefore joins God and human beings inseparably. Human beings are the only creatures who fashion *theo*-logies. By keeping to their specific distinction of asking why, they inevitably come to "God." Even "primitive" peoples, whom Westerners long despised, come to "God," for, as Mircea Eliade has shown, their concern with the sacred is a quest for the *really* real—for the ultimate power on which one can fully depend, from whose assurance one can finally feel secure.[5]

Mystery alone, however, would make Rahner only a philosopher of religion. It is one thing to say that human beings raise questions, or even to interpret our raising of questions as a listening for **revelation.** It is another thing to describe reality through faith that revelation has occurred, that divine mystery has shed its veil of obscurity and spoken a word. What makes Karl Rahner fully a Christian theologian is his complete embrace of the traditional faith that God did in Jesus Christ speak a privileged, definitive word. There the mystery that our questioning human constitution always implicitly pursues gave flesh to its self-expression. There the human questioning and the divine answering met in a full symbolizing of both what God is most like and what human beings are best called to become. Karl Rahner is a thoroughly Christian thinker because faith in Jesus' utter centrality motivates all the analyses in his system. Insofar as such a faith is both "traditional" (long handed down) and "catholic" (universal, proper to Christians everywhere), it makes Rahner riveted to the Catholic core.

Behind Rahner's probing analyses of how human beings strive toward divine mystery stands the philosophy of Martin Heidegger, one of his teachers at the University of Freiburg. Behind his final understanding of both human nature and divine reality stands the Christian tradition. Neither of these background influences, however, explains the creativity by which Rahner has reworked Christian theology. Ultimately, of course, that creativity is as inexplicable as the creativity of an Einstein or a Picasso. One senses an important part of its dynamics in Rahner, though, when one reflects on how his faith in Jesus comes to color his "God."

In the quotation cited above, Rahner is saying, in effect, that faith in Jesus does not remove God's mysteriousness. No matter how strongly we cling to the Christian center, we still know dark abysses of noncomprehension. Indeed, in an article on Thomas Aquinas for the University of

---

*In fidelity to the traditional notion that God is beyond gender, we use either the masculine or the feminine pronoun.

Chicago's celebration of Aquinas's 700th birthday, Rahner has recalled and made his own Aquinas's view that even the **beatific vision** of God that constitutes "heaven" does not remove the divine mystery.[6] Nonetheless, despite all this stress on God's intrinsic exceeding of our capacity to understand, Rahner's most basic inference from faith in Jesus is that God has once and for all shown the divine mystery to be pure love.

We shall have full occasion to develop this theme, and to show how it recasts the traditional doctrines of grace, the **Trinity, salvation**, and more. Here the point is simply to introduce a few recurring notes from the mastersinger who will be our main guide. For Karl Rahner, God the mysterious is finally a creative love more intimate than we are to ourselves. If Dante was taken by the love that moves the stars, Karl Rahner is taken by the love that keeps the human heart from the hell of self-absorption. On the basis of Jesus' life, death, and resurrection, Christians can call the dark wilderness of their lives "Abba"—"Father," or even "Daddy." That is what Jesus called God. It is what Paul heard the Spirit groan in his depths (Rom. 8:15–16). We hope to show how such grace is no cheap emotion but rather the one energy that makes life good.

SPIRITUALITY AND POLITICS

If a Catholic theology such as Karl Rahner's centers in grace, it extends itself through **spirituality** and politics. This has been true in the past, since many Christian thinkers have reflected on the need for all believers to pray and help their neighbors. In recent years, however (partly in response to Rahner's theology and partly by going beyond it), Catholic theology has been making spirituality and politics reflect Jesus' own two-fold commandment.[7] The rise of books, retreats, and tapes focusing on **contemplative prayer** suggests a renewed appreciation of how Christian grace leads people into deep communion with God, while the parallel rise of books and movements concerned with embodying Christian ideals politically suggests a re-appreciation of Jesus' call to social justice.[8]

Spirituality is an ingredient in Karl Rahner's theology. Not only has Rahner himself written many works on prayer and **asceticism**, his understanding of both the Christian God and Christian theology stresses an experiential awareness of the divine mystery. If God is essentially mysterious, all our contacts with God lead into silence. As well, our theology always has to confess that it is but a stammering effort to point people in directions where they may meet the divine mystery for themselves. For Rahner, divine mystery defines the human person as essentially spiritual, unavoidably involved in a religious adventure. It is because God is at our beginning, in our depths, and out in front of us as our final goal that we are the special creatures we are. We do not gain independence by fleeing from this divinity that defines our condition, but by coming closer to it. Such coming closer is most of what one means by a "spirituality."

Consequently, one of our main interests, both in the chapters on **doctrine**, where we explain contemporary Catholic understandings of the traditional teachings about Jesus, the Trinity, the Church, Sin, Grace, and the like, and in our chapter on personal Christian living, will be to suggest the spiritual dimensions of the discussion at hand. Recent Catholic theology has tried hard to close the gap between scholarship and piety, abstract analysis and concrete living. It has begun to speak willingly of **mysticism**,[9] as well as to argue that a doctrinal theology not pointing to social justice is deficient. This does not mean that contemporary writers no longer have a place for **scientific theology**, in which a scholar simply attends to historical or philosophical problems. It just means that their renewed appreciation of the divine mystery has caused many theologians to lament the divorce between prayer and reflection that afflicted the theology they themselves were taught.

For the more politically oriented Catholic theologians, the ties between theology and the practice of social justice are equally close. Since they want theology to deal with human beings' real problems, and with God's most likely agenda, such theologians stress the poverty, sickness, political corruption, and war-making that disfigure the image of God in human beings, that daily make the **gospel** of Christ miscarry. The main obstacle to believing in God, they sometimes say, is the failure of believers to act as though they were saved, to show others the love that God has lavished upon them. In the freedom of Christ's grace, brand new political possibilities open up. Not to see these new possibilities is to suggest one has not appreciated Christ's grace.

Spirituality, of course, is not a purely private matter, and politics is not something only for groups. The Christian community is not fully itself, many contemporary theologians would say, until it engages in deep **worship**, and individuals are not fully themselves until they bring their ideas into the public arena. The individual is political—bonded to other people —through and through, while groups are through and through spiritual (faced with the mystery of God). Still, some of the issues that preoccupy a person depend upon special personality traits or home circumstances. For that reason, much prayer and suffering occur in solitude, away from others' eyes. On the other hand, most political causes force people to bond together, for only through concerted lobbying, rallying, publicizing, and the like can they have an effective impact. Thus it is not surprising that recent Catholic spirituality and politics have respectively stressed the individual and the group.

The faith that focuses on Jesus, spirituality, and politics comprises a core triad. In our view, dealing with this triad enables one to handle the major concerns of contemporary Catholic theology. As well, dealing with any one entails the other two, for recent Catholic reflection on faith has been linking them together more and more tightly. Thus, theologians concerned with Jesus or grace have been looking more to prayer and

liberation movements than they would have a generation ago. Writers on prayer and **penance** have been more concerned with making connections between solid doctrine and generous politics. And political thinkers have realized that social justice demands solid theological and spiritual foundations. The triad now seems well established, so we can use it with some confidence.

THIS BOOK

The main doctrines of traditional Christianity, spirituality, and politics— these are principal topics that a contemporary Catholic theology with ties to Karl Rahner will develop. To be true to Rahner's inspiration, however, these topics ought to unfold from a reflection on how human beings actually live. Therefore, following this Introduction we embark on what we hope is a thoughtful consideration of "the human quest." Misused, that title could suggest a noon-hour soap opera. But taken as a call to consider how people actually live, what they really seem to be seeking, it may make the mystery of God something quite familiar, not at all an exotic or foreign realm.

One of the main characteristics of human beings is the tendency (or at least the central capacity) to ask questions. At core, human beings *are* questions—vessels, capacities, for meaning. Sensitive scholars such as Michael Polanyi have rung many changes on "meaning."[10] In science, art, or just ordinary human interactions, these scholars show that we know more than we can say, are always probing the world, both its outside and its inside. "God" most really, most genuinely emerges from such probing, for "God" is the light, the illumination that lures it. Similarly, "God" is the love that draws the probing of our hearts, the sense we have that a quality of goodness most situations lack just *has* sometime, somewhere, to burst forth for our fulfillment.

Biblically and traditionally, Catholic theology finds the meaning and love of Jesus to be its interpretational key. Jesus so fits the mystery of God that faith in him swings open the treasures of Father-Son-Spirit. Father-Son-Spirit is so rich a symbolization of meaning and love that St. Paul's hope starts to become credible. In the wake of Jesus, it does indeed seem possible that where sin abounded grace abounds more. If so, the theology of Jesus is the nub of the theology of revelation and salvation. Ecological science asks whether Jesus can be the center of the eons of the universe, and some Catholic theology answers yes: in the revelation, salvation, and person of Jesus stands clear the intimacy with God for which *all* creation groans.

These topics will take us three full chapters to develop. By that time, though, we will have pondered rather thoroughly what Rahner calls the "cardinal" mysteries of Catholic faith: **Incarnation**, Trinity, and Grace. On that foundation, we can build a chapter called "Christian Realism."

It will be a pause to refresh our sense of the whole—especially our sense of what core Catholic faith gives as an orientation in reality. For instance, ought we more to trust our spontaneous instincts or distrust them? Is the nature we see in Yosemite Valley, or from the heights of Big Sur, or in the withered winter grasses of Kansas like a good mother, or a demon? Does the rush of desire a man feels for a woman carry God's voice or the devil's?

The theology of the Protestant Reformation has bequeathed us the solid wisdom that we are both "just" (right before God) and sinners. Catholic theology traditionally has added the slight wrinkle that grace perfects an already good human nature. It is true that many a Catholic **moral theologian** (both the professional kind that dominates a classroom and the practical kind that dominates a **confessional**) has seemed not to know this tradition. It is true that a solid Catholic school thought all sexual matters intrinsically serious. One of our small pleasures in representing the high Catholic tradition will be to correct such misrepresentations. In the best Catholic tradition, one deals with "sinfulness," or felt need of God, not by thundering about human corruption but by encouraging the best human drives to see what they actually reveal. [This can make a wry theology of **hope** (not optimism), a salty religion of good tears, showing that God is less our judge than the lover we need if we are ever to be fulfilled.]

Christian theology and religion (response to God) occur in the "Church." The Church is the community of Jesus' followers, the organic body that Jesus heads. In the best tradition, the authority of the Church comes from the genuineness of its religion and shows itself as a service. For the Church as a whole, honesty and love make a **mission** that "the world" cannot overcome. Recently, that sort of mission won Mother Teresa of Calcutta the Nobel Peace Prize. Simply by giving her life for the most wretched poor, she both testifies to God's intimate character and convicts "the world" of stupid heartlessness. Such heroic charity seems to be beyond the rest of us. Nonetheless, were we but honest in our work and kind in our human interactions we too would enlighten the world. Being the Church is not mainly a matter of heroism, as it is not mainly a matter of brains. Being the Church is mainly a matter of trying, day in and day out, to follow Jesus' plain rule: "You will love the Lord your God with all your mind, all your heart, all your soul, all your strength, and you will love your neighbor as yourself." That is the Church's constitution. All Church **office** should serve such love. All Church arrogance, or pomp, or pretense disserves it. The Church, then, is impossibly simple. It is merely the people who gather to remember Jesus and emulate his example.

In the chapters that follow our study of the Church, we try to concretize a program for personal and social living. What does Jesus' love entail for prayer, personal life, family life, work, play, and the like? What does it reveal about politics, social justice, the economy of oil, the hopes of the world's starving peoples? Do women and minorities have a special place in a Catholic social action faithful to Jesus' vision? Are the liberation theologians right when they make the poor the apple of God's eye? Such questions are not easy, but they are full of life. If Catholic religion—the actual daily living of Catholic Christian faith—cannot be sexy, creative, joyous, long-suffering, on the side that's right, what healthy person wants it? The grandeur of the tradition is that it *can* be all these good things —that it *can* shout with the early Greek theologian Irenaeus, "God's glory is human beings fully alive."

We conclude by dealing with some summary items: the heart of the Christian matter; distinctively Catholic themes; personal theologizing; a worldly horizon; and "the pope and the people." They are but final efforts to suggest how recent Catholic theology has been recasting the Roman church's vision. In an Appendix we deal with the history of Catholic theology, offering a brief sketch of how other ages have conceptualized their faith. The Glossary provides help with more technical terms, and the Annotated Bibliography suggests leads for further study.

SUMMARY

We began our Introduction by considering some first impressions of the Catholic church as it heads toward the year 1990. One of the first impressions is that it is split between liberals and conservatives, due to their different interpretations of the Second Vatican Council (1962–1965). For liberals, the Council was a breath of fresh air, and the Church ought mainly to further conciliar initiatives. For conservatives, the Council was a dangerous swing toward things Protestant or worldly, and the church ought mainly to control conciliar initiatives. Ordinary Catholics, however, probably evaluate their church mainly in terms of its impact on the bread-and-butter issues of family life. When the message of Jesus seems to make life at home rich and cheerful, ordinary Catholics will applaud their church.

The theologian on whom we shall draw most heavily in trying to show how recent Catholic theology has been presenting the message of Jesus is Karl Rahner. Rahner's influence on both the theology that led up to the Second Vatican Council and the liberal developments that flowed in the Council's wake stems from his deep concentration on the mystery of God. Because he finds the mystery of God at the center of human existence, and finds Jesus to be the richest revelation of this mystery, Rahner's work rivets onto the heart of any given topic: work or politics, prayer or poetry.

Our explanation of Rahner's (and other theologians') thought will first deal with the traditional doctrines of Jesus, God, and the Church and then pay special attention to spirituality and politics. Spirituality and politics have received much attention lately, since many writers see them as summarizing the key demands of contemporary Christian faith, and they will serve us as a contemporary version of Jesus' twofold command. Thus our book will develop a triad of doctrine, spirituality, and politics, hoping that by the Conclusion what contemporary Catholic theologians have been saying about both faith and practice will make a clear whole.

STUDY QUESTIONS

1. Why did the 1968 papal encyclical on birth control lead to a crisis in Catholic circles?
2. What does Karl Rahner mean when he calls God a "wilderness"?
3. How might spirituality and politics summarize the main obligations of Christian living?
4. Should we trust our spontaneous instincts or distrust them?

NOTES

1. See Andrew Greeley, *Crisis in the Church* (Chicago: Thomas More, 1979).
2. Rosemary Radford Ruether, "A Religion for Women: Sources and Strategies," *Christianity and Crisis*, 39:19 (December 10, 1979): 308.
3. See Leonard Swidler, ed., "Woman and Communist, Senator and Catholic: A Discussion with Giglia Tedesco," *Christianity and Crisis*, 39:19 (December 10, 1979): 311–15.
4. Karl Rahner, *Foundations of Christian Faith* (New York: Seabury, 1978), p. 2.
5. See Mircea Eliade, *A History of Religious Ideas* (Chicago: University of Chicago Press, 1978).
6. Karl Rahner, "Thomas Aquinas on the Incomprehensibility of God," *The Journal of Religion*, 58/Supplement (1978): S107–25.
7. See John Carmody, *The Heart of the Christian Matter* (Nashville: Abingdon, 1983).
8. See, for example, Rosemary Radford Ruether, *To Change the World* (New York: Crossroad, 1981); John Coleman, *An American Strategic Theology* (New York: Paulist, 1982).
9. See Harvey Egan, *What Are They Saying About Mysticism?* (Ramsey, N.J.: Paulist, 1982).
10. See Michael Polanyi and Harry Prosch, *Meaning* (Chicago: University of Chicago Press, 1975).

The Human Quest

THE CENTRALITY OF QUESTIONING

In our introductory chapter, we suggested that a major force behind the reshaping of Catholic theology that occurred in Vatican II was the work of neo-Thomists. Perhaps their strongest wing was what came to be called "**transcendental**" Thomism. It derived from the research of European Catholics, many of them at the University of Louvain in Belgium, who tried to reconcile the philosophy of Thomas Aquinas with such modern thinkers as Kant and Hegel. The focal point in that work was the dynamics of the human spirit, especially of the human intellect. By a careful study of how our mind stretches toward reality, wants to know more broadly and more deeply, neo-Thomists such as Joseph Maréchal gave new precision and vigor to the medieval dictum that the human mind is able to "make" and "become" (imagine and understand) all things.[1]

Potentially, through its abilities to imagine and conceive, the human mind rises to the horizon of all reality. In principle, the mind is proportioned to (made for) anything that exists, for to be (to exist) is to be intelligible, understandable. Because of this quality, the neo-Thomists called the human spirit "transcendent." It is always "going beyond" (that is what transcendent means in its roots) present achievements, always stretching out to "more." Indeed, if we except the death that stops this process, we can say that the human spirit is "equal" to the entire universe, ready to appreciate whatever can occur.

Now it may seem a far journey from this rather abstract analysis of human intelligence to the *aggiornamento* (bringing up-to-date) that John XXIII hoped Vatican II would achieve, but in reality it is not. The conflict that "modernity" had brought between the Catholic church and European culture, the gap it had created, largely pivoted on the rights of human intelligence. In the **Enlightenment**, of which Kant was an especially prominent representative, European intellectuals had proclaimed their independence of external, what they called "heteronomous," authority such as that of theology and the Church. It was their own reason that would form their consciences, would map their world. The spectacular successes of this attitude in the physical sciences, above all in the work of Galileo, Copernicus, and Newton, made the independence of human reason modernity's prize. Any Church wishing to be up-to-date, up to the measure of the best human aspirations, had to contend with human reason.

Rather belatedly, Catholic thinkers took up this challenge. As we show below, they pointed to the limits of human reason (which today's scientists are more willing to admit than post-Enlightenment scientists were). But more importantly, they accepted the positive values of modernity's experiences and strove to appreciate how the human drive to understand is good. Aquinas was a great help in this, for he had seen the value of Aristotle's highly positive interpretation of human reason and brought it into his own theological system. Before long, the neo-Thomists were going beyond Aquinas, learning what they could from Kant, Hegel, Darwin, Einstein, Freud, Marx, and other pioneer explorers of modern human consciousness.

This process was by no means a smooth one, and it continues to bump along today. Nonetheless, renovating the Catholic intellectual tradition by a vote of confidence in humanity's God-given powers was what drove those who prepared Vatican II's innovations. As late as 1950, Pope Pius XII was still casting a dark eye on the theory of evolution and existentialism. However, priests such as Teilhard de Chardin and laity such as Gabriel Marcel had used evolutionary and **existential** insights with such obvious profit that only repression, or simple dishonesty, could deny the impact such insights ought to have on contemporary Catholic faith.

Perhaps a few concrete examples will sharpen the issue here. Consider, for instance, the modern scientific laboratory. Having worked in one, I (John) can report that there is much to admire—much to admire on precisely theological grounds. The Worcester Foundation for Experimental Biology, where I worked in the mid-1950s, was already acquiring a fine reputation for research on such disparate phenomena as cancer and schizophrenia. It made its biggest popular splash, though, in developing an oral contraceptive—"the pill." Ironically enough (for a Catholic school kid), I helped develop this contraceptive, by systematically frustrating a cluster of laboratory rats. (The chairman of the biology department at Holy Cross College had offered the opinion that such work would not be immoral.)

Despite the cheerful atheism of most of the scientists I encountered at the foundation, and despite the use they made of poor women in Puerto Rico, or indeed of all sorts of women, who in a sense were chemical guinea pigs, the work of the foundation was basically a very moral, high-minded affair. Essentially, the people assembled there were highly intelligent, highly trained, and dedicated to understanding. What neo-Thomist Bernard Lonergan's book *Insight* calls "the pure desire to know" was fundamental to their motivation.[2] Further, they directed their desire to know toward the service of what they considered human betterment. That is, they strove to understand the dysfunction of cells so as to cure cancer, to understand the chemical imbalances of schizophrenics so as to cure mental disease, to understand the intricacies of female hormones so as to give people control over their own fertility.

In hundreds of laboratories, where science is both pure and applied, this sort of mentality prevails. It does not necessarily remove arrogance, egotism, or even the desire for money. It does not exhaust the ways the human spirit can be great. But it does manifest something so human, so representative of men and women at their best, that it conjures up the Genesis story of God making men and women in the divine image. Indeed, the creativity of a great scientist such as Linus Pauling or Max Planck reflects the Johannine God in whom there is no darkness at all (1 John 1:5). Moreover, the very structure of science—its central gamble that human light can illumine physical data—seems to the religious observer a vote of confidence in God. Whether believers see it or not, scientists assume, stake their every day on, God's having done good work —good work in the universe, good work in their own minds. Stanley Jaki has recently shown the connection between the rise of Western science, and faith in the world's intelligibility, and while not all his fellow historians of science accept his theological interpretations, the data that he assembles and the light that his theory sheds are impressive.[3]

What Jaki and the neo-Thomists share is a willingness to look beyond scientists' words and investigate their concrete assumptions. Albert Einstein agreed with this attitude, for he counseled those who would understand scientific creativity to study what scientists do more than what they say. Many scientists, as many people in other kinds of work, are poor interpreters of their own activity, indeed of their own lives. There is often a great gap between what we "know" in a tacit or intuitive way, and what we can express conceptually, in clear ideas and words. There is, in other words, a whole realm of preconceptual knowledge—many things we know but have not brought to clear expression. As Michael Polanyi has shown in the case of physical science, the best way to get access to this sort of knowledge, to learn the creative intuitions and techniques by which productive research actually proceeds, is to apprentice oneself to a master.[4] As common experience tells each of us ten times a week, there are things we "know" about a friend or spouse long before we clarify them in conversation or reflective analysis. To anticipate a bit, it is a key principle of the transcendental Thomists' analysis of God's presence to us human beings that we "know" divinity preconceptually, recognize the Spirit intuitively, long before any formal theology gives us the "right" words.

Therefore, from our ordinary questioning, our quite commonplace efforts to get a better handle on the world around us, there arises the issue of "God." Probe any of the implicit or explicit moves of human intelligence, look for its assumptions and implications, and the issue of a final cause, an original source, or a guarantor of meaningfulness will emerge. Bernard Lonergan has put this issue of God very precisely, linking it with his careful analysis of human knowing.[5] From our ability to *understand,* to have insights, there arises a confidence that the universe is intelligible, and from that confidence there arises the question whether the universe could be intelligible unless it had an intelligible ground or basis. From our ability to *judge,* to weigh evidence and conclude that something is or is not so, there arises an awareness of *necessity* and non-necessity, and from that awareness there comes the question whether a non-necessary world could exist without a necessary source. Finally, from our ability to *decide* between the worthwhile and the trashy, to love things that are good and hate things that are evil, there arises a sense of moral calling. But that moral calling becomes a cruel deception, a destructive revelation of absurdity, unless there is a guarantor of the lovable and a judge of the hateful—unless an imperishable goodness finally holds the world.

The preceding is a full, slightly technical elaboration of the preconceptual assumptions people make as they go about the business of living. It is clearest in those people whose living depends on a vigorous exercise of their wits, such as scientists, judges, and mothers of six, but it can be teased from the humdrum life of John Q. Public. The drives to know, to make, to be fair—they all assume that intelligence, reasonableness, and justice are worthwhile. The teacher assumes that it is worth long years of schooling to master a body of knowledge and the skills to communicate it. Moreover, the "worthwhile" in the teacher's case is not the paycheck or the social status. Rather it is the experience itself of understanding, the experience itself of helping another to understand. We do not mean that all teachers are so idealistic, so realistic about the genuine heart of their matter. But we do mean that the good teachers, those who show what the profession ought to be (and so in a directive sense "is"), are idealistic/ realistic in this way. To teach with any flair, success, manifestation of real humanity, one has to assume that things can be understood, people can understand, understanding is worthwhile. One has to assume that the light that flashes when a math problem is solved, the light that flashes when a child says "Wow!"—is a nearly pure treasure, a nearly sure indication of what we are made for.

One could write a similar analysis for doctors, lawyers, engineers. Good police work contrasted with bad, good politics opposed to shabby —these too would show what decent human living entails, assumes, postulates. Why bother to raise children, if the world is the tale of an idiot? Why feel any outrage about environmental pollution, government corruption, inner-city crime? Racism or sexism are but meaningless evolutionary accidents if the world has no ultimate judge. Constitutional rights, international law—they are but breakable conventions. The alternative to faith, hope, and love for a world that ultimately depends on light and love is cynicism so sheer that most of us have never seen it, and the monstrosity of people so self-destroyed that their own lies and lovelessness no longer pain them.

Perhaps a Hitler or a Stalin achieved this degree of perversion. Perhaps the Vietcong who drove chopsticks through children's eardrums achieved it. But even they had to appeal to the world's sense of "right" and "justice" to give their causes some decency. National Socialism, Stalinist Communism, and Vietnamese Communism all had to present themselves as systems that would bring more reason and goodness. None could blatantly sell sheer cynicism or evil, for the majority of even their own followers knew from within that human life concretely is "made" to move toward being rather than nonbeing, what is intelligent rather than what is stupid, what makes for justice rather than what makes for disorder. If "God" be the term of all the positive options in these sets of choices, then "God" clearly is not outside human living. Rather, God is the very soul of good human living.

THE DEMANDS OF LOVE

So far, then, we have tried to show how the dynamics of the human mind, the demands of the human being for meaning and goodness, inevitably raise the question of God. In this section we focus on the dynamics and demands of the human heart. Of course, no sensible anthropology (analysis of human nature) separates the mind from the heart. When Pascal (1623–1662) spoke of the reasons of the heart that the mind may not know, he reminded a rather rationalistic time of a truth that common sense has always held. One place where mind and heart frequently hold together especially well is in the artistic personality. There, mediated by imagination, they concentrate a whole human person on creative work. Since all of us have to work, if we are either to survive or to prosper, and since creative work is the happiest kind of labor, perhaps a little reflection on the implications of artistic spirituality will serve our present purpose well.

We don't personally know a first-rate artist well enough to discourse on how such a person actually proceeds. However, in the Australian Nobel Laureate Patrick White's remarkable novel *The Vivesector* one can find a splendid literary account.[6] Hurtle Duffield, the main character of this novel, was to the artistic manner born. From the dawn of his childhood intelligence, he realized that he had to draw and paint. A dazzling chandelier, the dance of the sun on clear waters—all species of light and color absorbed him. So, he became a pure case of someone called to a life of art, a life of fresh seeing. To be sure, such pure cases are easier to find in novels than in real life. Nonetheless, we can occasionally find the real historical equivalent in the child prodigy, such as Picasso, who picks up crayons at the tenderest age and only lays them down after seventy, eighty, or even ninety years of pursuing new forms and radiance each day.

What is fascinating to the religious observer of Hurtle Duffield is the way his art completely dominates his time. As soon as he can, he frees himself from home and school, in order to get into his work full time. The early years are hard going, both financially and psychologically. Though his childhood was a romance with light, early adulthood was a harsh education in human darkness. It is not that Hurtle himself is especially mistreated or abused. His own direct bruises are rather slight. But he sees the torpor, the economic depression, the confines in which most of the people of his city live. The person who summarizes much of this lesson is a young prostitute, whom White only slightly romanticizes. She stands for the dozens of ways in which people who are neither heroic, nor blessed with genius, nor wealthy—the majority of us—get cornered into squalor. It may be the squalor of a low-rent part of the city, or the squalor of a spirit with no window for light. Either way, it makes an impact on sensitive observers. If they are politically minded, it probably makes them socialists of some stripe. If they are artists like Hurtle Duffield, it keeps them probing human darkness in search of ultimate light.

For his grave, brooding, twisted paintings of human sufferers, Hurtle wins a small initial notice. That gets him money enough to purchase a house (which he comes to share with a dotty sister-by-adoption) and so concentrate on his work that he becomes increasingly eccentric. White emphasizes this eccentricity through a variety of tragicomic social encounters that Hurtle has through his middle years. He is always discovering, through some *faux pas*, that normal society considers him an outsider. The most penetrating examples are his several love affairs, where his strangeness makes even simple sex very complicated. Slowly, Hurtle realizes that he himself is partly to blame for this. His true spouse is his work. So much of his self goes into semihuman forms and colors that he has few of the notions or words by which ordinary people render love doable, manageable.

At the end of his career, Hurtle's work takes him directly into mystery. If we adopt the language of the mystic's journey, he has walked the

purgative way and learned about human limitation, walked the illuminative way and learned about his own peculiar character, and now he must
walk through a dark night toward union with ultimate reality. So his final
canvasses are huge, dark indigo paintings. Reversing the common sense
notion of progress, he proceeds from lights to shadows and barest imagery. As a counterpoint, to keep the landscape somewhat familiar, White
shows us Hurtle's increasing critical acclaim—and the bemusement this
brings him. Critics babble about his native Australian genius, museums
hold special exhibitions of his work, and he walks through it all with egg
on his coat. But now he is resigned to the egg, and resigned to the
craziness of "ordinary" life, of what the world calls sane and well appar-
eled. For he "knows," in a very basic way, that the full light for which his
creative heart hungers is too bright for human bearing. To creatures in
skins and heads like his, it must appear as pitch blackness. At his very end,
his speech jumbled by a stroke, he teeters between despair and the
self-surrender that makes the purest love: "Too tired too end-less obvi
indi-ggoddd."

Of course, we choose Hurtle Duffield because he serves our purposes
well. Patrick White so reads the human quest that it comes to term at
"ggoddd." Were he to write Hurtle a "wake," as James Joyce, whom the
jumbled language recalls, wrote a "wake" for Finnegan, it probably
would mock a good deal of Christian religion. But it would be untrue to
the dynamics of Hurtle's story if it mocked that, or any religion's real
God. For any religion's real God is inseparable from the light and darkness, the *chiaroscuro* that frightens its best artists and fascinates them. Like
science, art seeks a fresh way of seeing the real, and all the really real is
holy. Because art separates emotion and reason less than science, art's
strivings for the holy more clearly nourish the heart. Furthermore, significant art is as religious in its tacit assumptions as significant science. If
there is no secure beauty, no fully satisfying light, the vitality of art stands
unexplained. The peaceful pauses that creativity experiences, its joy in
giving birth, is a harbinger of God's glory. For God the Creator takes
glory in our dappled things, in beauty that is pied.

The heart of an artist such as Hurtle Duffield wants a love affair that
renders experience orderly, fruitful, beautiful. It searches for a love that
nourishes good work. But even nonartists, people who consider themselves uncreative, people whom society considers drones—even this
great mass of the rest of us have hearts of lonely hunters. What do our
hearts, our capacities for love, demand? Do we, too, restlessly search after
God?

It is easy to say that we do, yet hard to show convincingly how. Human
passions and affections are so tangled a skein that few "proofs" of their
"Godwardness" are smooth. Still, it does not seem overreaching to say
that human passions and affections more imply a mystery of holiness,
more hope after God, than they imply hope after a void. Let us try to show

this in the case of sexual love, where traditional Catholic theology often has felt uneasy.

In its Christmas issue a few years ago, *The National Catholic Reporter* published several articles on teenagers' sexual experience. The general drift of the articles was grim: poor information skewed first experiences; unwanted pregnancies and abortions resulted. People physically capable of sexual relations, physically able to reproduce, were in most cases still children emotionally, still far from ready to handle sex. Since some of the cases dealt with young people only thirteen or fourteen years old, that is hardly surprising. In our complicated society, thirteen or fourteen years is hardly time enough to learn the rudiments of what one's body is for. But, as droves of troubled teenagers testify, it is time enough to wonder, painfully, how that body's desires and needs can make sense.

If we translate that a bit, it seems to say, first, that even the youngest loves ask protection against abuse. It may be the abuse of being treated as just a thing, an instrument of pleasure. Or it may be the abuse of being frustrated by elders who have forgotten their own early needs. Either way, even the youngest loves cry out for understanding, peace, and fulfillment. They say, with considerable confusion, that having this tangle of wants and hopes and angers and fears is a painful way to have to live. If there is no achievement of intimacy and integration, adolescent longing can make teenagers think that love is a painful cheat. So, even the early teens are years when the scheme of things comes in for intense scrutiny. The scheme of things that parents and teachers propose may seem thoroughly ill fitting. The scheme of things that peers mumble about may seem equally unsuitable. And living between the two, sailing back and forth, is like Odysseus trying not to sink. Between the rock of official "morality" and the soft place of quick comfort, the young person can be badly confused.

There is a wholesale therapy demanded by such an early striving for love, and perhaps a retail redoing of our ethics. On the therapeutic side, Catholic theology could bring forward, in quite concrete ways, the element of suffering that love constantly reveals. For ancient peoples, the rites of passage into adulthood often took the form of physical suffering. Adulthood meant having to endure the jungle hunt or the arctic cold, and sterner tribes sometimes drove the price of adulthood home by knocking out a tooth or lopping off a finger. That does not mean that the Catholic ceremony of Confirmation should include lopping off a finger. It could mean that when people enter adulthood they become candidates, catechumens, for straight talk about ordinary suffering. To follow Christ is to take up his cross. To gain adulthood is to fight for it. It might clear the air and delineate the real situation to put such things on the line.

Of course, doing so would cast a light on the whole suffering or non-suffering, maturity or immaturity, of Christian adults. To be credible to confused adolescents, adults preaching sacrifice would have to show it in their own lives. Further, they would have to show, to evidence by the total configuration of their own sex, love, and work, that their real sacrifices brought real fruitfulness and joy. With such demonstrations, and a little sympathy, fewer adolescents would feel lost, without a coherent view of the world, a community, a band of fellow sufferers who understand.

On the ethical side, a hard look at the heart of the Christian matter might show us that God is less nervous about sex than we are. Other cultures have arranged for love's sexual needs less repressively than American Catholicism has. They have also been more savage. But the full experience of human societies, for all its consensus that sexual love needs control for the common good, shows considerable creativity. Though early marriage has often proved quite harmful, as it was for Gandhi and other Eastern masters, forms of engagement that allowed sexual relations seem to have worked fairly well. The implications of this for our time are not clear, but it suggests that we relax our fears about adolescent eros a bit, remember that all hunger for love is ultimately hunger for a beautiful, incarnational God.

Our point is not to make ethical pronouncements. It is not to slice away the traditional identification of the self with the body that the apostle Paul used to discourage fornication. It is simply to describe a real aspect of the heart's drives and confusions and show that tussling with them calls for an ultimate, religious point of view. Simply to say that past ages have vetoed premarital intercourse does not prove the ethical case against it today. Few past ages have found their own sayings completely satisfactory. One only gets to the heart of the issue of premarital intercourse, as one only gets to the heart of marital contraception, when one appeals to "the way things ought to be"—to the divine order that human love demands.

Those arguing against premarital intercourse usually say that the human person is such that sexual intimacy without marital commitment violates or devalues it. Those arguing against marital contraception by "artificial" means usually say that the human person is such that intervening in its reproductive processes violates or devalues it. Behind both arguments is a view that claims to understand the person and morality quite exactly. That leads to an exact kind of religion and an exact kind of God. Behind the opposing arguments of those who see circumstances in which premarital intercourse and marital artificial contraception could be good is a view that sees the person and morality as a matter of our own human responsibility, something not wholly laid out in advance. Either viewpoint, pushed to its limit, comes up with an assumption about the nature of the world and the human person. Either viewpoint suggests (does not prove) that the heart's loves reveal a lot about ultimacy, and so about God.

PERSONAL AND SOCIAL DISORDER

We have been considering the implications of the most important human drives, those of knowing and loving. In the main, our analysis has been positive. People do pursue truth, people do want to love well. It is characteristic of the Catholic view of human nature, in opposition to the pessimistic view that some followers of the classical Protestant theologians Luther and Calvin developed, to take this positive position. That does not mean, however, that any sane view of human history—Catholic, Protestant, or Zulu—can dismiss the tragically full bins of evidence that personal and social life often misfires. At the end of a long life spent studying human history, Arnold Toynbee wrote what was for him a "short" narrative (600 pages) of the whole story.[7] It deals mainly with wars and rumors of war. Toward the end of an energetic career spent studying human fulfillment, psychologist Abraham Maslow estimated that only about one percent of the population realize a significant amount of their potential.[8] From the sorry story of history, theologians have long discoursed on original sin. From the personal experience of inner division, their early captain and poet, the apostle Paul, cried out to God for help. There is nothing in the current headlines, nothing in the average personality one meets, to let us judge that Toynbee, Maslow, the theologians, or their captain describe a reality we have outgrown.

In the earliest days of the 1980s, Americans watched the ordeal of their compatriots held hostage by Iranian students. Night after night, the television news reported this drama, well beyond the limits of easy patience. In essence, it revealed the massive disorder of the prevailing world political and economic system. Part of the dysfunction was rooted in opposing legitimate claims. America wanted its relatively innocent embassy personnel to receive the civil treatment that international law and solid custom guaranteed them. Iran wanted recompense for its suffering under the Shah. Minimally, then, politics and diplomacy run the risk of stalling on legitimately conflicting claims.

Maximally, social interactions reveal a deep disorder in the interactors. The United States' presence in Iran had for decades been self-serving and impure. The Shi'ite Muslim revolution that gave the students their chance showed many signs of fanaticism, ruthlessness, and a leader more power-mad than his predecessor the Shah. Thus, innocent parties were few and far between. Western allies who rushed to the United States' support kept an eye on their own fuel reserves. Russian invaders of neighboring Afghanistan did their best to profit from the confusion. For far too long, the world has enjoyed spectacles like this of its own uncivility. After nearly half a billion years of experience, the human species has not learned how to share the one earth. By any reckoning, that shows a pretty low intelligence quotient.

So low has been our practical intelligence, in fact, that deeper analysts have said that we must remake human nature. Thus in many traditional societies one finds a ritual pattern of death and rebirth. The classical Siberian shaman, for instance, dies, is transported to the gods, receives from the gods new organs, and revives as a fresh, holy being.[9] The modern sellers of technology, if one reads between the lines of their ads, see themselves as providing equally new organs. By probing the world of business with their new computers, the world of weekends with their new sports equipment, one will rise above present weaknesses to snatch gusto and new good life.

Christianity has its own view of disorder and the need for a new human nature, analogous to those cited above. It speaks of dying to sin and rising to Christ, of new faculties come from the Spirit. But it also speaks of human inability to sustain moral development, human impotence to be human without God. In other words, it reads the disorder we all know and lament as a clear indication that human resources alone are not enough. Left to themselves, without clear direction and new motivation, human beings largely make a mess. Generation after generation, we bring children into a game we ourselves received tilted. Year after year, we persist in our personal vice. Unhappy people that we are, who will rescue us from this bondage? "Liberation" is such a rescue, and it has become a major theme of our theological time.

We shall study this theme at some length in the chapter on politics. Here we need only note that analysts of the human situation in Europe, the United States, and Latin America see so much disorder, so much injustice, that they search desperately for a faith that could rework the whole social condition. In Europe this search has gone under the name of "political theology," and it has raised the hackles of traditional Europeans. In the United States the search has dominated black theologians, and more recently women. It has raised the hackles of traditional Americans as well. In many countries of Latin America, liberation theology has tried to fuse Marxist analyses of class oppositions with Christian sources of renewal. There it has both raised the hackles of repressive governments and become the main issue of meetings such as the Puebla Conference to which John Paul II hastened in the fall of 1979.

Put rather simplistically, these and other examinations of the human social condition find that wealth and power regularly corrupt us. For instance, in Brazil during the period 1960 to 1970 the top 5 percent of wage earners increased their share of the national income from 27.4 to 36.3 percent, while the bottom 80 percent saw their share decrease from 45.5 to 36.8 percent. The Southern Hemisphere of the world now accounts for about 80 percent of humanity's poverty, most of it among rural peoples. Those peoples have the highest birth rates, and about 40 percent of their population is under 15 years old. From figures such as these, economists predict that by the year 2000 the earth will have about 6 billion people, 1.5 billion of whom will not be able to earn enough to live.[10]

Nor are the figures comforting at home. The millions of Americans who live below the poverty level, the gross percentage of black youth who are unemployed, the number of women who are paid less than comparable men—they too witness that present society malfunctions. It is more unequal, more unjust, the cause of more suffering than it has any right to be.

Such a judgment carries several potent implications. One may be that human beings are so equal in their basic natures that they make the present American use of the world's raw materials obscene (we, 6 percent of the world's population, consume about 40 percent of its resources). Is this implication foolish or deeply wise? Do we Americans, who use about nine times the resources per capita that people of India use, merit this disproportion by our greater intrinsic worth, or our greater service to the world community, or a special election from God that Indians do not have? A few analysts of the situation, such as right-wing capitalists, imply that it is simply a survival of the fittest. In their dictionary, no profit is "obscene," because part of any profit fattens the Gross National Product. The Gross National Product says something (a rather vague something) about jobs, bank accounts, consumption—about the quantities of an economic life. That it says little about the quality of a spiritual life goes by these capitalists like a greyhound.

The above may seem a liberal or radical view of the implications of economic disparities, but it has impressive conservative credentials. In the Catholic tradition, socioeconomic injustice is an index of human disorder, human greed, for which "sin" is a proper name. From Leo XIII to John Paul II, with high points in John XXIII's *Pacem in Terris* and Paul VI's *Populorum Progressio,* the writers of papal encyclicals have hammered this judgment home. Their God made the world for *all* human beings, and a radically imbalanced use of the world's goods violates their God's creative intentions. In other words, they see a direct link between social order or disorder and "God," the world's origin and end. Insisting on the dignity of all human persons, they call the profiteering of some from the flesh of others an insult to the holy.

All sorts of people claim not to accept this connection between order and God, but few of them do not suggest it in their lifestyles. How a woman in Japan reacts to the male chauvinism (in Western terms) of her economy and culture, what a Chicano child thinks when she compares her migrant life to that of the large-scale grower[11]—these are exercises in theology. More precisely, they are exercises in *theodicy*—the search to find a meaning deeper than the world's manifest injustice. From the side of the less oppressed, or even of the oppressors, thoughts and actions that connect economics with God are equally numerous. During a Barbara Walters special we watched four interviewees describe their living quarters. They were all currently hot properties in show business, and the least expensive of their houses went for three-quarters of a million dollars. That two people would have to work full-time to use a thirty-room house seemed to escape all of them. That their lifestyles contradicted all the spiritual masters of humanity's past was never even suggested. What must the world be, for such things to happen? How must "God" and "humanity" be related? Does inequality sing forth that our basic law is from the jungle? Or does inequality sing, by the suffering it causes, that the hot dog of today fries in hell tomorrow?

We could continue this sort of inferring, puzzling, drawing of lines, using more personal disorders. If a child is brain-damaged, or a teenager overdoses, or a good father ruins himself with alcohol, or a good mother has terminal cancer—if these disorders and evils are questioned, what do they say about "life?" At the least, they say it is painfully trying. At the most acute, they say it either moves according to a pattern we cannot comprehend or simply is without meaning. Either way, they push our hearts and minds beyond mere food and clothing. Either way, they fuel a search that soon becomes religious.

RELIGION

"Religion" conjures up images of ceremonies, churches, and interior acts such as prayer, but its core is being "bound" *(religatus)* to the holy, the mysterious source of meaning. In terms of the disorder that we have been discussing, a clear case of profound religion shines forth in the life and teaching of the Buddha. Raised to wealth and security, the legendary sources say, the Buddha became serious and sad when he discovered old age, sickness, and death. After trying various regimes that claimed to solve this composite problem, he found light and peace in an experience of insight whose conceptual expression is the "four noble truths." Together, the four noble truths explain the cause of suffering and the way to overcome it. First, there is the bedrock fact-truth: "All life is suffering." Second, there is its source: "The cause of suffering is desire." Third, with the active acceptance of this analysis a therapeutic program comes into view: "The removal of desire removes suffering." And fourth, the way to remove desire is to follow the eightfold path of right views, right intention, right speech, right action, right livelihood, right effort, right-mindfulness, and right concentration. Thus, from personal combat with disorder and the suffering it causes, the Buddha won through to a re-formation of how we view the world—a re-formation that has brought meaning and peace to millions.

We could write similar analyses of the other world religions. Unless they face the problem of suffering and offer a plausible solution for it, they do not survive or prosper. Equally, unless they show themselves compatible with the tendency of the mind to keep raising questions, and the tendency of the heart to keep seeking a stable love, they win no great support. It may be that they reset the terms of those tendencies, as Zen Buddhism does in trying to undercut ordinary thinking, or as Christianity does in elaborating "faith." But to serve any significant number of human beings who have deep problems, a religion has to illumine and guide their questioning, address their demands of the heart, and grapple with their widespread disorder.

Indeed, before the rise of Western modernity, which first cast the world in a secular or nonreligious horizon, the general population of all societies lived in a religious culture. Actually, there was no distinction between their general culture and their religion, for the whole culture was quite directly tied to the peoples' view of ultimate meaning. That was true in ancient or "traditional" societies of Africans, Australians, American Indians, and Eskimos. It was true in Hindu India, Confucian China, the Muslim Middle East. Christian Europe made no great distinction between its culture and its religion, nor did its scattered Jewish ghettoes. To be a people was to live with a common set of values that quite directly folded into a common mythology or world view based on the gods, or the scriptures, or the ancestors' traditions about the "way." The human quest, through both prehistory and most of the recorded story, took its direction from privileged tales or seers who formed a common culture around the way that holy being gave the world meaningful patterns.[12]

Today civil religion—culture formed around a common consensus about the holy—is a more complicated affair. The societies that call themselves "advanced" tend to be pluralistic: allowing a variety of different world views. As well, they tend to be secularist—to deny the cultural significance of the holy. It is not our desire nor are we competent to analyze this newer phenomenon, which sociologists still struggle to unravel.[13] We merely point to the view of theoreticians such as Max Weber, Edward Shils, and Clifford Geertz that societies continue de facto to depend on charismatic personalities, people who make life seem meaningful. John F. Kennedy, Martin Luther King, Jr., and Pope John XXIII come to mind. They, along with effective symbols and myths, offer at least a minimal sense of how to get in harmony with a cosmic order. The alternative would be such a massive lack of norms or hope that social interactions would grind to a halt. Thus, the traditional social functions of "religion" continue to be powerful today, even when some of their traditional forms have fallen by the way. We may not be fully satisfied with our Memorial Day and Fourth of July, but we still feel the need to celebrate.

Discourse about society in general, however, tends to be unsatisfying. "Society" is such an inclusive term that few of its features are clearcut. Of course, the "individual" is a concept almost as variable, since all of us realize it differently. However, at least there is a definite personal reality to which any reader can refer—him- or herself. Let us therefore try to bring this reflection on religion to bear on the individual human person.

For a society such as the current American one, it is not clear that most individuals understand themselves as religious, at least in the most common traditional senses. True, better than 90 percent of Americans report some of the traditional marks of religion, such as a belief in a supreme being or a final order of things. This sort of report, along with the evidence that a solid majority of Americans occasionally pray, gives the lie to an easy reading of American secularism as irreligion. But neither church attendance nor a firm commitment to a full program of religiously based morality seems to dominate the average American's daily life. Rather, an unanalyzed mixture of hope, comfort-seeking, ambition, and fear shepherds most of us along. In no clear way does the average undergraduate in a large public American university rivet each day's time on the question of God. In no clear way does the average business person place his or her work in the horizon of a golden rule such as Confucius', a twofold commandment such as Jesus', a passionate hope for the Messiah such as that of premodern Jews. At best, the reliance of the typical contemporary American on religion is tacit or implicit.

On the other hand, we do not know the core motivations of most people very well, including, perhaps, ourselves. The things going on inside the "average" person are so complex that it is legitimate, even wise, not to pass judgment too quickly. Thus, there is the folk wisdom that the typical young buck becomes quite quiet after sowing his wild oats. Who would have thought that Bill Walton, the superb and radical basketball star, would take to vests and three-button suits before he turned thirty? And, along the same line, there is the stereotype that the wild filly will become quite the madonna when she nurses her first child. The life cycle has a certain gravity toward responsibility. Becoming accountable at a job or accountable for children tends to increase one's respect for the laws and sense of order that one's elders have developed. They do not immediately make one religious, in any sense that a Catholicism close to Jesus wants unreservedly to applaud, but they do make one serious.

Being serious is half of religion. It is not the same as being grim, and it does not supply the other half of religion, which is free-spirited and close to play. But being serious does express the tie to ultimacy, the drive to fit oneself to a larger pattern, that all the religions have seen as an energy close to their cores. If so, part of the question of whether God is relevant to a given individual's life pivots on his or her seriousness. Is this person someone who thinks, at least now and then, about how "it all hangs together"? Is he or she pressured by some sense of obligation to use time well, to treat other people fairly, to take care of the goods of the earth? When we answer yes to such questions, as we would in a majority of cases, the "religiousness" of the average person becomes considerably more impressive. For all its neglect of deeper things, all its mediocrity and worship of **mammon**, Western society shows more to admire in the case of the average individual than secularism really explains. There is a seriousness, a regular if not steady move toward basics, that confutes "eat, drink, and be merry." Both students and shopkeepers feel the tugs, the attractions, of more.

Sometimes we bolster a commonsense, descriptive argument such as this if we take on the least promising cases. For some commentators, the hellish shouting of the Chicago Commodity Exchange, or the queer emotionalism of the Super Bowl, are quite unpromising cases. We do not find them so, because the Commodity Exchange seems clearly to be religious (ultimate) passion in the service of the false god of profit, while the Super Bowl seems to be but new myth, ritual, and distraction. Much less promising as cases for religious analysis, religious arguing that the human person is set for God, are the brutish types on whom ultimate things make virtually no impact. Gross in their pleasures, such people show so little humanity, so little soul, that evolution seems wasted on them. The habits of animals would satisfy them.

One of the early films that established the Italian director Federico Fellini's reputation was a modest production called *La Strada*. It featured a very brutish circus performer who went through life in a haze of lust and alcohol. He had little redeeming social value. He caused other people considerable pain and took away considerable decent pleasure. If ever one saw an unpromising candidate for religion, it was the male lead of *La Strada*. At the film's end, however, things changed rather revealingly. Finally disgusted by his own disorder, finally realizing the pain he had caused an innocent woman to suffer, the man (who made his wretched living by displays of strength) was brought to his knees by an idea. On the beach, it struck this brute that not even a pebble, a senseless bit of sand, could *be* without some meaning. Not even the lowest bit of creation could lie there except mysteriously. Reeling with this perception, the strong man turned his eyes toward the sky. If the pebble cried out for explanation, how much more so did he. If the pebble's dirty "being there" was a pledge that there could be more, how much more was his own dirty "being there" an invitation to look for bigger answers.

There aren't many films that can manage to make philosophy from a pebble, and Fellini's presentation, though it does much better than our skeletal sketch can suggest, is less than fully convincing. Still, one knows that even the people who watch daytime television have pains and struggle to soothe them. Even Joe's bar on the corner, or Marie's sewing circle, buzzes with low-grade philosophy. In a half serious, half time-wasting way, the places where we congregate show us turning over the order of things. We may gossip more than philosophize but we seek some sense of comfort, even if it is only the comfort, the diminishing of upsets and conflicts, that comes from realizing that others share our pains. Thus, in the suburban stereotype, women become friends by sharing confidences. Each has a clear enough window on the other's life, maybe even on the other's bedroom, to feel both compassion and nakedness.

Men tend to be less self-revealing, at least without alcohol, but they too work into their conversation considerable reflection. About two-thirds of the time we've traveled on airplanes we've been unwilling parties to time-killing conversations. Beneath their pomposity and drone, the business people we've overheard have been groping after order. More than their obvious efforts to impress one another, or their attempts to appear wise and grave, the speakers have been seeking some confirmation that another person finds life sane. Business, let alone international politics, is insane enough to make such seeking both reasonable and touching.

At core, religion is the search for an ultimate, stabilizing meaning. Its fringes may show hysteria or boredom, revolutionary newness or conservative mold. But its core is the search after ultimate meaning. In ecstatic mystical fulfillment, or plodding daily pain, religious people answer the call of their bones to find and make the world good. Conveniently (for our purposes) but nonetheless really, religion turns out to be the centerpiece of being human. Whoever has a heart restless for more being, more explanation, more love is by our definition religious. Whoever is seriously irreligious is seriously inhuman. Such restlessness can derail badly, as it has in many Nazis and many followers of Karl Marx. It can suggest that "atheist" Albert Camus may have more religion than Cardinal Krol, Billy Graham, Jimmy Carter, or others born again, who do not manifest his passion for full meaning. Thus, our definition has the advantage of riveting the question of God or ultimacy to the dynamics of being human. God and genuine religion are nothing apart from our struggle to endure and grow. Rather, they are the innermost aspects of such struggle.

GOD AS MYSTERY

In Karl Rahner's summary reading of the human situation, we who search after meaning and love soon run into an undeniable mystery.[14] Wherever we go in our quest, the totality of things escapes us. For the astrophysicist who studies the stars, the totality of the universe remains an unsolved problem. For the microphysicist who studies subatomic particles, the end of the infinitesimal dances well out of sight. Within the realm of natural biology, staggering numbers keep us from full understanding. Annie Dillard, for instance, reports that a single grass plant of winter rye sends forth 378 miles of roots with 14 billion root hairs. One cubic inch of its soil contains 6000 miles of root hairs.[15] That sort of power or creativity is staggering. It tells us very clearly that behind the world is a force far greater than ourselves.

"Mystery," then, is not the same as "problem," as Catholic philosopher Gabriel Marcel has explained.[16] A problem is something we do not understand right now but have good grounds for expecting to understand in the future. "Mystery," as Marcel, Rahner, and other theologians employ it, is intrinsically beyond us. No matter how much further information we obtain, we will not penetrate its core. It has a fullness of being or light or love or power that simply goes beyond our human capacity. To think of grasping it, comprehending it, is like thinking of carrying the ocean in a glass. Consequently, we better deal with mystery, better "understand" God, by simple acts of contemplation. If we open our "hearts," by which both the Bible and common usage often mean our integral selves, and somewhat disregard our step-by-step minds, we can appreciate things really beyond us.

This is a rather important point, so we beg patience to pursue it. To have experience of the real God, to locate divinity in one's own present time, normally requires some contemplation. God can step in and knock any of us over, as the story in the Book of Acts has Christ knock over Paul. But that is not how it usually happens. Usually, we get our intimations of God in moments that show us a mysterious "more." For ancient peoples, sunrise and sunset were two such regular moments, and sometimes they can be mysterious even for city dwellers of today. If you think a little about the total darkness that would come over the desert, when in John's time the desert had no artificial lighting, you may be able to imagine how the author could make "light" a primary designation for God: "The light shone in the darkness, and the darkness did not overcome it" (John 1:5).

Other mysterious moments occur between people. There are romantic moments, for instance, when one swells with feelings of love. They bring a fullness, a rightness, a harmony that tend to make us grow quiet, and wonder. Just being with another person in silent agreement is a primal experience our limited minds will never come near to explaining. The sexual expression of such romance creates a longing to spread the deep agreement along all the nerves of two complementary bodies. It succeeds about as often as the free, gratuitous swell of love itself flows through us, but that is enough. It shows us what sexually different bodies are for, and why marriage was a great mystery to Paul.

We could give other examples of peak experiences, and they all would flow out to a mystery that involves us personally. The aesthetic experience of overwhelming beauty, the intellectual experience of leaping to a higher viewpoint, the communal experience of real teamwork, the ecclesiastic experience of union in the Spirit—all are exactly mysterious. So, in a reverse way, are the negative experiences of failure, of bereavement, of brokenness—the times when the world seems flat and barren. The strain they put on us, the depression they threaten, suggest that two-dimensional, "mystery-less" living is the frustration of our spirit. Not to live toward a "more," not to stretch out in hope, is a retrenchment to telltale sadness. By speech no linguist can fully understand, it tells us that things should be different. If we listen, we hear a counsel to make a change, get some help, rest the body and ease the mind. If we listen, we get our first lesson in what the saints call the **discernment of spirits**.

One of the most famous cases of the discernment of spirits involved the founder of the Society of Jesus, Ignatius Loyola (1491–1556). Wounded in battle by a cannon ball, he sought to relieve the boredom of his recuperation with some interesting reading. The library available to him had mainly romances and lives of the saints. He alternated between the two, and before long he noticed a significant difference. The romances he took up with anticipation and lay down with a certain unease or sadness. The lives of the saints he took up rather reluctantly and lay down with a sense of peace, even an eagerness to do like deeds. That experience was the germ for Ignatius's famous and very influential *Spiritual Exercises.* Following the way to peace, puzzling out the alternation between what he came to call "consolation" and "desolation," he stripped away vainglorious ambitions and came to make **evangelical** poverty and humility food for his spirit.

We live in a different time, and most of us have vocations different than Ignatius's. Nonetheless, we can learn a great deal from reports such as his, because they greatly illumine the processes of any deep personal maturation. To become mature, we all have to move beyond what Freud called the pleasure principle (conceiving reality egocentrically) and come to accept reality as it is. By the common report of the people most societies have called holy or wise, reality as it is asks us to die to merely sensual gratification and ego. That sounds harsh, so the majority of us run away and block our ears. However, bit by bit, the years themselves etch in the message. If it does not carry much weight when we are twenty, or even when we are forty-four, it probably makes some sense by the time we are sixty. For by the time we are sixty we know in our bones, and not just in our minds, that we are soon to die. Clearly enough, there will die with us all the sensual pleasures we spontaneously pursue. Neither the good meal, nor the comfortable coat, nor the wavy orgasm stays with us permanently. On the other hand, the way we change through creative work, the way we change through creative love, seem to go to our marrow. Whatever of "us," of our "spirit," survives the grave is more likely to be colored by creative work and love than by our sensual pleasures.

In the Catholic contemplative tradition, these homely little lessons gain a sharp focus. For an Ignatius Loyola or a John of the Cross, who had extraordinary interior experience, God lures us through our sadnesses and joys to grow in religious understanding. So grown, we begin to deal with God not as a projection of our needs, not as a great father figure, but as God really is: mysterious, other, too bright for our minds. Such influential modern antireligionists as Feuerbach and Freud criticized Christianity (and religion generally) as being immature. They had eyes to see, and all around them was wish fulfillment. Living in fantasies of "heaven" and "hell," distracted from both self and the earth, religious people seemed like children. By Freud's criteria of good psychic health —the ability to love and the ability to work—few believers seemed healthy. Rather, their religion seemed a symptom, even a cause, of wide-spread neurosis. As Michael Buckley has recently shown, contemplative Catholicism largely seconds this diagnosis.[17] John of the Cross and Ignatius Loyola are more kindly than Feuerbach or Freud, but they too want fantasy to yield to sober realism.

That is the point to such close analyses of interior experience as those developed by John of the Cross as the "dark night of the senses" and the "dark night of the soul." The real God must wean us away from the images (often quite self-serving) that we interpose between ourselves and her. Slowly, in the Spirit's good time, we must come to *real*-ize, to recognize experientially, the long-standing Catholic faith that no matter what we say about God he is more unlike than like our description. In Thomas Aquinas's terms, that results in a teaching that says that while we can know *that* God exists we cannot know *what* God is (precisely how God exists). And even this revered teaching is but a small diminishment of God's mystery, for though the First Vatican Council (1869–1870) taught the natural capacity of the human mind to know God's existence, it neither affirmed that particular individuals achieve this knowledge nor separated it in fact from the work of God's grace—from God's own activity of revelation.

But how does all this "mystery" work out concretely? Rather consolingly, we believe. First it suggests that none of us human beings has a handle on the full plan of things, and so none of us has a diploma boldly to pontificate on God's inner doings. God is not a King who has made certain human beings his privy counselors. We are all in the dark, and the sufficient light that God gives us all, through either conscience or tradition, is a thing so modest we can trust it. Probably the most trustworthy catechetical volume of the past Catholic generation was the Dutch bishops' *New Catechism*.[18] It begins with the human orientation to mystery and maintains throughout that faith is a *wonder*-ful way to respond to the otherness of God, a way both humble and joyous. Equal in our being unequal to God, all of us stand needy. As the medieval artists saw it, we all are led by death to dance the same measures. King or jester, peasant or pope, none of us has ever seen God.

Second, however, most of us have felt God—have received some intuition. We may have been little able to appreciate what we felt, but our daily lives have borne us the divine. If only in small groups, we have had our version of T. S. Eliot's moments in the rose garden, in the draughty church at "smokefall," when a stillness brought us God's "more." Or we've learned a little wisdom through suffering. Detached by some pain, we've taken a fresh look at our time and resolved to get its next acts together. The mysterious, real God is the fullness into which our best moments go, the limitation on the world shown by most suffering. Close as the pulse at our throat, mystery lets all our being be. The most basic question in philosophy is, "Why is there something and not nothing?"

The most difficult question in most people's lives is, "Why are my hopes so often thwarted?" However these questions play out for a given person, in religious perspective they suggest that God is as objective, as ready-to-hand, as the most ordinary pebble. Similarly, God is as much a part of one's life as the most ordinary daily frustration. The pebble is not God, the frustration is not pure revelation. Catholicism teaches neither **pantheism** nor **magic**. But it does teach that, in Augustine's phrase, God is more intimate to us than we are to ourselves. Today, we suggest, the most real way to summarize this notion is to accept the mystery into which all human experience leads. Quite literally, we are nothing without God—we do not exist. And quite playfully, God is no thing, but rather a fullness of a different order.

None of this analysis, rhetoric, or playfulness *proves* that the human quest intends or attains God. At best it is a persuasive indication or suggestion. But it gathers together a group of experiences that surely keeps the possibility of God's existence open. As full religion finally is an option of **faith** that goes beyond experience because of personal commitment, so full **atheism** finally is an option of faith that does very much the same. The question for Jesus, then, is how persuasive he makes it that the mystery behind life is a saving parental love.

SUMMARY

The human quest is a search through daily life for a true, mysterious God. Catholic theology has in recent years focused its understanding of human nature by analyzing our drive for understanding, our drive for love, and our responses to personal or social disorder. In analyzing our drive for understanding, recent Catholic theology has solidly affirmed the rights of the mind, and so closed the gap between the church and modernity. If we follow them, the dynamics of the mind lead to an ultimate meaning that correlates well with God. So too with the dynamics of our love. Be they the artist's need for beauty and creation, or an adolescent's sexual yearnings, the dynamics of love show an ardent hope for goodness and intimacy that also bring God into view. From their experiences of breakdown or dysfunction, human beings also are primed for religion. In ways both formal and very humble, we all try to get a handle on injustice, to make some compromise with our pain. So doing, we all open the issue of God.

Religion, East and West, has traditionally organized these drives and experiences for people. The serious times in the average person's life continue to point toward religion, as do even the aimless philosophizings of the people in the local bar and grill. For religion is *but* the search for ultimate, stabilizing meaning. And the God of such omnipresent religion? This God ordinarily appears as mystery—as the ungraspable ultimate into which all our strivings and times lead. Consequently, the real God requires a certain contemplation. We will only mature to the potential of our own drives if we let God become real to us as the mysterious source of everything we know, love, and hope.

STUDY QUESTIONS

1. How does ordinary questioning suggest the issue of God?
2. How would you argue that human life is made to move toward justice rather than disorder?
3. Describe the development of Hurtle Duffield's sense of God.
4. What is the fight to become adult all about?
5. Why have deeper analysts of human history said that we must remake human nature?
6. Why should we not view international economics as simply the survival of the fittest?
7. Explain how the two halves of religion, seriousness and play, can be put together to make a whole.
8. What is the relation between mystery and a mature religious faith?

NOTES

1. See Joseph Donceel, ed., *A Maréchal Reader* (New York: Herder and Herder, 1970).
2. See Bernard Lonergan, *Insight: A Study of Human Understanding* (New York: Philosophical Library, 1957), pp. 636–39.
3. See Stanley Jaki, *The Road of Science and the Ways to God* (Chicago: University of Chicago Press, 1978).
4. See Michael Polanyi, *Personal Knowledge* (New York: Harper Torchbooks, 1964).
5. See Bernard Lonergan, *Method in Theology* (New York: Herder and Herder, 1972), pp. 101–4.
6. Patrick White, *The Vivesector* (New York: Viking, 1970). See also Anne Tyler, *Celestial Navigation* (New York: Alfred A. Knopf, 1975).
7. Arnold Toynbee, *Mankind and Mother Earth* (New York: Oxford, 1976).
8. See Abraham Maslow, *Toward a Psychology of Being*, 2d ed. (New York: Von Nostrand, 1968).
9. Mircea Eliade, *Shamanism* (Princeton, N.J.: Princeton University Press/Bollingen, 1972).
10. See Barbara Ward, *Progress for a Small Planet* (New York: W. W. Norton, 1979).
11. See Robert Coles, *Eskimos, Chicanos, Indians* (Boston: Little, Brown, 1977).
12. See Denise Lardner Carmody and John Tully Carmody, *Ways to the Center*, 2d ed. (Belmont, Calif.: Wadsworth, 1984).
13. See Robert N. Bellah and Phillip E. Hammond, *Varieties of Civil Religion* (San Francisco: Harper & Row, 1980).
14. See James J. Bacik, *Apologetics and the Eclipse of Mystery* (Notre Dame, Ind.: University of Notre Dame Press, 1980).
15. See Annie Dillard, *Pilgrim at Tinker Creek* (New York: Harper's Magazine Press, 1974).
16. See Gabriel Marcel, *The Mystery of Being* (Chicago: Henry Regnery, 1950).
17. See Michael Buckley, "Atheism and Contemplation," *Theological Studies* 40:4 (December 1979): 680–99.
18. See *A New Catechism* (New York: Herder and Herder, 1970).

Jesus Christ

THE BIBLICAL THEOLOGY OF JESUS

At the end of the last chapter, we said that the question for Jesus—the question we ought to put to his religion or theology—is whether he makes the mystery into which our lives lead a saving parental love. That question squares with a straightforward reading of the biblical story of Jesus. As the gospel writers present him, Jesus did not primarily preach or promote himself. Rather, he primarily preached and promoted a God whom he called "Abba"—"Father" or "Daddy." This God Jesus identified with the God of his people's past—the God of Abraham, Isaac, and Jacob. However, on the basis of his own experience, Jesus spoke more intimately about his God than his people's past had, and more insistently. Whereas the scriptural tradition had passages, such as those in the writings of the prophet Hosea, that depicted God intimately as a suffering spouse, in Jesus' time the God of the fathers was mediated by *Torah:* traditional guidance, "Law." Because of that mediation, some of the Jewish religious establishment did not take kindly to Jesus, for Jesus insisted that God cared little about past moral performance. Breaking into history to cure its disorders, God wanted wholehearted conversion.

We have packed a great deal into one simple paragraph, so it will be wise to step back and unpack the above at some length. Doing so we note, first, that all present-day New Testament theology assumes Jesus' Jewish-ness.[1] Jesus of Nazareth was a man of his times, as we are men and women of our times. He inherited a language and culture that shaped his thought, and he could only communicate his thought to his contemporaries in terms of that language and culture. Even to begin to understand him or his message, then, we have to grasp at least the rudiments of his Jewish cultural situation. Of primary importance, for instance, was the influence of Torah. On the basis of what they took to be God's revelation to Moses, Jews of the centuries preceding Jesus had elaborated a full program for religious living. Religious living meant being "clean" in one's dealings and so worthy of the holy God who had made a **covenant**, a quasi-contractual relationship, with the Jewish people. To have such cleanliness or purity, the good Jew would refrain from work on the Sabbath, refrain from unclean food such as pork, stay far from pagan idols and licentious games.

The people to whom Jesus preached his new conception of God, and his new sense that God's rule was rushing in, were trying to live a Torah-directed life in rather trying circumstances. Politically, they were not a sovereign people but subject to Roman authorities. Culturally, the Greek language, art, philosophy, physical nurture (gymnasiums, games), and the like—which comprise what scholars call **Hellenism**—dominated the Mediterranean world. This culture was greatly at odds with traditional Jewish ideals. Religiously, various cults from Greece and the Near East offered alternatives to the traditions of Torah. It is not surprising, then, that many of Jesus' contemporaries were confused. Some retreated to a stubborn conservatism and refused to have anything to do with "foreign" elements. Harkening back to a solution hammered out during the **Babylonian exile**, they kept to themselves and centered the community's whole life on the **synagogue**, or the Temple in Jerusalem, where Jews could pray, study scripture, and learn Torah while supporting one another in pure living. Other Jews found foreign notions attractive and so abandoned the traditions of their fathers and mothers. Taking part in **Gentile** culture, they tried to lessen the strangeness that Gentiles associated with Jews by downplaying dietary laws, Sabbath laws, and the physical mark of circumcision.

To those of Jesus' contemporaries who kept a strong sense of their traditional faith, at least four parties or groups presented different options. The group called Zealots were a politically oriented party dedicated to the overthrow of the Roman occupation, if necessary by force. The group called Essenes were separatists. For them the way out of the current conflicts was to withdraw to remote areas, such as the hills around the Dead Sea, where they could live a religious life of the strictest observance. The group called the Sadducees took a conservative position on Torah and political accommodation. For them only the written law, especially the Pentateuch (first five books of the Bible) comprised the revelation that God had given to Moses for the community's guidance, and only keeping peace with the Roman authorities could ensure the community's continued survival. The group called the Pharisees were largely lay people of middle-class status (in contrast to the Sadducees, who tended to be priestly and wealthy). Pharisees tended to be zealous for Torah rather than for political opposition to Rome, and to extend Torah beyond scripture, so that it included the interpretations developed by leading **rabbis**, who had labored since the rise of the synagogue during the **Exile** to adapt the **Law** to changed conditions.

Jesus associated himself with none of these groups. Rather, he responded to the appearance of a **prophet**, John the Baptist, who was preaching a message of repentance in preparation for God's coming judgment. In Jesus' adaptation and development, that message became the centerpiece of the preaching we find in the **synoptic gospels** (Matthew, Mark, Luke): the Kingdom of God. To one and all, Jesus preached that God was at hand, ready to overturn the present unsatisfactory state of affairs. A whole new order was dawning. With a personal *authority* that his observers found astonishing, Jesus drew together some of the most humane attitudes of the rabbis contemporary with him in order to reinterpret much of the Torah. Where it had been said in the past, an eye for an eye and a tooth for a tooth, Jesus said that God is such that we must love our enemies, do good to those who persecute us. Whereas in the past the Sabbath was made for God, in the sense that one was to do no worldly work, Jesus said that the Sabbath was made for human beings, in the sense that good deeds, such as healing the sick, were the genuine religion that God wanted.

In such ways, Jesus strove to improve upon restrictive understandings of Jewish religion. No longer could one feel secure that by keeping the precepts of Torah he or she stood right with God. Much more important than any precept-keeping was the traditional stress on love—of God, with one's whole mind, heart, soul and strength: of neighbor as oneself. Thus, those who refused to support their parents in their old age, by taking advantage of a law that allowed them to give moneys to the service of the temple, did not break a precept of Torah, but they did break the more fundamental duty of loving their parents. In much the same way, those who had the power to cure fellow human beings and refused to do so on the Sabbath were not, in Jesus' eyes, pleasing to God. God was such that laws, "rights," precise calculations of "justice" fell away. The parable of the prodigal son (Luke 15:11–32) put all this indelibly. A son who had brashly demanded his inheritance, and then wasted it in high living, found himself reduced to the disgusting occupation of tending pigs. So he "came to himself" and decided to return home and beg his father's forgiveness. But long before he could recite his little speech, his father spied him and ran out to embrace him. The father ordered rings for his fingers, a feast for his friends. When the son's older brother, a dutiful but cheerless type, grumbled about this celebrating, the father explained the logic of his heart: "This your brother was dead, and is alive again; he was lost, and is found."

The parables are our best indications of how Jesus actually taught, and in this parable he was teaching that God is so good, so loving, that he does not hold grudges. His love and concern for us all is such that he runs out to meet us, takes any indication that we have "come to ourselves" as reason to welcome us back and make merry. There is more joy in heaven over one sinner who repents than over ninety-nine just, because God is heartsore over those who ruin themselves by rejecting his love.

A similar sort of God emerges in another of Jesus' stories. The parable of the good Samaritan (Luke 10:30–37), who takes pity on a man beaten and robbed (after "good people" have walked by), shows Jesus' understanding of what sorts of acts imitate God. The judgment that Jesus makes on the pharisee and the publican (tax collector) who pray to God (Luke 18:10–14) (the one self-righteously, the other very humbly) shows that Jesus' God wants deep honesty. When Jesus associated with publicans and prostitutes—the despised of his society—he made concrete his God's unlimited love. When he told those who brought him a woman caught in adultery, "Let him among you who is without sin cast the first stone" (John 8:7), he showed the nonjudgmental, re-creative side of his God's love.

That love reset all human relationships. In a word, Jesus said that we should treat all others as we would have them treat us. We should forgive them, try to understand them, try to love them because this is what our own hearts most deeply crave. From our hearts' cravings, we "know" what a genuine, worthy God must be. It was Jesus' amazing gift to have no doubts about this worthy God. Through most of the gospels, Jesus moves with an utter confidence, an utter trust.[2] God his Father so centers his whole life, is so overwhelmingly real to him, that he has virtually none of the fears or inhibitions that keep the rest of us from being fully human. He can respond to nature, to fellow men and women, to even the despised rejects of his society—respond lovingly, understandingly, healingly. In that way he shows some of the best traits that the Hebrew Bible and early rabbis had urged.

It is this startling humanity, this transparent goodness, that rivets most of today's biblical theologies of Jesus.[3] What he says and does is fresh and challenging after nearly two thousand years. Despite the fact that all the New Testament accounts of Jesus filter the original historical happenings through at least a generation's worth of interpretations, he continues to breathe the dearest freshness. No tidy formulas capture him. No comparison with other world religions' founders detracts from his sublimity. Quoting an earlier scholar, the Jewish interpreter Geza Vermes concludes near the end of his study of Jesus: "In his ethical code there is a sublimity, distinctiveness and originality in form unparalleled in any other Hebrew ethical code; neither is there any parallel to the remarkable art of his parables."[4]

Fully human, able to get angry at evil and to weep for his friends, Jesus has fascinated not only his contemporaries but all the subsequent generations that have bothered to study him. A spate of literary and musical interpretations have captured Jesus' freshness in recent years. *Godspell,* for instance, captured the joy and liveliness that Jesus could have shown. *Jesus Christ Superstar* captured the countercultural quality of his mission. Such interpretations, along with the New Testament and any acquaintance with Christian history, show that few past times have understood Jesus very well. Most times have turned from his originality, his freshness, his challenge and tried to go on doing business as usual. So long as there are copies of the gospels, however, that will never be completely possible, just as so long as there is the Hebrew Bible (Old Testament) we will never be able to cut God down to comfortable size.

For his challenges to the establishment, political and religious alike, Jesus went to his death. His closest disciples deserted him; he was so alone he wondered whether even his God had gone. The first reading of Jesus' story, then, shows us a man faithful unto death. He gambled on God's nearness, God's total goodness, and he lost his very life.

THE THEOLOGY OF THE INCARNATION

But this first reading of Jesus' story is inadequate. There would have been no gospels, no New Testament, no Christian church had Jesus merely been faithful until death. The passionate conviction of his first followers was that God resurrected Jesus—took his death up into the divine life and made him present again in the disciples' midst. Since the Resurrection colored all the New Testament writers' understandings of Jesus, we find in their accounts a second story line. Even prior to his resurrection, Jesus was extraordinarily powerful. His cures and **miracles** (calming the storm, changing the water to wine, raising Lazarus) revealed him to be more than just a man. As the Gospel of John put it, before Abraham (the father of the Jews) came to be, Jesus was.

It is a tendency of New Testament scholars today to attribute the first reading to the historical Jesus and the second reading to the early community that came to believe Jesus was still alive. Catholic and Protestant scholars alike share this tendency. They remind us that the earliest portions of the New Testament (in its present form) are the epistles attributed to Paul, and that those epistles focus not on the historical Jesus but on the Christ, the risen Lord. Consequently, all of our reading of the New Testament runs into the "hermeneutical circle." **Hermeneutics** is the study of interpretation—how to determine what a text means. In the New Testament context, it is first of all a matter of gaining critical control of the fact that faith informs all the writers' declarations. None of the writers attempted an objective, detached history or philosophical analysis. All of them wrote "from faith for faith." The way that even the gospel writers, who do depict Jesus speaking and acting in historical situations, proceeded was determined by their faith, their theological point of view. Matthew, for instance, was a believing Christian, probably of Jewish background and writing for Jewish Christians, who wanted to show how Jesus fulfilled scriptural prophecy and perfected the Jewish covenant. He cast his materials so that they served this intention.

So too with the other New Testament authors. Each of them had a **Christology**, a point of view that assumed that Jesus was the decisive revelation of God. In various parts of the New Testament, such Christology reaches beyond titles and symbols to state rather directly that Jesus was the divine Son or Word of God. The beginning of John's gospel, the first chapter of the Epistle to the Colossians, and the first chapter of the Epistle to the Hebrews all exemplify this trend. In their view, Jesus' life represented a great circle. He existed with God before his earthly birth, assumed flesh to serve God's work of salvation, and then returned to God's right hand. Thus, the New Testament itself has a theology of the Incarnation, a conviction that in Jesus God's Word took flesh.

God's "Word" (as God's "Spirit") was a notion available from Jewish scripture. Thus, according to Genesis, God created the world by speaking: "Let there be light." Similarly, it was God's Word that came over the prophets, giving them their words of both accusation and comfort. The theologians of the New Testament took this conception and fitted it to the task of interpreting what this exceptional man, Jesus of Nazareth, meant. He was so full of power, so close to God, that he must have been God's very self-expression. From his words, his deeds, his whole bearing, God stood disclosed—made human, come into our terms as full of compassion.[5] Therefore, Jesus was the beginning and the end of God's alphabet—God's alpha and omega. Therefore, one who saw Jesus also saw his Father.

We need to stress that this conviction of Jesus' divinity, which has been central to Catholic faith from the beginning, is precisely an article of faith. As such, it is not something that historical data can ever clearly prove. Even if we had pictures of Jesus calming the storm or raising Lazarus, we could not "prove," in a scientific way, that he was divine. We do not understand natural phenomena well enough for that. Rather, we would still have to assent from the heart—go beyond the mind's persuasion to the full acceptance that only love brings. Indeed, Jesus' own sayings—the parts of the gospels that have the best title to be considered historical—make this very point. They do not present his cures, for instance, as displays of divine power that he himself possesses. Rather, they ask onlookers to believe in God, his Father, with whom all things are possible. In other words, Jesus almost always points away from himself to his Father. Almost always, it is faith—wholehearted trust—in God's goodness to which he attributes his success. To talk about what Jesus meant, or what Jesus continues to mean today, apart from this context of faith, is almost surely to misfire. Jesus speaks a language of faith, hope, and love. The understanding of Jesus, the estimation of who and what he was, has equally to proceed in faith, hope, and love. It is a requisite of good methodology that one fit one's procedures to the tasks at hand. Contemporary study of Jesus' Incarnation often shipwrecks on this requisite, for that study has the very difficult task of trying to extract objective, detached meaning from a wholly subjective, faith and love-laden set of reports.

This very difficult task has practical implications or applications at the present time. In early 1980, the bishops of the Dutch church met in Rome with Vatican officials and the Pope to try to solve some deep divisions that troubled their people. Those divisions had many causes and focuses, but the one that seemed to trouble Rome most was the Dutch effort to work out a truly contemporary understanding of Jesus' divinity. The progressives among the Dutch theologians wanted to reset the question of Jesus' divinity in the context of faith, love, and social justice. It is incumbent on us today, they said, to be more sophisticated than Christians have been in the past. Principally, it is incumbent on us to appreciate the results of biblical scholarship, and scholarship on the development of Christian **dogma**, and so to realize that often past ages underestimated the distinction between objective assertions and assertions of faith. That distinction does not make a complete separation (faith depends somewhat on objective reality, and somewhat intends to say "how things are"). It does, however, keep a proper distance between what one does in the laboratory and what one does kneeling in the pews.

Perhaps an analogy will help. At the time of the frightening accident at the nuclear reactor on Three Mile Island, we heard Helen Caldicott, an Australian physician who works in Boston, lecture on the medical dangers of radiation. In explaining the breakdown of radioactive materials, their half-lives and particle changes, Dr. Caldicott was a marvel of detachment. However, when she turned to the implications of these objective facts—to the possibility of wind currents bringing radioactive materials from Pennsylvania to Boston, where her children presently were—her detachment ceased. A great deal was at stake, and it clearly colored the "truth" of what had happened at Three Mile Island.

The same sort of bifocal vision occurs in other situations. The surgeon who operates on a cancer victim—for instance, to amputate a leg—has to suppress certain emotions and proceed rather mechanically. This is a rational, necessary choice, based on the judgment that the good of saving the patient's life outweighs the evil of taking a leg and causing great pain. However, if that same surgeon cannot change lenses and later see the patient as a suffering human being rather than simply a surgical problem, "reality" will be dishonored. The coolness that helps good surgery can ruin a postoperative interview. What the patient wants after the operation is some warmth and understanding. It is not a question of either/or—either competence or warmth. It is a question of both/and. There is a time to be cool and a time to be warm. There is a whole medicine, a complete enterprise of healing, that knows how to treat patients as both objective biological problems and subjective bundles of feelings.

The application to Christology is analogous. As an expression of passionate personal faith, the confession of Jesus' divinity tends to use symbolic, or **mythological**, or poetic discourse—to use language that is warm. In both the New Testament and the centuries of subsequent Christian faith, to call Jesus Savior, or Lord, or Son of God was to invest in him the great treasure of one's life. He was such a revelation and powerful realization of the way things ought to be that he was more than ordinarily human. Rather, he was a man singularly connected to the deepest and best power, a man actually identifiable with the creative love that makes all the best things be. Committing one's life to Jesus meant opening oneself up to this love. Because the love was so ultimate, it meant being "healed" (the root notion of "salvation"). Because the love was so profound, people could only talk about it rather paradoxically. Being seized by it, one felt that he or she was passing from "death" to "life," from unacceptability before God to acceptability.

That is the way that contemporary theologians such as the Dutch progressives tend to interpret much of the biblical and traditional discourse about Christ's divinity. They emphasize that it is often full of symbols struggling to express the deep impact that the real wonders of Jesus, and his real effects through faith, produced.[6] Very little of it was written with the mentality of a surgeon coolly operating on a cancer patient. There is another side to this issue, however, and it has an interesting history. Early in the fourth century, a number of Christians who had been educated in Greek analytic techniques pondered the question of Jesus' relation to the Father. They were of rather speculative temperament, and they wanted to know whether Jesus was of the same stuff (was *homoousios*) as the Father. The most important representative of this group, a priest of Antioch named Arius, put the matter succinctly: was there a time when the Logos (Jesus as the divine Word) did not exist? Arius answered his own question affirmatively: yes, there was a time when the Logos "was not" (did not exist). At the ecumenical Council of Nicaea (A.D. 325), the bishops assembled voted against Arius's position, saying that it did not represent traditional Christian belief. Their champion was Athanasius, who argued that the Logos was indeed of the same stuff as the Father and so existed eternally. Athanasius was certainly moved by a desire to defend truths he felt were crucial to people's salvation, but he admitted that if one is challenged by technical questions, one ought to try to give good technical answers.[7]

Few contemporary theologians have studied the **methodological** implications of this bit of dogmatic history more profoundly than Bernard Lonergan. His reading of what happened at the Council of Nicaea is that there the Church legitimized the rights of the mind to move beyond the horizon of scripture. Arius had raised a legitimate question, one that scripture itself had not posed (in his overtly metaphysical terms). By choosing to respond in Arius's terms, and not simply to repeat the non-metaphysical language of scripture, the council faced up to the challenge (itself seen by scripture: see 1 Pet. 3:15) of giving an account of its faith that would bring it up to date. The alternative would have been an anti-intellectualism or **fideism**. It would have been to deny a legitimate question about the divine nature.[8] Slowly and painfully, the Councils of Nicaea and Chalcedon hammered out the dogmas of Christology. At Chalcedon (A.D. 451) came the classical definition: there is in Jesus Christ one **person** and two **natures**. The one person is that of the Logos; the two natures are those of divinity and humanity. The precise mystery of Jesus' identity lies in the juncture, the **hypostatic union**, of the two natures in the one person.

Through the centuries, this classical definition gave rather abstract form to the Catholic understanding of Jesus. In the thirteenth century, Thomas Aquinas argued that we gain some understanding of the hypostatic union if we suppose that what Jesus' human personhood lacks (the reason why there are not two persons) is only and precisely the act of existence *(esse)*. The union of Jesus with God, the identity between Jesus and the eternal Word, is such that the Word's act of existence gives Jesus' two natures their being.

Now, this sort of scholastic development, which in its own way is a work of genius, has left rather far behind the solid reality of Jesus of Nazareth. For all that it resolutely affirmed Jesus' full humanity, scholastic theology dealt with him so abstractly that it left ordinary readers quite cold. If we were to consider it the whole of Christology, we would be back again to the surgeon with no care for the patient's emotional needs. Moreover, since the time of scholasticism speculative thought has moved from **metaphysics**, which give a rather wooden treatment of objects, to categories that derive from the personal intentions (drives, demands) of consciousness. Thus, both the needs of ordinary persons' faith and the advances in philosophy conspire at the present time to demand that theology rethink Jesus' reality in terms of **personalism**.

In part, this demand can be answered by a distinction. We can say that what one preaches on Sunday, or writes in popular books, ought not to proceed in the detached, analytic categories of the professional theologian. The professional theologian is like the surgeon at work. Insofar as his or her goal is the most lucid theoretical understanding, the professional theologian can be coolly objective. But, like the good doctor after the operation, the good theologian who would communicate theology to people with deep needs and hopes must find a language that is concrete, warm, and personally meaningful.

On the other hand, a vexing problem remains. What one communicates, even popularly, ought to be what one holds to be true. Insofar as the dogmas of Nicaea and Chalcedon, and the elaborations of those dogmas through subsequent Church tradition, represent something that the body of Christians has long believed to be true, we cannot lightly discard them. Insofar as their truth may be merely partial, or may be outmoded in its language, we must in all honesty try to update it. To deny that our understanding of traditional dogmas can, indeed must, develop is to deny that we human beings change—is to say we do not live in history, do not have an inbuilt need to grow. Poised amidst all these conflicting claims, the best contemporary theologians struggle mightily to honor all the truth they see. They make clear what the Church has taught in the past, what they find permanently true in that teaching, what they find inadequate or unintelligible by today's religious or intellectual standards, and how Jesus can continue to symbolize to common people God's unfailing love for every human being.

Religiously, we clearly need a Jesus who is fully human. As Gerald O'Collins's short survey of recent Christology shows, there is a solid consensus on this.[9] Intellectually, by thinking carefully about the great power of Jesus' teaching and person, we should be able to retain his divinity and show its credibility today. For instance, if we start from "below," with the rich humanity in Jesus' speech and then go on to analyze the implications of his singular authority and love, we may discover how all human beings seek union with God. In that case, Jesus will be "just" the full, unique realization of something the rest of us partially share. Were we as gifted by God as Jesus was, we too might be amazing expressions of divine love, amazing miniatures of God's eternal Word. This approach is rather hypothetical, but Rahner and others have used it to good effect.[10] By showing that we should not assume too quickly that we know precisely what "God" and "man" fully mean, they help us realize our own orientation to divine mystery, our own revealing of God. Then, in the space they have cleared, the possibility that God chose to take one man's capacity or orientation and so fill it that that man uniquely "incarnated" God's Word does not seem ludicrous.

From below, then, we can keep much of what the older Christology, which proceeded from "above" (from the Logos in heaven, who came down to take flesh), really wanted to say. And, to keep the basic intent of the tradition is all that contemporary theology rightly can expect to do. For theology is only faith seeking understanding. It can never substitute for faith, for the personal commitment that finds, based on all the aspects of the whole situation, that Jesus is the best interpretation of how human beings are called to live and the Christian tradition is the best explanation of how to be human. The dogma of the Incarnation is only one of the aspects of the whole situation. Equally important is the dogma of grace: God shows in Jesus that the divine intent is to befriend us in love. If a given person finds the dogma of grace, or other central aspects of the way of life that radiates from Jesus, more helpful or significant at a given time, there is no obligation to concentrate on less helpful, more problematic areas. In other words, one doesn't have to jam a traditional view of Jesus' divinity down people's throats.

As Rahner has argued, any person who honestly accepts the challenges that life sets us, especially the challenge of being honest and loving in the horizon of death, is so imitating Jesus that, in the context of a Catholic understanding of grace, that person is very likely a "believer."[11] Essentially, God invites us all through the experiences of every day. Those who respond with love anything like Jesus' make a commitment to God, an ongoing act of trust, that slowly draws their lives toward a goodness (and often a suffering) like that of the God-man. In that sense, all faith has a Chalcedonian "orthodoxy": those who meet life lovingly continue the Incarnation. For that reason, Christian tradition has long spoken of "the whole Christ"—Jesus joined with his followers.

JESUS IN AN ECOLOGICAL WORLD

Can we continue to speak of a whole Christ, or a unique Incarnation, or a definitive salvation today, when evolutionary science has so vastly extended our "world" (horizon of reality)? In our contemporary context, many find it difficult to think that the billions of evolutionary years center in Jesus. Yet Colossians 1:17 says: "He is before all things, and in him all things hold together." Is that a woeful anthropomorphism, a relic from benighted ages when people thought the world only a hundred generations old (and soon to come to completion)? Catholic interpretation of Jesus that mounts from his extraordinary humanity to his divinity, and that tries mightily to bring the conciliar traditions up to date, has to investigate this issue fully. In fact, it has to investigate whether one can have either a fully intelligible evolutionary theory or an adequate Christology without placing Jesus Christ at the center of global history.[12]

Let us begin this difficult investigation with a strategic detour. It involves a review of the writings of Teilhard de Chardin. Time was, not so long ago, when one could assume a general familiarity with Teilhard's main theses, but that no longer seems possible. So we have to note, first, that this quite original thinker was driven to try to synthesize his science (paleontology) and his faith.[13] He suffered for his boldness, in ways quite instructive, for both scientists and theologians took ready aim at him. However, when one considers how the logic of his detractors ran, his intent seems all the more admirable. The logic of his scientific detractors ran to a denial that the **biosphere** has any finality—any goal or terminal meaning. In many evolutionary scientists' view, the universe is a system accidental in its beginnings and purposeless in its developments. The logic of Teilhard's theological detractors ran to a denial that science should have any influence on the understanding of faith. If, for instance, paleontology suggests that the first human beings likely arose in several unconnected ancestral pools ("polygenism"), that ought not at all to impinge on the theological position ("monogenism") that all human beings derive from a single set of parents ("Adam and Eve").

Since Teilhard's day, in the years after World War II, considerably more sophisticated positions have arisen, and they mediate between these two logics of detraction. It is clearer now than it was then that the different orders of questions and interests that science and theology represent have to be brought into dialogue, and that with good will and imagination many of their differences can be whittled down. For instance, theologians can learn to appreciate the limits in the scientist's assertion that evolutionary mechanisms have no finality in view, and the reasons why the scientist's proceedings have to screen out the tendency to think that species develop organs (e.g., thumbs) for specific reasons (e.g., tool manipulation). On the other hand, scientists can learn why theologians are concerned about the unity of the human species (our solidarity in sin and grace), and their sympathy can help theologians rethink precisely what the biblical language is trying to say in its accounts of Adam and Jesus Christ (the new "first man").

We give Teilhard a prophet's honors, then, for being boldly concerned to make Christ relevant to the world of science and evolutionary nature. Influenced by his faith that Jesus is God's supreme revelation, Teilhard tried to look behind the face of things. Inside the things of nature, he thought he discerned a law of complexity-consciousness. Increased complexity, especially in nervous systems concerned with information, seemed to correlate with increased consciousness (self-awareness). By this law, *cosmogenesis* (the development of the natural world) seemed ordered to *noogenesis* (the development of thought). That was a rather macroscopic or large-scale inference, but it gave all the data of science and Christian faith a certain coherence. If one cannot speak of finality in individual subhuman agents of evolution, one certainly can speak of finality or design in the prime agent, the divine Creator. Everything in the Christian conception of God conspires to make us think that if he made the system we call the universe it was with deliberateness and purpose. Teilhard thought that his law of complexity—consciousness captured, after the fact, some of the coherence that the Creator intended in the fact.

Looking from this point of view, one who finds the traditional doctrine of the Logos credible and illuminating will infer that Jesus has an intimate function in the evolutionary process. If that process derives from the divine mind, and Jesus is the very Word of the divine mind, then that process correlates with Jesus from the outset. When God diffuses the divine goodness, so as to create, creation's "logic" partakes of the self-expression that a Father makes in speaking forth a Son. And if the Son be incarnate in the material world of evolutionary processes, then the communication of divinity to humanity in the Son becomes a primary channel or instance of the world's **divinization** (since the humanity that the Son assumes is not separable from the material world). By rather abstract reasonings such as these, speculative theologians have tried to make sense of the New Testament assertions about the Word's centrality to creation.[14]

For the Eastern church, such reasonings undergirded and derived from the doctrine of the *Pantokrator:* Christ is the ruler of all creation. For the West they combined with Greek science and philosophy to make the world open to rational investigation: the world is a product of divine intelligence. For us today, they sharpen the question of evolution's meaningfulness, linking Christ to the current ecological crisis.[15]

In the Christian view of nature, Jesus' full humanity receives the fulfillment for which all creation labors and groans (Rom. 8:19–22). The solid, material flesh that Jesus has from Mary so carries God's life that it becomes "God-with-us" (Emmanuel). For the Hebrew Bible, the God of Israel promised ("made a covenant") to be with his people through history. Indeed, "he" (for Israel God was largely a patriarch) revealed his divine nature in the people's experience of his hidden presence in time: "I am as I shall be with you" (Exod. 3:14). For the New Testament, Jesus was so complete a presence of the hidden God that he became the new covenant, new ark, new temple—the redoing of the old symbols of God-with-us. Through his flesh, all the expectation and longing of human hearts for wholeness and death-defeating life finds satisfaction. Through his flesh, the evolutionary processes that lead up to creatures who can have such expectation and longing also find fulfillment. That is how a contemporary Christology might advance the old theses. Doing so, it assumes that union with God, attainment of God's own life of love and holiness, is the "goal" or "end" not only of human beings, who can think about the implications of their strivings, but also of nonhuman creatures, who strive unawares. If we are indeed ecological with natural creation, it makes sense that we read into the "lives" of oceans and mountains, leopards and camels, a striving like our own. It makes sense, that is, that we take our Christology to ecological conclusions.

The kinship that human beings have with nonhuman creation has been put in popular, accessible form by such naturalists as Lewis Thomas and Annie Dillard. In his recent book *The Medusa and the Snail,* Thomas uses a story that we heard him tell during a lecture at Pennsylvania State University in 1977. He had a layover in Tucson, and he decided to visit the local zoo. It was a fine day, and as he wandered between the tanks that housed the otters and beavers, admiring the play of the sun on the waters, he was overwhelmed by the "perfection" of these animals' sport. They were larking to the sun and the waters, swimming and diving and turning flips. So wonderfully did they take him out of himself that Thomas knew they were his kin. Like a Saint Francis, who preached to the birds, he felt at one with the whole of animal creation. The same sort of vitality—response to sun and sparkling waters—coursed through his blood as coursed through the blood of the otters and beavers. Reflecting on this afterward in his study, Thomas added another unit to the **holistic** philosophy that his years as a cytologist (student of cells) had been developing for him. As the inside of human beings shows us to be "colonies" rather than isolated entities, since we house all sorts of viruses and parasites and quasi-independent subsystems, so the outside of human beings shows us to be parts of an organic whole, of a "nature" that is so intimately cross-related that it is *one,* more than just poetically.

At her hermitage near Tinker Creek in Virginia's Blue Ridge Mountains, Annie Dillard, a professional writer, found dazzling variations on this theme.[16] What she and Thomas share is a sense that we human beings cannot divorce our lives and fates from the incredibly energetic, profuse, and beautiful nature that has spawned us. Let "ecology" name this sense of the interdependence of all living things, and the old theses about Christ's pantokratorship become planks for an ecological platform and faith. Through the Incarnation, God has given not just human beings but all of creation a definitive (**eschatological**) promise that its processes and labors are not in vain. Where microbiology or molecular biology may see only random reactions, Christian faith "sees" a divine co-action that carries all that has been made toward the ocean of God's own love-life. If we humans have been saved, our world has been saved with us. The new heaven and new earth that scripture (Rev. 21:1) glimpses express, in an intuition that never cracks the mystery of *how* God's promises actually will be realized in time, the joyous hope that *all* will indeed one day be well.[17]

In Teilhard's language, Christ is an omega point of all creation where the fulfillment of the world already stands realized. In more pedestrian speech, the unification of the nations that economic interdependence and communication are achieving, and the unification of material creation that the evolutionary and ecological sciences are discovering, point to a call for unitary fulfillment that the cosmic Christ, who for Colossians (3:11) is all in all, already has achieved. In a truly evolutionary world, Jesus forces theology to upgrade its appreciation of nature, and forces biology to raise its sights to religion.

HOW DOES JESUS SAVE?

But is all this not impossibly high-flown? What does it mean for Jesus to be the peak point of all humanity, let alone of all creation? How do we bring these soaring assertions and fancies down to solid earth? Primarily, we bring them down to earth by recalling the analyses of human striving on which we labored in the previous chapter, and then by trying carefully, restrainedly, to correlate such analyses with a sober estimate of the Jesus of Christian faith.

The strivings of concrete human living, as we analyzed them in the previous chapter, and as we have extended them analogously to the rest of creation in the present chapter, demand an achievement that will give human living sense and completion. By sense we mean explanation: showing human time to have significant purpose and order. By completion we mean emotional satisfaction: peace and love. To "save" human beings is to furnish them sense and completion. Insofar as we human beings "demand" a sense and completion "right now," in the time before our deaths, salvation has to touch our biology, politics, history, and biographies. It has to be a vision and power that can bring us to harmonious relationships with nature, international cooperation, confidence that there is a solid path to the future, confidence that our individual stories report that it is good to be. Insofar as human beings "demand" more than what "right now" ever could supply—*lasting* sense and completion—salvation has to stretch beyond this earth and its history. It has to lead on to "heaven" and "eternity"—transcendent realities we can only symbolize dimly.

Traditional Christian **soteriology** deals with both "right now" and "eternity." It has a sense and completion for both our existence in time and our existence beyond time. When it has lost its balance, its tension between now and then, it has failed the Incarnation and the full Catholic Christology. For instance, when certain communities of the **apostolic** period (while eyewitnesses of Jesus still lived) so concentrated on the end of the world that they neglected worldly institutions such as marriage and government, they failed the incarnational truth that God really has joined divinity to our flesh and time. On the other hand, when present-day Christians so concentrate on reforming worldly institutions that they bracket or even deny the realities that traditional symbols such as eternity and heaven have sought to indicate, they fail the incarnational truth that God has offered humanity a fulfillment history alone never could. In the first case, where Christians neglect the world, they open themselves up to valid criticisms, such as those of **Marxists**, that religion is an opiate—something the powerful offer the oppressed to keep their eyes off revolution. In the second case, where Christians neglect the profound experience and meaning in their tradition's transcendent symbols, they open themselves up to valid criticisms that they have denatured the rich original vision.

The task for a contemporary Catholic soteriology, then, is to try to restore a balanced view, not simply by repeating old formulas but by creating fresh metaphors and applications. For instance, it might make Jesus' saving function more impressive and credible if present-day theologians tried to show how adopting Jesus' life and message can touch our very bodies. That would seem a powerful way of showing the significance faith has for our human experience "right now." Let us therefore attempt it, at least in sketch.

If God's own Word took flesh, as a Christology "from above" affirms, or if Jesus so made flesh a presence of divinity that one had to wonder whether he wasn't more than human, as a Christology from below affirms, then flesh—our embodied human being—is clearly valuable, good, divinizable. Catholic theology has often affirmed this proposition, but lately it has not affirmed it creatively enough to make it a powerful glad song. Two places where historically the tradition affirmed the goodness of bodily creation were in its opposition to **Gnosticism**, which called fleshly things ungodly (and so doubted the Logos' Incarnation), and in its opposition to **Albigensianism**, a heresy that denigrated the flesh and marriage. Further, in developing its sacramental system, the tradition made various material things "carriers" of divine grace. Thus, it gave bread, wine, water, and oil a solid vote of confidence. Impressing them on the bodily senses, and adding lovely music and words, the tradition echoed Psalm 150: "Let everything that breathes praise the Lord."

Nonetheless, Catholicism did relatively little to encourage physical regimes for the body of the average believer, and often it made marital use of the body a second-rate vocation (and so something suspect). Compared to some yogic regimes that developed in India and East Asia, Christianity was less than fully loving toward the body. It so stressed the soul that the body could become Saint Francis's "brother ass": just the beast of burden that carries us through the vale of tears that earthly life is bound to be. In such documents as Pius XII's *Sacra Virginitas* (1954), the tradition was interpreted to mean that religious abstinence from sexual relationships is the first class way to heaven. Today we still lack a satisfactory Catholic theology of health, exercise, play, and sex, as we still lack a fully effective solidarity with the poor. The result is that our lives are less beautiful, graceful, joyous, and self-sacrificing than they could be. We are less than fully saved, less than fully whole.[18]

Other important zones of contemporary life and faith connect to these we are discussing. For instance, we need not journey far to find a Catholic neglect of the feminine. True enough, Catholic veneration of Mary introduced a feminine factor that was powerful in popular faith. But for women it produced a rather impossible role model (virgin and mother), and for men it did nothing to alter a repressive view of sex. In another direction, the relative inadequacy of our theology of the body, our concern for the body's salvation, surely has played a part in our slowness to embrace a radical commitment to social justice and ecology. There has been considerable championing of the rights of workers, but not enough to make the Church a clear opponent of hazardous work, such as mining, laboring in mills, laboring in chemical factories. Until very recently there was virtually no popular or even scholarly attack on industrial pollution, the devastation of the oceans, or nuclear contamination. Catholic theologians have not clearly seen that, because we have bodies, nature is our home. They have not clearly seen that the Word's becoming flesh means that all natural and bodily things struggle to become whole and godly. For instance, in the eight years (32 issues) 1976–1983 the leading American Catholic theological journal *Theological Studies* published no articles on ecology or the theology of nature.

An important part of renewing Jesus' saving implications therefore lies ready to hand in theological reflections that apply the incarnational principles of a high Christology to current issues of nature, social justice, and the body. Two other dimensions also beg consideration. One is Jesus' salvation of our trans-worldly aspirations, and the other is his having saved us from sin. The first dimension takes us to the depths of human experience, whence cometh our best hopes. As historian Eric Voegelin has shown, profound human cultures everywhere have produced symbols of transcendence.[19] Greek culture, for instance, rode the wings of its great playwrights and philosophers to a high, transcendent imagery of justice. Thus, Plato gave to his political analyses of justice the ballast of an artful myth of the judgment of the dead. Egyptian, Iranian, and Muslim cultures, to name just a few, have had equivalent symbolisms.

In such symbolisms, a people expresses its intuitions of how things "must" be, if fairness and decency are not to be mere shadows. Unless we have lost all moral health, we "know," at the fine point of our spirits, that there ought to be some recompense for innocent suffering. The poor people of the slums know that life has dealt them a bad hand, and they struggle to hope that somehow things will change. The wealthy people who profit from the poor of the slums have to harden their consciences to avoid their own intuitions of what justice implies. So they tell themselves that the poor are shiftless, dirty, not worth loving "as themselves." When Jesus says that as we judge we shall be judged, he claims the center of this profound human sense of how things ought to be. Faith in Jesus therefore stretches beyond the realm of history, where full justice never obtains, to a realm of another order: the Kingdom of God. In the Kingdom, things will be as they ought to be, and even better.

We naturally think of justice in terms of people's dealings with one another, but it has analogous applications to nature's dealings with us. The people who suffer from plague, famine, flood, or earthquake all receive less than what a "fair" human life implies. It is true that, insofar as creation is from nothingness, the Creator "owes" us nothing. But our full instinct is that to make human beings, or other creatures, only for suffering or frustration is cruel and unworthy of "God." So we either abandon the very notion of God, which leaves us in a world without ultimate sense and hope, or we raise our eyes to further possibilities. "Eternal life" is precisely such a possibility. Believing in God, hoping for the fruition of the longings deep within us, we wonder whether there isn't true justice beyond the grave. For the Greeks, divinity was precisely deathlessness. For the Christians whom the Greeks influenced, the resurrection of Jesus symbolized the first fruits of a return to the deathless God

—a return to life as it ought to be. These are but symbols—arrows we shoot into mystery. But on occasions of deep suffering or joy, when we are especially human, they can seem more "true" than believing that human existence ends at the grave. For us present authors, who have seen three of our parents die prematurely, these suggestions from faith keep a salutary wonder alive. Would not a God as good as Jesus depicts his Father to be recompense his people who have been shortchanged?

Jesus' having saved us from sin is the final motif we consider. This part of salvation goes beyond the securing of our sense to the pardoning of our evil. For we human beings do miss the mark and fall short of the glory of God. We do abuse nature, hurt one another, injure our bodies and minds. We can be fools, saying in our hearts there is no God, no mystery that honesty must honor. We can turn our backs on the stories of Israel and Jesus, where mystery becomes steadfast love. We have our excuses, our reasons, our exculpations, but ultimately they are hollow. Some responsible irresponsibility so infects us that we no longer say thanks for the light of our eyes, the air we breathe. Stupidly, we turn to pleasure and mammon. "Original" sin is the generality of this condition, the social construction of a "reality" truncated and poisoned. Personal sin is the affirmation of this condition, the "I" joining in with the general perversion somewhat awares. So deeply is this sin the underside of human history, so deeply does it stalk all our hearts, that sense and completeness seem shattered. On the stones of human hardness, human forgetfulness, the best of our instincts fly apart.

We all know sin, so there is no point rehearsing its countless variations. From petty slights that keep blood relatives shunning one another for decades, to massive desecrations such as germ warfare and nuclear peril, sin is the good we would do and do not, the evil we would not do and do. It involves us in a terrible retribution, a jungle law of eye for eye. The salvation that Jesus offers us is the reversal of this jungle law. Instead of eye for eye he offers suffering love. Struck, abused, rejected, Jesus did not strike back. By the goodness of his God, he stayed uncorrupted by what we humans do—by the concrete evil the humans who killed him did. The cross of Jesus is a shout that God endures our evil. The resurrection of Jesus is a quiet assurance that God's love is stronger than our evil. Place that shout and assurance at the center of a human assembly, and you have what the "Church" ought to be. It ought to be the gathering that so opens to God's love that forgiveness is its middle name.

When forgiveness has been the Church's middle name, human beings have felt wonderfully saved. They have heard a scriptural word that stressed mercy, not sacrifice. They have experienced sacraments of baptism, eucharist, penance, and anointing that healed their festering self-hatred. Perhaps above all, they have become a community with a healed imagination. Most of what is possible to us human beings depends on what we can imagine. When we see the possibility of reconciliation, forgiveness, and renewal—grasp the scenarios they might assume—we take charge of healing our future. All things are possible with God, Jesus the preacher assured. The Christ makes all things new, the New Testament authors proclaimed. If we take a message like that to heart, embody it in our whole lives, we will reconcile estranged spouses, motivate enslaved alcoholics, fiercely oppose the unjust status quo. Basically, we all ask to be saved from lovelessness. The whole significance of the Word made flesh is that we have been saved from lovelessness—that even when our hearts condemn us, God is greater than our hearts.

THE CHRIST AND NON-CHRISTIANS

Through much of its history, the Catholic church has had only a fuzzy sense of its relations to non-Christians. The teaching of Saint Cyprian (ca. 300) that "outside the Church there is no salvation" crystallized a tendency toward exclusivism, while the biblical notion that Israel was to be a light to all nations (and so was not "elect" for itself) constrained the young Christian church, which thought of itself as the new Israel, to try to serve the world. In its doctrine of **baptism of desire**, which said that people who lead good lives implicitly want entry into Christ's Body, the Church later saw a tacit act of faith at work in the hearts of all people of good will. In its notion of **limbo**, the place where the innocent unbaptized would enjoy a "natural" happiness after death, the Church backed off from such generosity. Thus for centuries missionaries such as Francis Xavier rushed through foreign lands, believing that unless they got holy water on pagans' foreheads heaven would be empty. The God who desired the salvation of all people (1 Tim. 2:4) seemed to have done rather poor work. The millions who lived before Christ, and the millions after Christ who never effectively heard his name, seemed bound to perish.

Non-Christians' actual reality broke this pessimistic theology. Just about all the foreign cultures that missionaries visited showed some impressive moral achievements. They surely begged salvation, from all sorts of ills, but equally surely God had not left herself without trace in their midst. Thus, the dignity of many American Indians, the wisdom of many Hindus, the deep peace of many Buddhists, the ardent piety of many Muslims forced honest Christian missionaries to take their Christian pretensions down a peg. There were pagans more honest than many Christians. There were foreigners more refined. How could it be that God had not preceded the missionaries to such foreigners' culture? How could it be that they had no portion in Christ?

Nonetheless, it was only among European intellectuals of the early eighteenth century that a universalist sense of concrete history started to emerge. As late as Bossuet's *Discours sur l'Histoire Universelle* (1681), the Augustinian pattern, where history centered in the Church, continued.

With Voltaire and the discovery of the sublimity of Chinese culture, things began to change, and with that change the Christian doctrine of salvation came into crisis. That crisis continued, indeed grew, in the Catholic church to the middle of the twentieth century, only ending with Vatican II's *Declaration on the Relationship of the Church to Non-Christian Religions.* The Holy Office did denounce Leonard Feeney's "Boston Heresy" in 1949 (Feeney claimed that all modern people had, through modern communications, sufficient knowledge to realize that they should join the Catholic church, and that therefore all who did not join would go to hell), but it did little positively to show how Christ lives in non-Christians.

The Vatican II declaration points out the special relation that Jews and Muslims have to Christians, in virtue of the biblical background and faith that all three groups share. Jews and Muslims have themselves recognized this, for Jews have tended to look on Christians as a deviant Jewish sect that history treated kindly, while Muslims have considered Jews and Christians "people of the book" (and so distinct from other non-Muslims). It is with more distant peoples—Indians and East Asians, for instance—that the problem has seemed most acute. They apparently have had little historical contact with Christ, and so their virtue or wisdom seems not to derive from Christ's preaching or self-sacrifice. Have they then no salvation, or have they a salvation independent of Jesus? The divine desire to save all people, which we mentioned above, makes the idea of no salvation unlikely, while Acts 4:12 ("And there is salvation in no one else, for there is no other name under heaven given among men by which we must be saved") made the importance of Jesus plain.

Before turning to the most celebrated "solution" to this problem, Karl Rahner's theory of "anonymous Christians," let us try to specify the problem with cases even more acute than those of well-developed Hindus or Buddhists. Anthropologists furnish numerous such cases, and we can quickly take up three: Colin Turnbull's study of the Pygmies of the Congo Forest, his presentation of the mountain people (Ik) of the border area between Kenya and Uganda, and Napoleon Chagnon's study of the Yanomamo, who live along the border between Venezuela and Brazil.[20] The Pygmies are a literary delight. They show all sorts of human foibles, but their love of their forest, their close-knit tribal life, and the way they sing to their God (who takes the physical form of the forest) all make one think that "primitive" humanity is in good shape. The mountain people called the Ik have become infamous in anthropological circles, either as an instance of an anthropologist's distortions or as an instance of what happens to a people when extraneous politics disrupts its traditional way of life. The Ik come across as a horrible group: deceitful, loveless, avaricious, and cruel. Literally, they take food out of the mouths of children and the dying. Because they are no longer allowed to wander and hunt as they had for centuries, fighting starvation has made them give up most signs of humanity. Reading about them, one thinks of Paul's harsh verdict in Romans 1:28–29: "God gave them up to a base mind and to improper conduct. They were filled with all manner of wickedness, evil, covetousness, malice."

Nor are the Yanomamo much better.[21] They spend their days preparing for war, engaging in war, or recovering from war. Other tribes are simply the enemy; fellow members of the tribe are competitors to subdue or outwit. The men abuse the women. The women abuse the children. Religiously, the principal function of the Yanomamo shamans seems to be to sniff hallucinogenic powders, in order to induce visions of fierce little demons who will aid the tribe in its battles. Socially, the only way Chagnon could keep the Yanomamo from taking his food was to stock up on peanut butter, which they thought was excrement.

Human culture apart from Christ is therefore a very mixed blessing. In the main it probably shows more need of salvation than "Christianized" cultures have, but that is a judgment open to challenge. Many non-Christians are truly admirable (the old Pygmy Moke whom Turnbull describes comes to mind), and many aspects of Christian culture (its militarism, usury, and wastefulness toward nature) make it clear that Christ has not conquered the West. The ancient cultures of India, China, and Japan offered their people considerable wisdom, holiness, and comfort. India offered the Hindu program of the *ashramas* (life stages), as a well-marked path toward salvation *(moksha)*. First in India and then farther East, Buddhism offered the eightfold path as a high way to appreciate ultimate reality *(nirvana)*. For traditional China, Confucian ethics and Taoist aesthetics provided a high-minded spirituality. For traditional Japan, Shinto love of nature and Buddhist philosophy combined to form an exquisite taste. On the other hand, India burned widows, China bound women's feet, and Japan could be exquisitely cruel. The data on non-Christian cultures therefore invite several interpretations. Depending on what one is expecting, either God or Satan stands forth.

There is a parallel with Western peoples, including Western ex- or anti-Christians. A friend who worked organizing cooperatives among Jamaican field hands told us that the nominally Christian establishment there reacted to these efforts to improve the lot of the desperately poor with naked savagery, while the most dedicated reformers were ex-Christians now of Marxist bent. A similar pattern often occurs in the American professions. Some of the most dedicated scientists, doctors, lawyers, and social workers are repulsed by institutional religion, or even declare themselves atheists. Some of the most chauvinistic and bigoted politicians insist on prayer in the public schools. The blessings of religion on American soil are therefore also very mixed. When the Pilgrims went on their "errand in the wilderness," or pioneers headed West to establish "God's New Israel," they sometimes did not scruple to slaughter Indians like buffalo. When John D. Rockefeller and Andrew Carnegie modeled the role of Christian businessmen, the Bible became businesslike.

The heart of the matter of any culture, any faith, any personal religion, then, is not determined easily or from without. Any culture, faith, or personal religion is worth precisely the authenticity—the honesty and love—that it produces. Cheek by jowl, Christians are saints and sinners, as are Hottentots. From beholder to beholder, the presence or absence of grace is differently judged. Francis Xavier thought Japanese of the sixteenth century the most ethical people he had ever seen. Søren Kierkegaard thought Danes of the nineteenth century captives of an irreligious Christendom. Only by entering the theater of existential conscience can one come even close to the mystery of the real God's presence or absence. And in the theater of existential conscience, Christ's drama is persuasively the best interpretation of God's play for all people.

That is the point of Rahner's theory of anonymous Christianity. Convinced that the one God, in whom he believes because of Jesus Christ, has offered salvation in all people's lives, Rahner distinguishes between salvation (revelation, grace) that is "transcendental" and salvation that is "categorical." Transcendental salvation is the offer of personal love that God, the one mystery into which all lives go, makes everywhere. Because of his reading of Jesus, Rahner thinks that God the Creator, who must be present to all creation if it is to continue to exist, has freely chosen to be for all people God the intimate lover. In technical terms, Rahner speaks of this state of affairs as "the **supernatural existential**." By that term he means that the actual situation for all peoples is a world of grace —a world where God offers love, sharing, communion with the very divine nature.[22] Substantially, then, all human beings have an equal "chance" for salvation, because all people meet a reality whose mystery is God's own accepting and helping love.

The categorical side of salvation (revelation, grace) is the specific historical and cultural forms that mediate this supernatural existential. All human beings live within a language, a set of traditions, and a common pool of values. For Christians, the categories that derive from Jesus represent the most adequate express forms for transcendental grace. That is, what happened in Jesus is the definitive (once-for-all) declaration of the universal state of affairs. The way that Jesus related to God, related to his fellow human beings, went to his death, and was raised to divine life—all of this love persuades the Christian that Jesus is singular, unparalleled. Other religious geniuses may reflect other aspects of divinity. Individual Hindus, Muslims, or atheists may be holy indeed. But the mainline, most "privileged" categorical expression of God's universally saving will and action are for the Christian Jesus and his authentic religion.

To put all this reasoning in a short formula, Rahner has spoken of anonymous Christians—people who do the essentials of the authentic religion that Jesus inspires but don't use Christian forms or language. Anyone who really accepts the full challenge of human life, Rahner has said, takes on the outline of Jesus. In other words, Jesus, overall, is the best hermeneutic or interpretational key for what it means to be human. Wherever people become mature, Jesus is illuminating. Of course, there are problems applying this notion, and it can seem offensive—seem to carry the old Christian superiority complex. But other theologians who have criticized Rahner for the "diplomatic" abuses to which his theory is liable seem to have missed his main point. Principally, Rahner's notion is an attempt to make sense, within the orbit of Catholic faith, of how Jesus functions in the salvation of the humane non-Christian. The diplomatic communication of this sense is an important but secondary matter.

Rahner's notion that Jesus "saves" all who come to full maturity, by being the most adequate personal symbol of the divine grace on which all full maturity depends, seems to us a great elucidation of Catholic doctrine. It holds together both the generosity that God's care for all people implies and the stunning uniqueness that shone from the flesh of God's one Incarnate Word. For those who wish to maintain orthodox Christological and soteriological faith, that is a very precious accomplishment. For those who have a touch of humanity and common sense, it begets no undiplomatic chauvinism. All salvation is gratuitous—an excess from God's goodness. To receive salvation in specifically Christian categories is but a further excess. Those who appreciate generosity respond to it with a like generosity: "Beloved, if God so loved us, we also ought to love one another" (1 John 4:11). In the case at hand, that means calling all people of good will brothers and sisters in Christ's love.

CHRISTOLOGY AND POLITICS

Rahner's reflections on Christ's functions in saving human beings from senselessness, incompleteness, and sin have led him to speak of Jesus as the "absolute savior." In the singular life and love of this man, God has disclosed his "eschatological" (definitive, once-for-all) stance toward humankind. That stance is one of steadfast love (the quality that the Hebrew Bible often associates with **Yahweh**). More precisely, it is the steadfast love of a parent. As God is fatherly toward Jesus, so God is fatherly toward us all. (We consider shortly the development of God's "maternity" that current feminist insights suggest.) Insofar as God's self-revelation through Jesus goes to the depths of the human condition, furnishing the ultimate wherewithal to make life good, it does indeed bear us a definitive glad tidings (gospel) of salvation. For it shouts that the great disclosure and deed for which our hearts have been set has occurred, to a measure we could never expect. Thus, absolutely, without any restrictions, Jesus brings us our most exalted destiny. Without the substance of his message, of his love, we are a people sitting in darkness. With that substance, we are children of God, partakers of the divine nature (2 Pet. 1:4).

In a largely Third World context, the present generation of theologians, some of them students of Rahner, have given these theses about Christian salvation and eschatology a more social, practical, and often political focus. Two such Latin American theologians are José Miranda and Jon Sobrino, and it will repay us handsomely to attend to their interpretations of Christology and soteriology. Miranda is a philosopher and biblical scholar, quite influenced in both pursuits by Marxist thought. From his studies of the Hebrew Bible, he has concluded that the prime practical demand of the God of the prophets and Jesus is that we do justice.[23] From his studies of existential philosophy and the Johannine literature of the New Testament, he has further concluded that genuine faith in Jesus empowers us to do justice.[24] In both cases, Miranda opposes any notion of faith that divorces it from hope and love—from concrete **praxis**, or doing, where we put out bodies on the line. Biblical truth is not a matter of propositions. It is a matter of *doing* the truth (rendering others justice) and so coming to the light (see John 3:21).

Thus, Miranda's **exegesis** of the Johannine understanding of faith in Jesus ties directly to his social concerns. The Johannine understanding shows a longer period of development than that of most of the rest of the New Testament. It is therefore in some ways more mature. The Gospel and Epistles of John stress that salvation is not some distant, future event that will only arrive at the end of the world, when Jesus returns in full power **(parousia)**. Rather, salvation is really in our midst right now. The very coming of Jesus meant that God's glory shone from human flesh and made a sacrament of human actions. What will occur at the world's consummation is powerfully operative in the present. Faith is the mode by which we open ourselves to such transforming, fulfilling salvation. Were we really to believe, we could embody heaven and eternity for present earth and time.

Linking this interpretation of Johannine faith with the conditions of depressed parts of the world such as Latin America, Miranda forges a powerful chain. To transform the hellish lives of his continent's poor would be an act of salvation that would marvelously display the incarnation of God's love, the power of God's grace. Sobrino and other Latin American Christians, among them a number of Brazilian bishops, agree with this logical chain. Moreover, like Miranda, they are quite willing to name the enemy, the powers of darkness that conspire against the salvation of the poor and a chance for decent living. Phillip Berryman has recently translated part of the Brazilian bishops' message in these ringing words:

Capitalism must be overcome. It is the great wrong, the cumulative sin, the rotten root, the tree that bears us the fruit we know: poverty, hunger, sickness, and death to the great majority. For this reason the system of ownership of the means of production (of factories, of land, of commerce, of banks, of credit sources) must be overcome. . . . We want a world in which the fruits of labor are shared by everyone. We want a world in which one works not to get rich but to provide clothing, shoes, water, and light. We want a world in which money will be at the service of men, not man at the service of money.[25]

Those are not words of comfort for us who live in the prime capitalist country that exploits Latin America. But before we turn them aside, protecting our vulnerability, let us try to see their connection with the biblical and traditional Christ. The salvation for which human beings truly hunger, the Bible and tradition say, is a sense, completion, and freedom from sin that love of God and love of neighbor "legalize." The "law" of Jesus' followers is but his twofold command. Because God has loved us, we are to love one another, and the minimal sign of our love for one another is fair dealing. We know this from personal experience —from having been dealt with unfairly ourselves. Whether that occurred in the schoolyard or at home or at work, it told us that things incompatible with "God" (with the fullness of how things ought to be) were going on. And we were not only angered by such ungodliness, we were shamed. Read the literature of any exploited group and you will find that they are severely tempted to blame themselves. That of course compounds their suffering, by adding more internal struggle. When the Bible says that God favors the "poor," it goes to the heart of such suffering. God favors the poor because, in addition to their material wretchedness, they can easily think they are worthless. But, as the prophet sensed, God can no more forget or regard one of her creatures as unworthy than a nursing mother can forget her child. Indeed, like a good mother, God's heart goes out above all to the most fragile of her children.

This sort of justice compensates for the deep inequities in a world where it is easy to prosper from the pain of our fellow human beings. This sort of justice saves billions of people from cruel senselessness. For if "God" is not on the side of those who get a raw deal, they are of all born of woman the most to be pitied. In the beatitudes (e.g., Matt. 5:3–12), Jesus says that his fatherly God blesses those who get a raw deal. Their suffering wins a special pledge that one day things will be different. If we would but extend our own sense of how things ought to be different, but imagine our way into the lives of the world's most destitute peoples, we would start to see the changes that any Christian faith worth speaking about entails. For then we would verge on loving our neighbors as ourselves. The narrowed imagination of the American 1970s and 1980s, when the country retracted most of the new hope that the 1960s had spawned, makes it imperative that we get this message clear. If the Bible and Christian tradition have any wisdom, we cannot serve mammon and prosper. The evangelical call to sell all that we have and give it to the poor (Mark 10:21) may be utopian, but it symbolizes a powerful Christian truth. Utopias are the "no places," the ideal realms, where we imagine how things ought to be. It is easier for a camel to pass through the eye of a needle than for a rich person to enter God's utopia, because God's justice despises the disparities, the untruths, that make for "rich" and "poor."

Jon Sobrino, the Catholic theologian who has most fully mined the liberating implications of following Jesus, develops the original biblical truth existentially. Like Karl Rahner, who has written of the unreadiness of the Church to accept poverty,[26] he soberly discloses our practical unbelief. For what counts in Christian profession of faith, as we have already insisted, is not our sayings but our doings. The imitation of Christ most imperative in our time is following his law of love to justice, because in our time a great deal of human suffering is caused by humans. It is true that people have always been poor. It is true that there have always been inequity and unnecessary suffering. But today whole economies and cultures are warped because a relatively few people are extremely piggish. Properly, lovingly viewed, the world has enough resources to provide any reasonable amount of people a decent standard of living. Properly, lovingly used, the human community has enough creativity and drive to feed, clothe, heal, and educate any reasonable amount of people. The main reason we do not do these things is only partly a failure of imagination and energy. It is more a failure of will. Utopian as it may seem, therefore, Jesus' program is the only sort that cuts to the heart of the matter, because unless we have a new will like that which Jesus offers, to power a new economy and politics, the best we will produce is Band-aids.

So from the biblical Christ, through the theology of the Incarnation and of how Jesus saves, we come to term at the contemporary passion for liberation. Many of our contemporaries want a world free of grinding poverty, of racism, of sexism, of war, and profiteering. In Latin America, small cadres of liberationists have so upset governments that imprisonment, torture, and even murder have become the order of the day.[27] In Nicaragua, they have even gained power, launching an experiment in Christian socialism. Latin America is perhaps the most Catholic locus of the fight for liberation, but its fight is more like than unlike those struggles going on in other oppressed lands.[28]

The regimes of recent Chile, Brazil, Uruguay, and other Latin American countries historically Catholic will finally be judged by the Spirit. So will the regimes of recent Western military-industrial complexes, recent Eastern totalitarianisms, and recent Vatican power-politicians. "For freedom Christ has set us free," Galatians 5:1 proclaims, suggesting what the baseline of the Spirit's judgments is likely to be. The beginnings, deep tradition, and contemporary pointedness of Christian faith add but further overtones. A central measure of Jesus' "worth" is the freedom, the health, the strength, and the joy he brings. A central measure is his absolute salvation. For Paul, such a high pragmatism made Jesus God's power and wisdom. According to Peter it left us nowhere else to go. The

Catholic experience of following Jesus, of living out the gamble that he is life's treasure, testifies that Jesus sends the Spirit. In the Catholic view, there is no better utopia: Jesus is the very Word of eternal life.

FEMINIST ISSUES

The majority of feminist protests against Christian sexism takes aim at matters of *ecclesiology*. It is the underrepresentation of women in the assemblies of Church power, and the restriction of women's ministerial roles, that get the most news coverage. Behind this sociological focus, however, lodge Christological and strictly theological issues. We shall take up some of the strictly theological issues in the next chapter. Here it behooves us to attend to some of the Christological ripples that the feminist wave has been creating.

Rosemary Radford Ruether's recent work *Sexism and God-Talk* includes a brief section that gets to the heart of the feminist Christological matter. First, there are the questions that the actual development of Christian sexism poses: "A Christology that identified the maleness of the historical Jesus with normative humanity and with the maleness of the divine *Logos* must move in an increasingly misogynistic direction that not only ex-cludes woman as representative of Christ in ministry but makes her a second-class citizen in both creation and redemption. . . . Where does this leave the quest for a feminist Christology? Must we not say that the very limitations of Christ as a male person must lead women to the conclusion that he cannot represent redemptive personhood for them? That they must emancipate themselves from Jesus as redeemer and seek a new redemptive disclosure of God and of human possibility in female form?"[29]

In presenting these questions, Ruether summarizes the historical re-sults of a patriarchal Christological context. Most of the Christian Church's reflections on Jesus have occurred in a "socio-cultural" situa-tion in which the male was almost unconsciously considered the prime instance of humanity. The historical fact that Jesus, whom Christian faith took to be the central Word of God and exemplar of salvation, was male seemed to put a seal of approval on this male supremacy. Thus it made complete sense to assume that power-holding in the Church would be mainly male, that the best characterization of divinity would be in male terms, and that women could only be second-class members of the Chris-tian assembly.

Ruether does not think that **androgynous** Christologies are the solu-tion. All too easily the historical fact of Jesus' maleness can obliterate the supposedly equal feminine side. A better way is to recall the program of the historical Jesus, especially as the synoptic gospels present it. There we see a Christhood or *Messiahship* that calls for the overthrow of all forms of domination and so calls for a strict equality between men and women.

In fact, Jesus' criticism of the religious and social structures of his day makes him remarkably akin to present-day feminists.

For example, Jesus rejects the hierarchies of first-century Palestine and says that in the coming Reign of God the last shall be first. Indeed, we should not depict God as a sovereign Lord but as an intimate parent. Relatedly, we should think of the Messiah as a servant rather than a king. Accepting this Messiah, and his God, ought to make us consider our fellow human beings brothers and sisters. Specifically concerning women, Jesus makes it clear that the Kingdom or Reign of God is exactly for such lowly people as the prostitute and the female ethnic outsider. In story after story, it is a woman from the lower class or a group despised by the current powerholders who exemplifies the revolution in Jesus' message. The poor widow, or the mother of the mortally sick child, or the woman afflicted with a (ritually unclean) flux of blood becomes an occasion to show the changes that the Reign of God implies. In the new society that the Christ announces, the new set of power-relations that the Christ inaugurates (and, faith says, makes possible), there are no "outsiders," no underlings. With God the poor are not less than the rich, women are not less than men. With God all human beings are well-beloved children, no human being has the right to despise or abuse another.

So Ruether's answer to the question of whether a feminist Christology is possible relativizes or even dismisses Jesus' maleness: "The protest of the Gospels is directed at the concrete sociological realities in which maleness and femaleness are elements, along with class, ethnicity, religious office, and law, that define the network of social status. Jesus as liberator calls for a renunciation, a dissolution, of the web of status relationships by which societies have defined privilege and deprivation. He protests against the identification of this system with the favor or disfavor of God. His ability to speak as liberator does not reside in his maleness but in the fact that he has renounced this system of domination and seeks to embody in his person the new humanity of service and mutual empowerment. He speaks to and is responded to by low-caste women because they represent the bottom of this status network and have the least stake in its perpetuation. Theologically speaking, then, we might say that the maleness of Jesus has no ultimate significance."[30] Whether the Catholic church can come to agree to this feminist Christological principle likely will be the crux of its viability for liberated women.

SUMMARY

The basis for the Christian view of God and human destiny is Jesus Christ. To begin to assess this basis (who soon turns and begins to assess us), we take up the biblical theology of Jesus—how he appears in the New Testament. There we find innovations in the contemporary Jewish religion and a singular personal authority that together make Jesus remarkable, challenging, and intriguing. Indeed, so intriguing and powerful did Jesus' early followers find him that before long they read his unique degree of humanity into a case for divinity. A man so charged with the grandeur of God, a man resurrected by God—he must be God's very Son. Expressing simultaneously both Jesus' full humanity and his divine Sonship has never been easy, but it has become especially difficult in modern times. Today Catholic theologians prefer to begin with Jesus' humanity, letting the awe it provoked lead them to faith-language about divinity.

Modernity asks how Jesus can be central to an evolutionary world, and incarnational Christology answers in terms of God's desire to communicate divine life to creation. Insofar as Jesus is the omega or realization point of this desire, he both centers evolution and stands as the personal symbol of God's eschatological (definitive and final) will to save. Salvation implies giving sense, completion, and release from sin. Jesus models this divine work and desire (which works in all peoples' lives) so he clarifies the destiny even of non-Christians. When we take salvation concretely, both non-Christians and Christians show ambiguities. When we take salvation concretely, we ask Jesus to call forth forces of liberation and justice all around. Thus, the practical Christology that comes from following Jesus involves us in a programmatic commitment to justice. For all doers of justice, Christian or non-Christian, Jesus' blessing is rich. For feminist seekers, the crux of the Christ is not his sex but his program of liberation.

STUDY QUESTIONS

1. How does Jesus depict God?
2. Explain what Jesus likely meant by "the Kingdom of God."
3. What role did faith play in the development of the theology of the Incarnation?
4. Explain the traditional Christological formula: one person and two natures.
5. How does Jesus represent God's will to fulfill all of creation?
6. Why can Jesus mediate salvation to non-Christians?
7. What does it mean to say, "The cross and Resurrection of Jesus are soteriological symbols that clarify any human being's situation"?
8. Explain Karl Rahner's notion of the "supernatural existential."
9. Why does Christology inevitably entail politics?
10. How is an indifference to injustice a practical atheism?

NOTES

1. See Gerard S. Sloyan, *Jesus in Focus* (Mystic, Conn.: Twenty-Third Publications, 1983).
2. See Lucas Grollenberg, *Jesus* (Philadelphia: Westminster, 1978).
3. See Edward Schillebeeckx, *Interim Report on the Books Jesus and Christ* (New York: Crossroad, 1981).

4. Geza Vermes, *Jesus the Jew* (London: Collins/Fontana, 1973), p. 224.
5. See Monika K. Hellwig, *Jesus: The Compassion of God* (Wilmington, Del.: Michael Glazier, 1983).
6. See Edward Schillebeeckx, *God Is New Each Moment* (New York: Seabury, 1983).
7. See Jaroslav Pelikan, *The Christian Tradition*, vol. 1 (Chicago: University of Chicago Press, 1971).
8. See Bernard Lonergan, *The Way to Nicaea* (Philadelphia: Westminster, 1976).
9. Gerald O'Collins, *What Are They Saying About Jesus?* (New York: Paulist, 1977).
10. See Karl Rahner et al., eds., "Jesus Christ," *Sacramentum Mundi*, vol. 3 (New York: Herder and Herder, 1969), pp. 193–209.
11. See Karl Rahner, *Theological Investigations*, vol. 14 (New York: Seabury, 1976), pp. 280–94.
12. See Denise Lardner Carmody and John Tully Carmody, "Christology in Karl Rahner's Evolutionary Worldview," *Religion in Life* 49:2 (Summer 1980): 195–210.
13. See especially Pierre Teilhard de Chardin, *The Phenomenon of Man* (New York: Harper & Row, 1959).
14. See William Barclay, *The Letters to the Philippians, Colossians, and Thessalonians*, rev. ed. (Philadelphia: Westminster, 1975), p. 120.
15. See John Carmody, *Ecology and Religion* (Ramsey, N.J.: Paulist, 1983).
16. See Annie Dillard, *Pilgrim at Tinker Creek* (New York: Harper's Magazine Press, 1974).
17. On Utopian symbols see Eric Voegelin, "Immortality: Experience and Symbol," *Harvard Theological Review* 60 (1967): 235–79.
18. See John Carmody, *Holistic Spirituality* (Ramsey, N.J.: Paulist, 1983).
19. See Voegelin, "Immortality: Experience and Symbol."
20. See Colin Turnbull, *The Forest People* (New York: Simon and Schuster, 1962); idem, *The Mountain People* (New York: Simon and Schuster, 1972); Napoleon A. Chagnon, *Yanomamo: The Fierce People* (New York: Holt, Rinehart, and Winston, 1968).
21. See, however, Florinda Donner, *Shabono* (New York: Delacorte, 1982).
22. See Leo O'Donovan, ed., *A World of Grace* (New York: Seabury, 1980).
23. See José Miranda, *Marx and the Bible* (Maryknoll, N.Y.: Orbis, 1974).
24. See José Miranda, *Being and the Messiah* (Maryknoll, N.Y.: Orbis, 1977).
25. Philip E. Berryman, "Latin American Liberation Theology," in *Theology in the Americas*, ed. J. Eagleson and S. Torres (Maryknoll, N.Y.: Orbis, 1976), p. 61.
26. Karl Rahner, *Theological Investigations*, vol. 14, pp. 270–79.
27. See Penny Lernoux, *Cry of the People* (Garden City, N.Y.: Doubleday, 1980).
28. See Virginia Fabella, *Asia's Struggle for Full Humanity* (Maryknoll, N.Y.: Orbis, 1980).
29. See Rosemary Radford Ruether, *Sexism and God-Talk* (Boston: Beacon, 1983) pp. 134–35.
30. Ibid., p. 137.

The Christian God

THE CREATOR

In liberation theology, current reflection on Jesus' God finds a stimulus to determine how God labors for human beings' freedom. Doing that, it finds itself much at home with the God of the Hebrew Bible. For the God of Abraham, Isaac, and Jacob declared himself partner to the Hebrews' wanderings and time, and the prime moment of the Hebrews' time (whose memory was decisive in shaping the biblical form of the *patriarchal* legends) was the Exodus—the Hebrews' deliverance from Egypt under Moses. "Egypt" therefore became a prime symbol for slavery and bondage. It was the dismal "before" that preceded the "after" of entry into a land flowing with milk and honey. Settling in that land and establishing a monarchy came to have their own religious problems, for Israel did not fully resist the temptations to power politics and **civil religion**. As a result, the period of wandering in the "desert," when the Hebrews were free of Egypt and en route to their own land, became a religious model. Despite the physical difficulties of unsettled life, there were spiritual compensations. Primarily, there were the compensations of journeying with a living God in faith.

The distinctive quality of biblical religion, then, is its time-oriented faith. In contrast to the nature-oriented religion of both its neighbors and other Bronze Age peoples, Hebrew faith sought and found God in time —through history. There are qualifications to this thesis (nature orientations played their part in Israelite **cult**, and other peoples' religions contended with time), but they do not remove its core truth. The God that Jesus inherited from his people's beginnings was distinctively close and distinctively mysterious. That is the argument of Samuel Terrien, in his elegant volume on biblical theology, and it so organizes the data of the primal biblical texts that we find it persuasive.[1] The elusive presence of the biblical deity was the objective correlative to distinctively biblical faith—the "outside" reality that summoned the patriarchs and prophets to search for ultimate meaning in time.

Many indeed are the ramifications from this biblical center, but perhaps we should pause to develop a contemporary one. It has to do with forgiveness, which we found to be ingredient in the way that Jesus preached about his Father, and in the way that Jesus saves. How is it that so many situations develop in which justice and progress are lost because recrimination deadlocks the decisive parties? Internationally, the vacillation between cold war and detente that has marked Soviet-American relations since World War II is evidence that *homo internationalis* has far from come of age. Again and again, we have failed to muster the imagination and persuasive ability (the *peitho* that Plato made the catalyst of all successful politics) that would break vicious cycles, such as the arms race, and would begin to create cycles of cooperation and peace. So too in such stunning examples of mutual recrimination as Northern Ireland and the Middle East. In Northern Ireland the world has an object lesson in how hatred is passed down from generation to generation. Before they even know what the words mean, little children use *Catholic* and *Protestant* as terms of abuse. And while it seems that a major cause of this situation is the economic exploitation that finally is England's responsibility, there are no innocent parties. The biblical doctrine of forgiving one's enemies makes all the partners candidates for serious judgment.

So too in the Middle East. The breakthrough in relations between Egypt and Israel that occurred in the late 1970s was a welcome relief from unrelenting hatred. However, it has hardly come to full flower, and the rise of militant pan-Islam threatens to make Arab-Jewish relations a new focus of an old notion of "holy war" (*jihad*). As in Northern Ireland, mutual accusation, well buttressed by facts, goes back almost to time immemorial. Palestinians surely have a solid case against those who despoiled them of their land. Jews surely have a solid case that being without a land of their own has given them their modern history of ghettos, pogroms, and Holocaust. Neither Palestinian terrorists of the present generation nor Israelite terrorists of the past generation have much of a moral platform. Neither Arab nor Jewish "lawyers," haggling over the details of tortuous treaties, show the world a very magnanimous face. In the Middle East, as all around the world, we find "realism" often opposing forgiveness.

A principal reason this judgment can come to clarity is the alternative that the Hebrew Bible holds out. There Yahweh, the sovereign King of all that breathes, is a God slow to anger and quick to forgive. And that is astounding, for a stiff-necked people who meet a God (an *elusive* presence) clearly out of their control might well have found things thoroughly otherwise. Because of their stubborn selfishness, they might well have found God principally a King of wrath. But no, it is not so. The depths of covenant theology, where the poets push the lawyers aside, make God's fidelity to Israel a consequence not of Israel's good moral performance but of God's own consistency. Nothing so fragile as human "morality" determines relations with the living biblical God. Freely, that God who comes and goes as she wishes, who devastates all our idols and preconceptions—freely that God chooses to be slow to anger, quick to forgive.

Similarly, it was not because of any human comeliness that Yahweh chose ragtag Israelites to center a plan of universal salvation. It was because of Yahweh's own mysterious love. Were the people even to abandon the covenant, even to play the harlot and adulterate their faith, the God of Hosea would not give up loving them. Were individuals even to rise up in adolescent ingratitude, even to demand their expected "inheritance" and debase themselves to the care of pigs, the God of Jesus would rush out to meet them with forgiveness. From the free goodness of the biblical God, then, Christianity has glimpsed a rich potential for liberation. In our time, that could produce a theology of God the Creator that would truly be creative.

The gist of an imaginative theology of creation is the fruitfulness of love. It is true enough that God classically is the *ens a se* (self-sufficient being) who makes the world *ex nihilo* (from nothing). It is true enough that the world so made from nothingness manifests God's supreme power— the ultimate existential act that the Greek philosopher Parmenides expressed in a simple outburst: "Is!" But neither God's being nor God's power "explains" creation satisfactorily. Neither fashions an analogue that makes us humans care passionately. Better are careful elucidations of human creative powers that illumine divine creativity by analogy. If so, there is little divorce between the God slow to anger and the God quick to create. Either way, the issue is the divine love. God is slow to anger —to want to "destroy" aberrant creation—because God is constancy-in-love. Equally, God is quick to forgive (re-create) and quick to communicate in the mysterious way that makes nothing something, because God is constancy-in-love. Classical Catholic theology of God as One *(de Deo Uno)* long saw that creation is not a once and for all affair. God has to conserve creatures in their being, and to concur in their actions. Continually, then, the divine love hurls "Is!" against nothingness. Continually God helps the universe participate in *ens a se.* And the best "motivation" we can conceive for this generosity is nothing but God's own goodness. Creation comes from God's constancy-in-love.

A few homey parallels come to mind, to domesticate this biblical ontology (study of being). Consider, for instance, human work. Is it not the case that the labor we spontaneously call "creative" is largely labor of love? To make something, in the way that a creative artist or scientist does, is not a matter explained by nine-to-five. The artist or scientist may accommodate to "business" models, if only to appear less eccentric and odd, but models drawn from creative work itself make clocks and charts secondary. Primarily, creative work follows counsels and rhythms more internal. Thus, the sculptor has to "see" the form that begs to stand, the musician has to "hear" the melody that begs to be sung, the writer has to follow his or her characters, the theologian has to keep ascending to higher viewpoints. Even if these "creators" always take coffee at 10:15, always lock up at 5:30, the progress or stagnation of their work is nothing they can program. When there is no muse, the poet has to wait. When the muse appears, the poet has to work. "Sorry, the bank is closed," is not poetic diction—nor is it scientific or theological. Archimedes obviously did not plan to grasp specific gravity while he was in the bath. Luther obviously did not choose to grasp justification while in the toilet. Key insights almost always come unexpectedly, as the release of long months of ardent concentration. Almost always, they issue from a long gestation—from hiddenness, midnight kicks, false and then real pangs.

Remove the limitations, extrapolate the pure core, and you have a fragile tie to God's creativity. It is utterly interior, utterly self-controlled. For no external good does God create. Nothing outside the divine fullness lures God as a complement. Rather, God is intrinsically creative because, as the Johannine writers insist, God "is" love and love is intrinsically creative. We sense this in human love, whatever its kind. The heterosexual love that seeks marriage aims toward procreation. The love of friendship creates likemindedness and puts a glow on all the hours. The self-sacrificing love of *agape* makes the old order of Adam the new order of Christ.

So too in our work. Empirically, the farmer who deals with his or her fields personally, lovingly, gets a per acre yield that no agribusiness can. The teacher who most loves the children brings out their best. Robert Pirsig, author of *Zen and the Art of Motorcycle Maintenance*, has described the mechanic to whom you should bring your machine.[2] He is the one *not* distracted by hard rock, *not* jabbering about Sunday's game. For in good work there is absorption. One treats the fields, the children, the engines with respect—pays attention to them, listens for their needs. When the Taoist sage Chuang Tzu wanted to describe artful living, he told of a master butcher. A bad butcher wears out knives right and left—he hacks. A mediocre butcher can get by on a knife a year, but he still saws and chops. A master butcher keeps a knife a lifetime, so subtly does he carve. The sinews and ligaments seem to part of their own accord. At one with his materials' needs, in love with his materials' prospects, the master butcher creates works of art.[3]

Love has a different "temperature" in the West, going among us less "coolly" than it does for Taoists, but its effects are similarly artful. Does that signify anything for the work-a-day world? It does indeed, E. F. Schumacher says, for all good work needs tender loving care.[4] To be creative—whether in human relations, scientific research, or the world of art—we have to nurture understanding with what finally can only be called love. For that reason, many of the most creative enterprises have long entailed apprenticeship. To know how technique and information turn creative, one must learn the *care*-ful atmosphere of front-line developments. Front-line developments move by the lure of elegance, of harmony, of exactitude. They love the formula that just fits, the shape that just catches, the language perfectly apt. So too, we may think, with God's front-line developments. So too with God's creativity (God's DNA, quasars, particles, and frontal lobes). What a dazzling display of light and power! What a tribute to mysterious love! And the heart of it all, Christian faith holds, is the communication of divine love-life as it is in itself—the communication called "Incarnation" and "Grace."

THE FATHER

The supreme instance of creativity, then, is divinity's presenting us with its own inner life. For Catholic theology, that inner life is trinitarian: a commonality of Father-Son-Spirit. Thus, in addition to its treatises *De Deo Uno* (On God as One), Catholic theology regularly spoke *De Deo Trino* (Of God as Three). In the popular mind, unfortunately, the Trinity seemed the most difficult to understand of the divine mysteries. Little children learned of St. Patrick's shamrock, or of the symbol of the triangle, but both children and adults found little help in structuring their faith toward a trinitarian God. Practically, as Rahner has noted, most modern Catholics have grown up as "monotheists," meaning in this case people who so concentrate on the single ultimacy of God that they neglect God's intrinsic community.[5] The alternative to "monotheism" is not "tritheism" (having three gods). It is an interpretation of the traditional symbol of God's plurality or community that will keep unity and trinity in balance.

As a negative introduction to this interpretation, it may help to present the reminder that *all* our discussion of God is halting and imperfect. For God really to be God, mystery must come to the fore. For "God" names the totality of beginning, foundation, and beyond that must ever recede from our sight. Thus, *theo*-logy in the strict sense (reflection on God herself), perches at the edge of our "world." The reality it would name always lies beyond, is always across the border. Indeed, it is "God" that gives us our borders, that defines our world. Thus, God and meaning run in tandem. At every turn where meaning heads into ultimacy, "God" appears. At every turn where "God" appears, meaning becomes mysterious (too full for our mastery).

A good illustration of this is the controversy about predestination and divine help *(De Auxiliis)* that preoccupied both Reformed and Catholic theology in the sixteenth and seventeenth centuries. In their rush to balance God's omniscience and human freedom, many of the controversialists forgot that divine action moves on a different plane than human action does. There is no "before" and "after" in divine knowledge, and so much of the problem of how we can be free if God knows "ahead of time" what we shall do is simply bad imagination.

So too with trinitarian reflection. None of it should aspire to making a blueprint for the inner divine life. All of it is frail analogy, puny symbolization. For the Catholic tradition, we can get *some* dim sense of the divine nature, enough to clarify our way, but we can never remove the great mystery. After revelation as well as before, God remains hidden—the ultimacy that eye has not seen, ear not heard, it has not entered the heart to conceive. Still, the "negative theology" that these religious truths sponsor has to leave a small part of the stage for a positive theology that marches human reason a few steps forward. Out of the Bible's theologies, Catholic tradition has speculated on the energies and relations of the Godhead, coming up with several privileged analogies. In presenting them here, our goal is mainly to suggest some of the helps to personal faith that a trinitarian imagination may offer.

For instance, building on the clear speech of Jesus himself, Catholic faith has long begun its conception of God's inner life with the imagery of the "Father." Jesus called his God "Abba," and the first reflections of the Christian community that gained general approval conceived of Jesus as God's Son.* There originally was some ambiguity about this title "God's son," since its predominant meaning in the Old Testament had been something like "one favored by God," but in time Christian theology took it quite literally: Jesus was the strictly divine offspring of God. God the Father "generated" a Divine Son; Jesus was the Divine Son generated by God the Father. Thus, the bearing of God and Jesus to one another was relational: origin to originated.

The tradition tried to avoid any sense that this process took place in time or was a creation. The Father did not produce the Son as an artisan produces an artifact. The Father also did not produce the Son by something like sexual generation. There was no divine couple mating in eternity. Thus, by a negative (not this, not that) sort of process, the early Church fathers groped after appropriate analogies. Continually, they agreed, the Father generates the Son—expresses himself in the Son substantially. It is the very active nature of divinity to have this outflowing character. Moreover, the outflow is not a giving that diminishes or parcels out the source. All that the Father is flows over to or out into the Son. Generation communicates the Father's totality. So much is this the case

---

*This imagery does not contradict the notion that God strictly has no gender, if one remembers that all imagery is only analogous to the Divine reality it seeks to clarify—only somewhat like it (and bound to be somewhat different from it).

that Father and Son differ only as two terms of an identifying relation. Father is origin and Son is originated. Apart from this difference, they are identical.

Now, what in our human experience comes closest to this sort of perfect relation and communication? Procreation and marital love come to mind, but for a complex of reasons, some good and some bad, the early fathers preferred not to use procreation and marital love. The bad reasons tie into the fears of sexuality and the body that warped patristic theology not a little. The good reasons tie into the realization that certain intellectual or spiritual processes are less finite than our bodily processes. Linking this realization with the biblical clue that God made men and women in the divine likeness, the early theologians located the image of God in our capacities to know and love. Influenced considerably by the Greek discovery of mind,[6] they stressed what happens when we know. Influenced by the biblical forms of Hebrew anthropology (theory of human nature), they stressed what happens when we love. The most articulate result of these stresses was the Augustinian-Thomist "psychological analogy."

For Augustine of Hippo (A.D. 354–430), the most influential of the Latin or Western fathers, our intellectual light is a participation in God's light. God's light, as it were, reaches down into our minds and hearts to provide our illumination, our spirituality. This is a prime way that Augustine concretizes his general statement that "God is more intimate to me than I am to myself." Meditating on my own light, therefore, I can glimpse its source. Meditating on the structure of my light, I can glimpse the structure of its source. Through the tour de force meditation called the *De Trinitate,* Augustine probes the trinitarian God's structure. He takes guidance from the Johannine writings, which brim with references to God's light, life, and love. He also takes guidance from neo-Platonic philosophy, which developed the theme of **participation.** But the powerhouse of the *De Trinitate* is Augustine's own introspective genius. That genius leads him to profound analyses of memory, understanding, and love, which become his symbols for Father, Son, and Spirit.

To grasp the sense of Augustine's trinitarianism, one must make at least part of the journey with him. So, start to go back in your own mind, to remember. For instance, go through the past few hours, before you began reading these pages. Make a trail of bread crumbs from now to the time that you arose. Then try to jump farther back, to a week ago today. What was the most memorable thing that happened a week ago today? Dwell on that thing long enough to reproduce its rich circumstantiality. For instance, if your most memorable thing was buying a new coat, recall the way the coat first caught your eye, the way it felt when you first tried it on, the way you debated whether your budget would allow it. Then add some of the surrounding details: the other two coats you tried on, the perfume of the salesperson, the glaring neon light, or the streaky triple

mirror. Do you see how profuse are the circumstantial details that consti-
tute even the most ordinary of our daily actions? Do you start to wonder
at least a little about this extraordinary faculty called "memory," which
can retrieve even how a past place smelled?

Were you to keep at your "anamnesis," your bringing the past into the
present, you might be able to reach things that happened when you were
two years old. Indeed, psychologists might insist that you have memories
from the womb. Memory, then, is a rich thesaurus, a vast treasure trove.
It holds a quasi-infinity of individual items; it recedes to "time out of
mind." Appreciating this, Augustine let memory symbolize God the Father. As the creative source of all that exists, God is somewhat like an
inexhaustible treasure trove. Whatever has come to be participates in
God—issues from the divine font. Thinking along this line, Buddhist
philosophers spoke of the *Tathagatagarbha*—the "womb" of cosmic "Bud-
dhanature," from which all things are born. For Augustine, though, the
special focus was memory's symbolization of precisely the Father. The
Father was the unoriginated, primal partner in the Trinity. Outside of
time, he was the "first." Where the Son derived from the Father, the
Father did not derive. Were you to travel the divine Fatherhood, you
would never reach a beginning. Rather, the Father was the beginning, the
origination, the dynamic ground zero. The memory of the divine mind
is like an infinite universe. The most one can say about it is negative: it
has no boundaries.

We have tried to take Augustine's drift and put it in more modern
terms, but the general accent is his own. As the last books of the *Confessions* reveal, time (which of course correlates with memory) always fascinated Augustine. That is one reason that he often sounds very modern,
very existential. Trying to purify his insights into time, he associated the
Father with the foundation of his own mentality. The Son he associated
with his own act of understanding. Dependent on memory, understanding is in some ways its issue—its child and word. However rough the
conception, it catches something of what the procession of the Son from
the Father might be. The infinite regress of the divine paternity is so
progressive as well that it generates a perfection expression. If one accents the whole life that the expression holds, then one tends to speak
of the Father having generated a Son. If one accents the intelligibility of
the process, its meaningfulness, then one tends to speak of the Father's
having spoken forth a Word. Either way, the effort is to grasp how the
Second Person is a perfect replication or image of the First. In language
dear to Eastern Christianity, the Second Person is the First's eternal icon.

We shall keep at the psychological analogy through the next sections,
spinning out Aquinas's variations on Augustine's beginnings and focusing on the Word and the Spirit. Let us pause briefly, however, for a
contemporary annotation. One of the more radical portions of current
feminist theology is the effort to gain for women a full share in the notion

that human beings are images of God. From forays into world religions, feminists know that many cultures have symbolized divinity as male-female. They have done this by having both gods and goddesses, or by having bisexual, hermaphroditic deities. In some of the more developed theologies, the Goddess is as powerful as the God.[7] That can be said, for instance, of much Hindu theology. It can be said of Mahayana Buddhist theology, insofar as the *Prajnaparamita* (the Perfection of Wisdom) is "The Mother of all Buddhas." It can also be said of Chinese theology, insofar as the Tao is a cosmic mother. Is it purer theology, or stronger patriarchy, that has removed the feminine from the theologies of the West?

Jews and Muslims (who in this simple division are "Western" religionists) can answer for themselves. Christian feminist theologians find the problem knotted. Patriarchy clearly has been very potent, but it is a patriarchy that goes back to Jesus himself. He may have treated women largely as men's equals, but as far as we know he did not call his God "Mother." Whether we can change Jesus' diction, for instance, by beginning his prayer, "Our Mother, who art in heaven . . . " is a more than interesting question. If we do change it, we have to take care not to crack the keystone of the whole Christian arch. If we do not change it, we have to explain how it is compatible with Christian freedom and love to insist on a language that contributes to many people's inferior treatment. The problem would be less acute if the Catholic church did not abuse Jesus' diction and person by making them props for male superiority. Even without such abuse, however, an important symbolico-conceptual issue would remain.

In our opinion, the Christian community ought to begin expanding its theology strictly so called to include God's motherhood. There are biblical hints of such a doctrine, for instance, in Isaiah (46:3–4) and the Genesis account of creation. They might best be appropriated to the Spirit, but the First Personhood ought to be considered as well. It would *not* take much experience for feminine pronouns and references to God to become familiar (we know this from liturgical experiments). It *would* take much experience for all the implied reconceptualization in those pronouns to emerge, but the growth and practical gain latent in such a reconceptualization seem worth the big investment. For though women surely have fathers, and can relate to Jesus' God, both women and men ought not to have their religion determined by a less than full symbolization of the parental relationship (which surely is one of the most formative for both the self and theology). Julian of Norwich, a marvelous medieval English solitary, sensed this and spoke freely of God her Mother. Pope John Paul I sensed it and offered the opinion that we might with more justice call God Mother than Father. There is enough evidence, then, to warrant a serious reconsideration. The historical limitations that follow upon Jesus' real humanity ought not to freeze our theology to the cultural sensibility (that is, the patriarchy or male-domination) of first-century Palestine.[8]

THE LOGOS

Let us return to the psychological analogy. Before our discussion of the male-female aspects of God, we had begun to deal with the Second Person. Perhaps because he was more dedicated to **intellectualism** than Augustine, Aquinas developed this part of the analogy more precisely. He had studied the doctrine of Aristotle that there are two prime acts of intellection, understanding and judgment, and he had pondered carefully Aristotle's view that insight comes from grasping form in matter, intelligibility in phantasms or imagery. Appropriating his own profound intelligence, Aquinas realized that human acts of understanding issue an "inner word." The issue of Aristotle's first act was the concept. The issue of Aristotle's second act was the judgment. Concepts deal with *what* something is. Judgments deal with *whether* something is. (Today we see concepts in the form of scientific hypotheses, judgments in the form of scientific theories.) But both involve a process that Aquinas called "emanatio intelligibilis"—intelligible emanation. In that emanation he saw the most perfect analogy to the Word's procession from the Father.

For the sake of brevity, we shall illustrate only the emanation of concepts (the first act). In the interpretation of Bernard Lonergan, which we follow here, Aquinas resolutely made understanding ("insight") preconceptual.[9] That is, we understand before we generate inner (and then outer, spoken) words; the subsequent word is the expression and result of the prior understanding. Consider, for instance, the following number sequence: 17–34–32–16–18–36–   –   . Assume that it has an intelligibility, study it, and fill in the last two blanks. The odds that you can fill in the last two blanks correctly simply by guessing are so remote that we can discount that possibility. If you have filled in the last two blanks correctly, you have understood the intelligibility of the sequence and so can give its "formula."

The two numbers that ought to go in the two blanks are 34 and 17. The formula is $\times 2$, -2, $\div 2$, $+2$. What intercedes between your first acquaintance with the series, when it remains just a senseless string, and your confident expression of the last two numbers and the formula, is an act of understanding.

The issue of the Son from the Father is like the issue of the concept (whose outer expression is the formula) from the act of understanding. Thus, the Father is like a constant, endless, ongoing act of total understanding. The Son is like a constant, endless, ongoing conceptualization of that understanding. The "generation" is like a constant, endless, ongoing **emanation** of concept from act of understanding. That is a poor man's version of Aquinas's basic analogy for the Father-Son relation. He liked it because it was an instance of act from act. The act of conceptualization flows from the act of understanding. It involves no movement from potentiality or lack to actualization. If you regulate your thought about God as Aquinas did, using assumptions of Greek philosophy, you want to have no potentiality, no lack, in God. For your God is Pure Act, infinite perfection, being that lacks nothing. Your God does not change, suffer, or become. So utter is the divine "Is!" that there is no unfilled divine capacity or potentiality, no basis for change. There is no perfection for your God to acquire or to lose, for your God *is* all perfection. Therefore, intelligible emanation, act from act, appeals to you strongly.

Recently this conception of God has received strong criticism, most pointedly in what is known as "process theology,"[10] and we shall take up such criticism below. For the moment, though, let us linger with Aquinas's view and achievement. Think again of that little insight you found in deriving the formula of the number sequence. It was a small flash of light, nothing monumental, but it is a precious clue. For in Aquinas's analogy, that light, magnified to the status that "divinity" implies, is what God is constantly being and doing. Thus, the divine "light" is not like a giant bank of bulbs over a football stadium. It is not a thing of physical wattage. It is more like the nearly instantaneous flash of meaning that comes only in highly developed brains. God's primal procession is an overflowing flash of meaning. The Word's expression of the Father is primitive intelligence.

Many indeed are the implications or extensions of this basic motif. For instance, the Logos (Greek for "Word") was glimpsed by pre-Socratic philosophers, who were unaware of Christianity, while they were pondering the relations between mind and nature. When they suspected a parallel, they took a momentous step. In theological clarification that step reads: All creation has a mental, logical aspect. All creation reflects the divine mind. If human beings, by virtue of their rationality, are "images" of divinity, subhuman beings are yet "vestiges" ("footprints"), for to be is to be mind-related. That is the truth in all **idealism**, all philosophies that most prize mind—Western and Eastern alike. The Mind that founds this truth expresses itself in the Second Person. The Divine Logos is a cosmic Word. It would be overstepping the sure evidence to say that the authors of Colossians and John's gospel had a full **ontology** of the Logos, but they did move in the direction of the Logos as cosmic Word. For instance, they said, "All things were made through him, and without him nothing was made" (John 1:3). It would not be overstepping the sure evidence to say that Church theologians, from the second century on, thought in terms of a cosmic Logos. From Justin Martyr to Origen, they were fascinated with this theme. Precisely how the confidence in the world's rationality that this theme sponsored contributed to the rise of Western science (which is a unique cultural phenomenon) would be a complicated historical question. Surely, however, it supported such confidence. When Einstein expressed his passionate conviction in the world's rationality ("God does not play dice"), he merely stated a centuries-old faith in the modern context of quantum mechanics.

It would take us far afield to show that such a faith remains tenable despite such epistemological (concerning the theory of knowledge) developments as Heisenberg's principle of indeterminacy and such political developments as the Nazi Holocaust of six million Jews. At its strongest, Heisenberg's principle concerns what we can know, not whether creation is parallel to the divine mind. At its strongest, the Holocaust concerns whether human beings may act absurdly, not whether God's logic is ruined beyond rescue. There are enough workable theories about nature, enough hypotheses that have led to spaceships and nuclear explosions, to show that nature is intelligible. There are enough good political experiences to show that madness is not the biblical God's first name. So we prefer to stress that the whole thrust of our minds is for sense and meaning. The way that human beings spontaneously think of nature and history assumes intelligibility. In such thrust and spontaneity, we think that human beings validate the basic analogy behind the classical Catholic theories of the Divine Logos.

Let us bring this closer to home. Can a potter, whom we can take as an instance of human creativity, make pottery without intelligence? Does there not have to be some "sense," some "plan?" However intuitive, holistic, or aesthetic, an artistic work such as pottery demands understanding. There has to be some sort of picture or feel of the intended final product. There has to be some knowledge of one's materials, one's wheel, one's kiln. The temperature at which to fire, the temperature at which to glaze, the way to obtain the patterns, the way to obtain the colors —all these must be understood. The Logos is the inclusive understanding of the global, divine artifact. In the divine artifact, as Paul saw (Rom. 9:21), we are the pots, not the potter. That we have been made proves that we could be. Our "could be" depends on the divine mind, as our actual existence depends on the divine will.

Another instance of how we move within an ultimate "logic," how we reflect something of God's Son, is human language. Tied inextricably to our "world," our sense and outline of reality, is our language. For that reason, Wittgenstein (the premier philosopher of language in recent times) made his often quoted statement: "The limits of my language are the limits of my world." For that reason, the decline in language skills among students is deeply threatening. If students cannot read, write, and speak precisely and clearly, they cannot *think* well. If they do not love their native language, they do not love their native *reality*. Manifestly, many students, as many citizens generally, do not read, write, speak, or think well. Manifestly, many do not live realistically. It is arguable, if not obvious, that those two propositions are intimately connected.

Not to live realistically, of course, is to condemn oneself to daily frustration. Ultimately, it is to drive oneself toward mental disease and sin. The jargon that rules government bureaucracies shows that their collective mind is largely diseased. The prose that one finds in insurance policies, leases, or canon law suggests that its authors have a sinful intent to obscure. During the summer of 1973, the nation received a soap-opera-like lesson in a sinful intent to obscure. The parade of witnesses in the Watergate hearings "stonewalled": muttered and equivocated and "mis-spoke" themselves. Ultimately, they abused the Logos. More than a decade later, too little has changed.

The "language" of God, of course, is richer than human logic or syntax. The Word of God, become flesh, has a multifaceted significance. For John, every gesture of Jesus spoke eloquently. The first half of his gospel, in fact, is a book of "signs": changing water into wine, multiplying loaves and fishes, giving sight to a man born blind. Incarnate, the intelligence of God is subtle, powerful, much richer than deductive logic. It teaches by deed and silence as well as by word. Therefore, we must not make the Divine Logos **rationalistic.** We must not divorce it from its heavenly context of love. Within the divine nature, the Word is an intelligence that breathes forth love. The "logic" of Christian religion therefore entails hearts as well as minds. The Word we accept in faith, and join ourselves to, is Truth for freedom and life. All this brings us to the Spirit.

THE SPIRIT

The Spirit is the Third Person of the Trinity. As is true of both the Father and the Son, it is a "Person" only analogously to the way that we humans are persons because, like the Father and the Son, it is unlimited. Further, the Spirit "proceeds" within the active life of the Trinity, as the Son "proceeds." Where the Son's procession is called "generation," the Spirit's procession is called "spiration." Father and Son spirate (breath forth) the Spirit. (This is the doctrine of the West; for the East, the Spirit proceeds from the Father.) The Spirit is the substantial fruit of the mutual knowledge of the Father and the Son, the love that their knowledge issues. No more than the Son is *other* than the Father is the Spirit *other* than the Father and the Son. It is *other* only relationally. Where the Father and Son spirate, the Spirit is spirated. Where they issue it is issued. Otherwise, Father, Son, and Spirit are completely one. They are three "persons" in one divine nature. Each is wholly God, wholly knowing, wholly loving. None is independent, a separate God. So there are not three gods. There is only one God who is a single community of three relationally distinct "persons."

Both Augustine and Aquinas agree that the Spirit parallels our inner psychology of love (as the Father and Son parallel our memory/understanding and conceptualization). Once again, however, Aquinas has the more exact analogy. For him, the best likeness to the Spirit's procession from the Father and the Son is the procession of our acts of love from our acts of judgment. Parallel to the way that concepts flow from acts of direct understanding ("insights"), acts of love flow from acts of reflective understanding or judgment. Acts of reflective understanding grasp a sufficiency of evidence. They occur when we realize that we have the grounds for saying that something is or is not so. A prime example of this process is scientific method. On the basis of intuition and experimentation, scientists form hypotheses—reasoned explanations of how things may be. It may be that certain kinds of viruses cause cancer. It may be that a bodily substance called interferon can fight some of them off. The critical work of science is to cross the gap from "maybe" to "is." That work goes on by testing one's hypotheses—verifying or disproving them.

When one achieves verification, a judgment follows spontaneously. Looked at as a final product, verification is the act of understanding that one does have grounds for saying something is so. Similarly, disproving is the act of understanding that one does have grounds for saying something is not so. That "saying" is a judgment, a committed assertion about reality. It is where truth or falsity occur. Perhaps putting this in more commonsense imagery will make it clearer.

Consider the proposition, "People in Somalia have pink hair." (It is hard to imagine where one would get that proposition, but suppose that someone saw an issue of *National Geographic* where the colors had run, so that natives of Somalia had pink afros.) On the face of it, there is nothing intrinsically contradictory in the proposition. People can dye their hair pink and live. Genes do strange things, as albinos demonstrate. So there "could be" people in Somalia with pink hair. But, would you bet your paycheck on it? Could we tempt you with 100 to 1 odds? Not likely. For you to take this proposition seriously, we would have to verify it, probably by showing you hundreds of pink-topped natives. Your skepticism shows that your mind has reflective demands. When you are acting responsibly, you demand solid evidence for your committed judgments of reality. Rightly, you distrust untested or untestable propositions. You know that all sorts of people have lost their shirts in the stock market—because they took "maybe" for "is." If you read Shakespeare, you know that Othello ruined several lives because he took plausible evidence of his wife's infidelity for actual proof. Hang on to your skepticism, your distrust, your Shakespeare. Hang on to your demand for reasonable proof. It is a prime mark of God's image in you.

When we issue judgments, we intend, push forward toward, commit ourselves to "truth"—to how things are. And as we have a natural, spontaneous orientation toward truth, so we have a natural love for it—a natural respect, regard, benevolence. This is perhaps clearest in judgments we make about people or important issues—in "value judgments."

Here's an example of a value judgment. Jack meets Jill. At first she seems a thin, pale, wishy-washy type, unable to climb the smallest hill, let alone fetch a pail of water. But Jill has started a program of physical conditioning. Soon she runs five miles a day, fills herself out on Nautilus machines. When Jack meets her again she is climbing mountains, hauling huge vats of water. She has become lissome, lovely, graceful. Along with the improvement in her physical condition has come an improvement in her attitude toward life in general. She is no longer wishy-washy, will say a firm "yea, yea" or "nay, nay." To Jack she says mainly "yea, yea." Jack admires her taste. Before long, experience and reflection convince Jack that Jill is a terrific person. He has sufficient data, adequate grounds, for committing himself to the proposition: "This Jill is a good one." In that commitment, as act from act, Jack loves Jill. He goes out to her goodness as Pooh goes out to honey. A judgment of real being and goodness develops an inclusive flow of love. That is an analogy for the Spirit. (In concrete reality, of course, love is not so programmed. It comes as a suggestion early on, suffers anxieties in the middle, and by the end is a warm contentment. Jack may start to love Jill from the first, "yea, yea." But the main point seems valid: judgments of goodness issue love spontaneously.)

On to the Holy Spirit. The experience Father and Son have of one another, their mutual acquaintance, involves something like a value judgment. Knowing one another, they "judge" that they are good. From this judgment flows an act of love. As was the case with the flow of the Word from the Father's self-understanding, the act of love passes directly from the act of value judgment. There is no potency involved, no lack of perfection. As fullness to fullness, divine knowledge passes into divine love. This passage is the procession of the Spirit. Like a breath of benevolence, joy, and delight, the Spirit proceeds from the relational unity of the Father and the Son. In the imagery of some of the early fathers, it is as the kiss of their love.

Further, there is a certain completion or roundness that the Spirit's procession brings. Images do not come easily at this point, but the Catholic tradition has talked of *perichoresis:* the mutual indwelling or coherence that the three persons have. The love that the Spirit personifies helps to enable this mutual indwelling. It is like an atmosphere or suffusion, except that it is as real as the memorial Father and the logical Son. Memorial Father, logical Son, suffusive Spirit of love—each is wholly in, with, through, for the other. We can't imagine this sort of thing very well, since all our experiences are structured by limitation. But perhaps the suffusion of love that goes through a good family situation, or a good marriage, or an ardent friendship, or a warm parent-child relationship catches something of the Spirit. Such suffusive or atmospheric love is as real, and as important, as the partners it joins. Without it, they not only are not joined, they also are not "themselves," not their full "I" and "you." The suffusive Spirit, then, is a sort of "We"—a sort of three that one and one make when they add in love.

The Spirit, therefore, saves the Christian Trinity from any appearance of being a merely intellectual affair. Where the Greek elements in traditional speculation led to a stress on mind and "logic," the Hebrew elements related presence and word to the "heart." Suffusively, the divine life that the three persons share is a blending of mind and heart. It is clarity and warmth conjoined. As such, we can appreciate its splendor, for our own best moments, our own peak experiences, are clarity and warmth conjoined. For instance, when we are in love (as we can be sure the three persons are), all is different. We perceive differently, associate differently, understand, and judge differently. Thus, a land that appears rocky and barren to an outsider is for a native the prime site on earth. A child that to an outsider is wrinkled and red is for a parent cute as a button. The shyness that a stranger finds too great a burden a lover finds mysteriously attractive. The colleagues that a fledgling finds doddering and boring an old-timer finds comfortable and shrewd. Perhaps, then, the Spirit draws lovable particulars into the universal divine splendor. Perhaps divinity itself plays to join heart and mind.

Further, it would be fairly easy to write the Spirit a feminine persona. One could begin with biblical cues. There is the figure of the Spirit brooding over the waters of creation (Gen. 1:2). There is the Spirit's care for a creation in labor for fulfillment (Rom. 8:22–23). The work of our sanctification traditionally associates with the Spirit, as though she mothers divine life in our hearts. Whatever the original force of these tendencies, and whatever their utility today, they tell us that God can and does move subtly, indirectly, by persuasion as much as by force. Chinese thinkers saw this when they contemplated the Tao. The "Way" of nature is subtle, actively passive, gentle. As water wears the rock, as an infant rules its parents, as a woman persuades a man—so does Tao move. There is no reason not to credit these insights to the Spirit. There are many reasons for thinking that the Spirit moves by *wu-wei*—passive action, light guidance of the flow.

Last, we probably do well to insist that the Spirit is most analogous to our *rational* loves, or that our love is at its best when it is rational. By rational we do not mean cold or unfeeling. The reasons of the heart that Pascal praised unforgettably are both clear and warm. But so much current American culture debases love to sentimentalism that we have to warn that the Spirit's love fires the mind even more than the senses. This is clear both positively and negatively. Positively, the reports of those who most profoundly experience God and instruct the tradition in God's deepest ways insist that mystical love purifies the senses. It is not a love that waxes sentimental. Rather, it burns away our illusions, in dark nights and clouds of unknowing. In time it goes beyond our imaginations, asking that we take God's existence as a simple invisible fact. Eventually, even, it goes beyond ordinary intellection, helping the mind to give God a blank check to satisfy reason. In these ways, deep love of God promotes the nicest, and sometimes the starkest, realism. It calls us to honor all evidence, to test all inspirations. It is sober and watchful, for its adversary (godless selfishness) is like a prowling lion, seeking whom it may devour.

Negatively, the shipwreck that regularly comes to those who base their religion on pure emotion testifies to the Spirit's rationality. In apostolic times, Paul had to remind ecstatic Corinthians that only a love which edifies the community is a completely desirable gift. Through most ages of Christian history, overly emotional types have stirred crowds to frenzy, bizarre behavior, or certainty that the world would end in the next round year. One of the healthiest traits of the Catholic tradition is the tendency of its mainstream to tame such emotional excesses. At core, Catholic tradition respects reason. The Spirit promotes sweet reason. Sweet reason, peaceful intelligence, a joy that gives lucidity—these are marks of the Spirit. The best Catholic charismatics make these marks the crux of discernment.

EXPERIENCING THE CHRISTIAN GOD

The specifically Christian God is trinitarian, incarnational, and saving. In the next chapter, we shall consider the realistic world view that faith in this God promotes. We shall also consider the theological virtues (inner strengths) that a gracious share in this God's life develops. Right now, however, we want to give a little description of the religious, or ultimate, experience that makes the Christian God credible. It is true, of course, that our approach to such experience is directed by our Christian convictions. Nonetheless, we think we can make a good case that the ultimate experiences that all people may receive, or that they have reported historically, suggest the portrait of divinity that Jesus and his followers have painted.

Concerning the "fatherhood" of God (which today we would prefer to render the "parenthood"), we suggest that many people experience it when they move in spirit toward the depths of their selves or their world. In moments of quiet contemplation, for instance, one can travel recent memories or one's current spate of images down to the depths of the "I." There, perhaps under the questioning form, "Who really am I?," one can sense that personal identity passes out of our sight. The different parts of personal identity are like links on a submerged chain. What anchors them to the bottom we cannot fathom, for the base of who we are lies deep in mystery. It involves a beginning and a term we cannot clearly see. That beginning and term is the unoriginated originator. It is the self-sufficient first that alone keeps our regress from being ad infinitum—endless, without surcease. So does the Father appear in our midst. As Jesus drew all of his identity from his relation to his fatherly source, his progenitor, so can we. Ultimately, we are children, offspring, of the prolific love that, as Dante saw, moves the stars. In our case, however, such love is personal. All that is uniquely human in us argues for that. Indeed, our best works image a fathomless capacity for creativity and effective self-expression. The artist and generator in us reflect God the Parent.

Concerning the Sonship of God, the Logos whom the Father speaks forth, we suggest that our experience of reason in nature, history, and the self moves in the train or pattern of the Logos. When God speaks forth the divine primordiality, it flows as a light or intelligibility that may be participated in by finite forms. As we have tried to illustrate, that light flashes in each of our insights. Therefore, whenever we turn a "eureka" or a grasp of judgmental grounds toward ultimacy, we raise our minds toward the divine procession of God's Word. Playing variations on this elevation, early philosophers such as Pythagoras and Plato entertained the proposition that the world is formed by numbers. Physical scientists run in their tracks today, when they chalk on the board equations that they hope to verify as patterns that stars or particles follow. For, to think of the world mathematically, and to find some of one's thought verified, is to experience profoundly the "logic" of creation. Warm that logic to a possible service of love and you have the universe participating in the first infra-trinitarian procession.

Third, concerning the procession of the Spirit, the religious experiences that weigh most heavily for us (as we take guidance from Karl Rahner) are those in which we are drawn to faith that God has given us divine love (the essence of our salvation) once and for all.[11] That is, the Spirit pours forth in our hearts a love such that we can find our divine childhood—our being carried to the bosom of God—solid and unillusory. The tradition reports this experience, calling it an *arrabon* or downpayment on the life we shall enjoy in heaven. The gift of the Spirit, then, is an earnest or marker that God will pay off the "debt" she has contracted in making us creatures who hope for a total fulfillment in interpersonal knowing and loving. The French Catholic existential philosopher Gabriel Marcel wrote in the grasp of such hope when he extrapolated from the experience of intense human love the spontaneous conviction, "You at least will never die." In his reading, when we fall profoundly in love we deal with something (a relation so good, or a soul so beautifully naked) that begs to survive the erosions of time. The Song of Solomon was on the trail of this inference when it described love as "strong as death." Explicitly Christian conviction finds God's resurrecting love to be stronger than death. It is a work of the Spirit in human hearts to make the resurrection credible or strongly anticipated.

These three modalities to religious experience, which we argue suggest the trinitarian persons, may emerge most clearly when one probes with convictions formed by Catholic theological tradition, but they are by no means limited to Christians. We have advanced such a proposition in another work, comparing Jesus' religious experiences with those of the Buddha.[12] From that comparison, we have further proposed that future

Catholic theology ought to do more with comparative religious studies than past Catholic theology has done. Thereby, it would remove much of the parochialism that makes it unattractive to a contemporary "global" consciousness—a consciousness that realizes that we all share but one worldwide "village." Raymond Panikkar, whose own biography blends a Hindu with a Catholic background, is the prolific author in whose works you may find this thesis developed extensively.[13]

When the three persons communicate *ad extra,* to creatures, they communicate "for us and our salvation." That is the nearly incredible conclusion to which the message of Jesus and the interior witness of the Spirit lead. The backward reach of the "Father," the outward reach of the "Word," the circling return of the "Spirit"—they all, by God's free choice, enter space and time, become incarnate with the Word, for our benefit. Aware and unaware, Christians have long expressed their faith in this saving grace in simple attitudes of affirmation. By "simple attitudes of affirmation" we mean saying yes—to the world, to other people, to one's self and one's given life. The rather extraordinary spiritual journey that the famous United Nations diplomat Dag Hammarskjöld recorded in his *Markings* pivoted on a day when there broke through his dark depression a deep and forceful "yes." From sources within him that played almost out of his control, he and the Spirit mustered a core word that overturned his whole outlook. Perhaps because he and Kierkegaard shared a common background, it is tempting to read his transforming act as a "leap" like that of Kierkegaard's knight of faith—a leap of nearly pure grace.[14]

In less dramatic terms, the prime psychologist of the life cycle, Erik Erikson, has spoken of the human person's terminal virtue as the ability to love life in face of death. The view that Erikson develops of human time sees it as passing through age-specific crises. Thus, the adolescent years typically foist on us an "identity crisis" (this famous phrase comes from Erikson). Similarly, the years of middle adulthood tend to bring a crisis of generativity: Is our time, now fairly well along, showing us to be fruitful or barren? The terminal virtue or strength that the human psyche needs for maturation is "wisdom." By the time we come in sight of our approaching end, we face a critical task of mustering the wherewithal to call what we have done and become good—necessary, fitting, something with which we can die.[15] It is not pure wish-fulfillment to find the Spirit at work in all these crises, and at work especially in the terminal one. As she who "presides" over our experiences of God's love offered and effectively received, the Spirit groans the prayers of our depths, keeps the flames of our hopes flickering. For those who do make an effort to answer God's calls in conscience—who do, for all their failings, keep trying to be honest and to love—the Spirit brings support and consolation. Where "the enemy of our human nature," as Loyola called Satan (and we may call whatever wills our destruction), tries to lure those who keep trying to depressions and discouragement, the Spirit is encouraging, supportive, a bearer of possible ways through.

The God of Christian experience also is communitarian. That is, the Three Persons' own sociability and relatedness overflow into our human experiences of togetherness. We are most ourselves when we are in significant relationship to other people (and to nature). The best societies or political groups are those that value the individual differences of their members. In the network of these truths shines forth an expression of the Christian God. Rugged individualism is not the Catholic Christian way. Neither is a legalism that goes blind before individual circumstances. These are cardinal theses for the theology of the Church, as we shall see below. We flag them here, however, because their ultimate warrant is the very nature of the God whom Church life ought to bear into the world. Father, Son, and Spirit say "We," not "I, I, I." Their identities are bound together. Would that our Christian identities were the same. Then the old patriarchal dictum would illumine a present golden goal: a brother helped by a brother is like a strong city.

The last observations we want to make about Christian religious experience of God deal with our creaturehood and God's suffering. Prompted by the whole story of salvation, Catholic theologians such as Rahner have read out of our experiences of **contingency** and limitation, which force us to the truth that we have neither made nor controlled ourselves, a religious paradox. It is that we are *more* ourselves the *less* we stand apart from God in supposed independence. True self-realization, in other words, is finding one's destiny in the mystery of one's origin, and Jesus puts this all concretely. Insofar as Jesus is signally human, signally a rich personality and free spirit, he argues powerfully that closeness to God empowers rather than destroys individual selfhood. From humanistic psychology we get a complementary message. The most "realized" personalities have come to grips with the "nothingness," as Erikson calls it with reference to Gandhi, that bounds all human life.[16] They have cast themselves upon the oceanic waters, made their peace with things out of their control. Doing so, they have been truthful to their creaturehood.

All creatures suffer—undergo, are done to as well as do. Most creatures also suffer in the sense that they endure pain. Does the image of God in us argue that divinity too suffers? Does the way that suffering seems intertwined with our creativity or deep loves give us warrant to place "passion" in God? Traditional theology said no: God the Pure Act dwells outside the realm of suffering. True, God's Word assumed a flesh that could suffer, but divinity itself did not suffer. In condemning *patripassianism* (a theory that the Father suffered with the Incarnate Son), the tradition made this denial of suffering in God explicit. Recently, "process theology," a loose school that owes much to the thought of Alfred North Whitehead and Charles Hartshorne, has contested the tradition on this point. It finds suffering so intrinsic to love, growth, caring, and other things we call positive that it wants to extrapolate suffering to God. As well, it points to the biblical portrait of God, for instance that of the prophet Hosea, where God grieves, is heartsore, makes himself vulnerable. Process theologians read the Bible as saying we do make a difference to the biblical God and so can "hurt" divinity.

Because of its convictions about this point, most process theology is willing to have a finite, limited God. That is the problem we see with admitting suffering in God: it implies God's limitation. But the consensus of the overall tradition, we believe, is that God is unlimited. The Catholic tradition says, overall, that a limited "God" is no real God. For that reason, we would prefer to take the indications of God's sufferings that either biblical texts or prime human experiences suggest with a careful qualification. Perhaps we can so analyze them that either vulnerability does not imply need or lack in God, or we can so correlate them with the mystery of the Incarnation that we can speak of God's having chosen to take a form in which the divine personhood *can* suffer. However, developing either of these responses would take us away from the proper focus of this present work, so we leave you more alerted than fully satisfied. You should know that some current Catholic theologians, such as David Tracy, look favorably on the effort to place suffering in God, and that it remains to be seen whether they can dispose of the problems this view causes and win the general agreement of their Catholic peers.[17]

SUMMARY

The liberationists' concern with a God who makes us free springs from the biblical perception of divinity. At the end of its conceptual chain, the biblical perception arrives at God our Creator. The hidden God, who makes all human pretensions relative and demands that we live by faith, makes everything to be by his "I am." We glimpse something of such divine creativity in our own best works—enough to lift our gaze to a comprehensive work produced by artful love. The specifically Christian variations on the being of God the Creator focus on the trinitarian processions. Developing scriptural hints, the early Church fathers clarified descriptions of Father, Son, and Spirit. Probably the most powerful tool that the tradition developed, however, was the psychological analogy that first Augustine, and then Aquinas, elaborated. Both of these giants worked with their own consciousness, appropriating the biblical and patristic doctrine that human beings are "images" of divinity.

For the psychological analogy, the Father is the fathomless divine understanding, the Son is the Father's expressive word, and the Spirit is the substantial love that proceeds from their mutuality. These glimmers are valid still, though today we must strip them of rationalistic overtones. To do so, the indications that Rahner and others have given of how the Trinity enters our own experience are enormously helpful, for they spotlight God's love and work on our behalf. Finally, from the Trinity's communal existence, we can better see our own communal calling, while from our own creaturehood and suffering we can ponder God's pure perfection.

STUDY QUESTIONS

1. Explain the relation between love and creativity.
2. In what sense is God's self-communication in grace the peak of the divine creativity?
3. How is God the Father like our memory?
4. How is God the Father like our understanding?
5. How is God the Son like a concept?
6. Explain the place of mind in the Christian view of the physical world.
7. Why does the mutual knowledge of the Father and the Son lead to their breathing forth the Spirit?
8. Give three examples of sweet reason that might hint at the presence of the Spirit.
9. How does persistently asking "Who am I?" lead one to God?
10. How does the Christian God offer us a model of community?

NOTES

1. See Samuel Terrien, *The Elusive Presence* (New York: Harper & Row, 1978).
2. Robert Pirsig, *Zen and the Art of Motorcycle Maintenance* (New York: Bantam, 1974).
3. See Thomas Merton, *The Way of Chuang Tzu* (New York: New Directions, 1965).
4. See E. F. Schumacher, *Good Work* (New York: Harper & Row, 1979).
5. See Karl Rahner, *Theological Investigations*, vol. 4 (Baltimore: Helicon, 1966), pp. 77–102.
6. See Bruno Snell, *The Discovery of Mind* (New York: Harper Torchbooks, 1960).
7. See, for example, Christine Downing, *The Goddess* (New York: Crossroad, 1981).
8. These limitations, however, should not be taken too narrowly. See Caroline Walker Bynum, *Jesus as Mother: Studies in the Spirituality of the High Middle Ages* (Berkeley: University of California Press, 1982).
9. See Bernard Lonergan, *Verbum: Word and Idea in Aquinas* (Notre Dame, Ind.: University of Notre Dame Press, 1967).
10. See John B. Cobb, Jr. and David Ray Griffin, *Process Theology: An Introductory Exposition* (Philadelphia: Westminster, 1976).
11. See Karl Rahner, *The Practice of Faith* (New York: Crossroad, 1983).
12. See John Carmody, "A Next Step for Roman Catholic Theology," *Theology Today* 32 (1976): 371–81.
13. See Raymond Panikkar, *The Intra-Religious Dialogue* (New York: Paulist, 1978).
14. See Dag Hammarskjöld, *Markings* (New York: Viking, 1964); Soren Kierkegaard, *Fear and Trembling* (Princeton, N.J.: Princeton University Press, 1941).
15. See Erik H. Erikson, *The Life Cycle Completed* (New York: W. W. Norton, 1982).
16. See Erik H. Erikson, *Gandhi's Truth* (New York: W. W. Norton, 1969).
17. See David Tracy, *The Analogical Imagination* (New York: Crossroad, 1981), pp. 439–40.

CHAPTER 5

Christian Realism

GRACE
SIN
SOBRIETY
FAITH, HOPE, LOVE

GRACE

"Grace" is the primary reason that Christianity is a gospel, a glad tidings. It puts into a single word the relationship that God has chosen to have with us. By ancient definition, grace means "favor." God grants us her favor—chooses to consider us children, friends, loved ones. Substantially, grace means divine life. It has not always meant this in Western Christian history, so let us begin our exposition with an Eastern Catholic theme. As developed by the Greek fathers, and modernized by Karl Rahner, it renders what we have said about the trinitarian God historical —"for us and for our salvation."

Early Eastern Christianity took from Greek philosophy and culture what we can only call an ontological bent. Ontology is the study of being —the effort to understand how things are, what reality is. It is the core of philosophy. In classical Greek times, philosophy—the love of wisdom —could be a whole way of life. Socrates, Plato, and Aristotle effectively made it a religion: a way to encounter ultimate reality.[1] Ontology, then, originally was a thing of passion and personal significance. It was not the arid "metaphysics" that later periods knew.

For Christians influenced by classical Greek culture, what God is like, how God exists, whether we participate in God's being were exciting, pregnant issues. Chroniclers report that there were brawls in barber shops over the difference between saying that the Logos is *like (homoi-ousios)* the Father and saying the Logos is the *same (homoousios)* as the Father. The difference was a single letter, a small Greek iota, but it had vast implications. Ultimately, it implied the difference between Nicene (orthodox) Christianity and **Arianism.** Since Arianism spread to the West and was powerful well into the sixth century, one iota marked a lot of history.

The temperament of the age of the Church councils such as Nicaea and Chalcedon was ontological (though also pastoral—concerned with how to live out the Christian faith) because most of the early doctrinal debates took place in the East. As a result, patristic Christianity (the early period dominated by the *patres* or fathers) came to think of grace as divinization. Building on such clues as 2 Peter 1:4, which speaks of our becoming "partakers of the divine nature," and on Johannine writings, which speak of our "abiding" with God (as branches with a vine), the fathers conceived of the life of faith as a participation in God's own life. Where the West, because of its Roman bent toward legalism, thought in terms of what we do, the East thought in terms of what we are. What we are in grace is participants in God's divine life. For the East the "new covenant" became an intrinsic transformation. When God writes the new covenant of grace on the fleshy tablets of our hearts, he wonderfully transforms us. Principally, he makes us immortal *(athanatos)*, because immortality is divinity's prime attribute. God simply is; God simply lives. Thus, the radical new creation that Paul proclaimed became in Greek minds a transformation of mortal human nature into divine deathlessness. As God resurrected Jesus into deathlessness, so God will resurrect the members of Jesus' "body." Grace—the faith-life we begin in baptism—stretches out to heaven, but it begins to make us deathless in time. The *arrabon* or downpayment of the Spirit was for Greeks exactly the beginning of immortality.

This may seem rather abstract speculation, but it merely shifts some concrete biblical motifs into a new key. For example, the relationship that the God of Hebrew religious experience established through Moses led to a pledge of sharing life through time. When Moses receives the divine name (Exod. 3:14), it turns out to be indefinite and future-oriented: "I am who I am—who I shall choose to be." In other words, the Hebrews will learn Yahweh's "nature" by living with him through time. He is not a god of natural seasons, not a god of sacred places; he is a God humans come to know through time. The covenant attempted to formalize this relationship somewhat, but of course it largely failed. Yahweh is the creator of all order. No little treaty can bind or constrain him. If he chooses to swear or not repent, to be faithful through all times, that is a form of his sovereign freedom. It never removes the need for Israel, his partner in the covenant, to find and follow him by faith. It never gives a contractual guarantee that removes the need for enduring his mystery. Only a distorting, idolatrous god could be so guaranteed.

Through the prophetic period, Israel struggled to learn this prime lesson. By the time of Isaiah (ca. 700 B.C.), it had become clear that for the majority the lesson was too hard. Only a remnant could bear the carte blanche that a living God demands. Only a small remainder had the heart and soul for deep faith. Christian experience has not been very different. Numerically, the fraction of Christians who have not run to laws, not hidden behind canons or indulgences or ritualistic prayers, has been rather small. The carte blanche of deep faith so coincides with profound humanity, with significant sanctity, that most of us do not keep giving it. In terms of the famous battle line that Dostoeveski drew in *The Brothers Karamazov*, we side against Christ, side with the Grand Inquisitor who wanted to trim faith down to human weakness. The price of Christ's freedom is stark (but joyous) faith. Not willing to pay this price, we let Grand Inquisitors, priests, theologians, neighbors—any "rescuer" we can find—give us tidy laws, tell us what to do. Thereby, we depreciate grace to something medicinal—make it God's syrup for our little cough.

Not so was grace for the great Eastern fathers. Not so is it for Karl Rahner. For them and him, grace is God's free love-life in us, the Trinity's processions taking up our minds and hearts. Technically, Rahner calls this state of affairs the "supernatural existential." Everywhere, by God's free choice, the Trinity offers human beings interpersonal communion. In place of the possibly impersonal relationship between a creator and a creature, the Trinity of persons has become for us as they are in themselves. Using Rahner's terms, we can say that the "immanent" Trinity is the "economic" Trinity. The immanent Trinity is God actively interrelating through the divine processions—God the personal community complete in itself. The economic Trinity is the God of the plan or dispensation that we humans indwell (the Greeks called this an *economia* or "order"). Just as an individual human person need not disclose his or her inner self, so God need not. God could have been for us only a somewhat objective, detached Creator, as we can be for other people only bosses, waiters, or token vendors. When we deal with other people that way, we show them but masks of our selves. On the other hand, when we open up, significant things can happen. God has "opened up" for us—made it possible for absolutely significant things to happen. If we but respond, we can participate in God's very own life.

How this actually occurs remains mysterious, as do all relations that open up and proceed heart to heart. But the biblical theme of sharing time prompts us to propose the analogy of a marriage. In a marriage, people try to open up, to live heart to heart, to share time, resources, bodies, selves—life itself. They are bonded, for better or worse, for richer or poorer. Ideally, their bonding increases their individuality. Though older spouses may look alike, may slurp their tea the same way, in good marriages each partner grows as an independent personality. Analogously, the relationship of grace does not collapse the self into God. It further advances the faith-truth that we find our real selves in the divine mystery. Perhaps Paul thought of this when he set the relation between Christ and the Church in marital imagery. Perhaps it was this that the mystics had in mind when they discussed the nuptials of the soul with God.

At any rate, the sharing of life that marriage seeks is precisely what substantial grace entails. God and those whom she graces enjoy a common enterprise. More and more, their interests flow together. The Spirit so purifies the human self that it increasingly says, "I must decrease, God must increase." The Spirit so convinces the human self of God's care that the self can pray confidently about any of its hopes or fears. This is an important lesson, which any who want to pray deeply and regularly have to learn. There is nothing that can separate us from the love of God in Christ Jesus (Rom. 8:39), so there is nothing we cannot bring to God in prayer. If God really shares our life and time, then our worries about a job, our hopes for a child, our pain from a separation—all these are common property between us and God. Those who pray regularly learn how to share common property with God. They learn how to change distractions into renewals of the love bond. Like Abraham, who haggled with God to try to save Sodom, they fight for causes they think right. Like Job, who accused God of injustice, they pour out their grievances. And like Jesus, who brought the Father his cup of sorrow, they finally say, "Thy will be done." For they want, in their best parts, to let God take care of their lives.

If the story of Christian salvation is credible, God's care of our lives is total. The Father numbers all the hairs of our heads. Therefore, like the lilies of the field, we shall prosper. Grace is the depth of this sort of confidence. It shows its presence in a holy abandon. The end of our lives, our sort of "prosperity," like the bottom of our selves, passes out of sight. No worry of ours can change it a cubit. We all have finally to rely on God's goodness, whether we like it or not. We all have finally to trust that we shall breathe tomorrow. Gracious Christian living makes this necessity an occasion of gratitude. It thanks God for the light of its eyes, for the air it breathes. The **Eucharist** is precisely the primary Christian focus of such thanksgiving. Remembering Jesus, each Eucharist expresses heartfelt thanks and praise.

In the next section, when we consider sin, we shall deal with the problematic patches that mar such a gracious scenario. Here, though, the accent is wholly positive. And the accent here is finally more important than any nuances that our reflection on sin may force. For the Catholic tradition takes deeply to heart Paul's conviction that where sin abounded grace has abounded more. There is no equality between the sin of the world and the grace of God. There is no question which is the victor. The light shone in the darkness and the darkness did not overcome it. The weakness tempted each heart but all hearts felt help for salvation. God, then, is a God on whom we can rely. However obscurely, the God of Jesus does only good work, operates only from love. Christian religion is as simple and as difficult as believing that. Its God is not too strange to be believed but too good. Again and again, our cowardice, our small-souledness, causes us to doubt God's goodness. We cannot believe God is generous to those who come at the eleventh hour, as well as to those who work the full day, because we would not be so generous. We cannot believe God is a prodigal father, rushing out to welcome back his churlish son, because we would not be. As Paul Ricoeur recently has shown, the logic of God is for us "excessive."[2] God is so much more gracious than we that we balk at believing in him.

The core meaning of grace, then, is sharing God's life. Western Christianity, however, has also discussed God's "operational" favor. That is, the West has underscored the fact that the Spirit helps us respond to opportunities and overcome temptations. Perhaps the simplest way to correlate this activity-oriented view of the West with the ontological view of the East is to emphasize the fairly obvious truth that an inert divine life would be both a contradiction in terms and a treasure little worth participating in. If divinity really does draw us into its life, the new sharing that that produces has to influence our behavior. When we are responsive, it soon produces a new horizon that orients everything differently. The "change of mind" that the New Testament calls *metanoia* is just such a new horizon. When we translate *metanoia* into "conversion," we ought to mean a restructuring of basic orientations. The dialectic (back and forth relation) between sin and grace that Paul describes depends on a conversion to the "mind," the horizon of Christ. Those who have entered the new, gracious life of Christ have a whole change of horizon. Whereas in the past their sinful minds could focus on little besides themselves, in the newness of their commitment to Christ they open themselves to a God of pure love. Whereas in the past they viewed their neighbors competitively, as opponents in a race after one small pie, in the present the Spirit lures them to love their neighbors as themselves. Paul's famous hymn to charity (1 Cor. 13) shows what this love looks like, as his contrast of "flesh" and "spirit" (Gal. 5) dramatizes the differences between a sinful mind and a mind of grace.

We shall see more of the mind of grace below, when we consider the theological virtues (faith, hope, and charity). For this first description, however, we can conclude by stressing gratitude. Grace above all produces gratitude. In the summer of 1976, for example, the United States put aside briefly its squabbles and greedy business-as-usual to celebrate its bicentennial. Against the backdrop of Watergate, which massively portrayed a sinful mind, July 4, 1976 was a day of grace. We watched this celebration from a far distance, in a hotel room in Hong Kong. When the regal clipper ships moved in stately order up the Hudson River, the tawdry junks of the past months withdrew to the mind's sidestreams. It was the one day of a six-month tour around the world when we were absolutely sure God blessed America.

SIN

Our description of grace has focused on the way that faith says things are between us and God. It has tried to report the traditional radicalness Catholic theology has seen in Jesus' eschatological (definitive) salvation. Were we human beings generously to open ourselves to God's gracious self-offer, the world would shine as a global sacrament. In this section we have to deal with the way things are in a different sense. Without subtracting anything of the radical transformation that Jesus' salvation has accomplished, we have to deal with the human frustrations of God's tremendous offer—with the absurd self-frustration traditionally called "sin." So doing, we complicate somewhat the view of human nature developed thus far. Thus far, we have been stressing how human beings come from a good Creator and are offered rich shares in the Trinity's inner life. Thus far, we have been opposing any doctrine of human depravity. Such an opposition became rather dogmatic for the Catholic tradition at the Council of Trent (1545–1563), where the Roman church reacted to what it considered abuses of the Protestant reformers. From the mid-sixteenth to the mid-twentieth century, Trent dominated Roman Catholic religion. Through that period, Catholic theology tried to maintain a view of human nature that was moderate or median. It wanted to be to the left of pessimistic views, which saw human nature as corrupt to the core. It wanted to be to the right of humanists who thought the whole notion of sin ridiculous. Catholic theology often failed to hit its graceful mean, especially concerning sexuality, but on the whole the balanced goal it sought is something of which it may be proud.

The doctrine of human depravity proves itself false *pragmatically.* Live by it and you will increase, not decrease, the fund of human woe. Stereotypically, the doctrine of human depravity is associated with the Calvinist wing of the Protestant Reformation. Closer to the stereotypic Catholic view is Luther's *simul jusus et peccator.* In this phrase ("at once just and a sinner") Luther encapsuled his twofold sense that: (a) human beings have been the recipients of a "justification" (being made right with God) that they can make their own if they open their hearts wide in faith; and (b) that this justification does not remove the daily need to recognize and confess one's distance from the all-holy God. Catholics can and should repeat most of this, for it is both an acute observation of human behavior and close to the biblical texts. But the ontological view of grace that we stressed in the preceding section leaves the overall Catholic position with a different nuance.

The great influences on Luther were Paul and Augustine, both of whom had a somewhat moralistic or operational (action-oriented) bent. The Johannine writings and the Greek fathers have been the sources for a recent Catholic desire to go beyond moralism to the new being that grace implies. Since such a new being is more substantial than moralistic changes could be, it gives a clear rationale for a Catholic desire to avoid the notion that grace is only "imputed" (entered in our account book) to us because of Christ's merits. Luther's writings encourage that notion. By contrast, a Catholic theology of grace that knows what it is doing makes the Holy Spirit a true renovator of human beings. Therefore, when Catholics repeat the formula "at once just and a sinner," they should make it clear that the formula does not mean schizophrenia. The "justice" that the Spirit gives is the good being that God sees and loves in our cores. The sin that we all too evidently manifest is merely our unwillingness to let the Spirit invade us totally, merely our unwillingness to love.

This leads to the hypothesis that sin principally is lovelessness. Lovelessness often shows itself as a prejudicial sourness that can abort colleagueship. A group can never become a circle of fellow workers, let alone a circle of friends, if a majority hold back from the fair dealing and good will that collaboration and friendship demand. Tuck away in your mind's side corridor, then, the notion that sin often shows itself as a lack of **community.** Socially, it is at work in the disorder, the fractiousness, the antagonism of people who refuse to cooperate. One advantage of this reading is that it links up nicely with traditional reflections on evil. For a line of Catholic thought that goes back at least as far as Augustine sees evil as the privation of good—the lack of an order, being, or value that ought to exist. Sin essentially is moral evil—evil that we choose. Contrasted with such natural evils as earthquakes or cancers, it lodges in human responsibility. Socially, then, much of our sin is a culpable privation of good. We refuse to go out to others in the love that would bring community, cooperation, justice, and mutual support. We refuse to be humane as we ought to be.

It is hard to develop all this as systematically as we would wish, because an understanding of sin is more a ramification and appreciation of how lovelessness branches out in all directions than it is a tidy deduction. Before we go very far, however, we want to make sure that the previous discussion of stereotypically Calvinist, Lutheran, and Catholic attitudes toward human nature does not leave a false impression. In actuality, individual members of those traditions very often "cross lines." For instance, one of the most loving, community-building couples we know have solid roots in the Calvinist tradition. Their home is a powerhouse of good will. By contrast, we have sat in Catholic educational committees that effectively viewed students as weak and depraved. For example, we once heard a prominent Catholic scholar deliver two jolting observations on education. First, he had suffered considerably in his own education, so he saw no reason why his students should find learning a thing of joy. Second, in his mind's eye the degree process was like entering a large room through a small door, being soundly beaten as one crawled along, and then exiting through a larger door at the far end. This from a distinguished heir of the "optimistic" Catholic view of human nature.

Such attitudes develop neither education nor community nor joy. Rather, old cycles of lovelessness keep returning. That is sin's most depressing side. Our fathers ate sour grapes, so we sons and daughters have our teeth on edge. Perhaps this is the most basic significance of "original" sin. It is not the tendency of current Catholic theologians to take the story of Adam and Eve literally. That story, in all the likelihood that literary and historical analyses can muster, is a subtle myth. As recent studies of human consciousness have amply shown, "myth" need not be a term of contempt. In this case, it simply says that a reflection on the human condition assumed the form of a story. The Genesis writers wanted to say that our human disorder is aboriginal. It goes back to any first "parent," any **corporate personality**, we can imagine. From the beginning, human beings have been unable to keep sensual appetite under the control of reason. From the beginning we have been "concupiscent": divided, attracted by false gods. We have had to struggle to obey the light of God in our consciences, the promptings toward honesty and love. We have botched our relations with nature and our sexual relations as men and women. Like Adam, we all tend to foist responsibility off on Eve. Like Eve, we all tend to foist responsibility off on agents outside us. The result is suffering—a painful life outside the garden, outside intimacy with nature and God.

Original sin, thus, is something we all share. We all live, move, and have our being within it.[3] Institutionalized, it erodes our money and banking. Given a code, it criminalizes our law. The Chinese sage Lao Tzu wanted to abolish all law, because he thought it made people criminals. Lao Tzu had glimpsed something of original sin. The average person of good will who confronts a tax form, or an insurance policy, or a contract to write a book finds Lao Tzu's intuition welling up again. He or she knows instinctively that what should be simple and straightforward has become complicated and twisted for bad reasons. Those who praise our American legal system, arguing that at least it gives some protection against pure might and greed, miss the point of this theological argument. The very fact that pure might and greed are rampant possibilities shows that we are a species disordered through and through. Our wars, our economies, our politics, our religions repeat one sorry story. None of them expresses a humanity fully pure, loving, honest, or good. None of them can stand confidently before Jesus or his God.

And, of course, we participate in these institutions, we benefit from some of their abuses, and often we promote their disorders. White-collar crime, for instance, goes along with a nearly standard, accepted tendency to gouge or cheat. Commonplace adultery goes along with a nearly universal tendency to seize a bit more gusto. Money is the root of a hundred political disorders. Power drives all sorts of people crazy. We all know these nearly banal truths because they deface our own apartments. In our own neighborhood block, sin has cracked many a foundation. More precisely, most of us also know sin because we ourselves more than once have done wrong. Some way or other, *we* have cut corners: stolen, cheated, been unfaithful, ridden roughshod because of our ego. Even the apostle Paul moaned about the good that he should have done and did not, the evil that he should not have done and did. Sin, therefore, is the dreary business of the ever-grimy conscience. It is the heavy weight of being without the peace of God.

Even great saints have regularly denounced themselves as sinners, which shows that sin has layer upon layer. Those who find no gross evil on their conscience will learn, if they reflect more carefully, that their motivation regularly is impure. Pleasure in another's downfall, joy in a cutting word—most of us collect many such ugly little toads. The way we expand when someone flatters us, or the way we flatter others is similarly toady. Christian moralism of the past had little difficulty compiling lists of such deficiencies. As Diaz-Plaja has shown in the case of the Spanish, the capital sins can even illumine a national character.[4] But moralism bakes little bread for the massive hunger we suffer. The root of our sin is our failure to love. Socially, we need only love God with our whole mind, heart, soul, and strength, and love our neighbors as ourselves, to have a holy community. Individually, we need only fulfill this great commandment to have the substance of human prosperity. The size of our income, the height of our social status—they are unimportant. Were the great commandment to love God and neighbor our common law, we would find all our times precious, all our gifts things to be shared.

"Sin," then, is a many-sided symbol for the fracture of humanity we suffer. It comes not from our finitude, not from our creatureliness, but from our freely chosen failure to love. Insofar as it means fixating on idols rather than on the living God, sin is irreligion. Insofar as it means profiting from the disadvantages, or even the sufferings of others, sin is deep injustice. But the constant in all instances of sin is our closing up to God or neighbor. Where love would keep us open, would insist that we try to see and help, sin narrows us to the moment—the moment of pleasure, the moment of profit, the moment of "couldn't care less." The percentage of human suffering that comes from our closure is depressingly high. Most starvation and despair depend on human sin. Sin, therefore, is the deepest core of the slavery from which we beg liberation. Christ the Liberator, therefore, is Christ the Savior from sin.

SOBRIETY

When we traveled the heights of the traditional understanding of Jesus, we glimpsed wonders and splendors. Jesus shows God to be better than we could ever conceive. But when we turned to the concrete human condition, the splendor gave way to deep darkness. From the gross sins of recent history (the massacres of Jews and Armenians, the torture chambers of a dozen dictatorships, the genocidal madnesses of Cambodia and Uganda) to the petty selfishness we all know, sin snatches away our joy. A mother who watches her child take its first steps on a ghetto street can rejoice only if she refuses to imagine the child's realistic future. An Oriental mother who watches her Eurasian child has even less joy: simply for having a half-Western face, the child can have no warm place in Vietnam, Korea, or Japan. At home, black people remind us all of our deeply sinful national history. Red people do the same. American Orientals tell of detention during World War II. Chicanos tell of the sinful way we get our lettuce and grapes. Look carefully at any patch of American society, or of global society, then, and you will turn quite sober. It takes great faith to believe that sin has not abounded more than grace.

As we mentioned in the beginning, sobriety is a hallmark of Karl Rahner's theology. Though he yields to no contemporary in his penetration of God's worldwide grace, Rahner is not your neighborhood consoler. He broods over the scene he surveys, and one often catches a groan. Realistically, judged on their performances, human beings are a trying lot. In the Church, which is Rahner's most immediate society, human stupidity and lovelessness make religion repulsive to millions. In the recent history of his German nation, there is guilt for many lifetimes. The grace of God, come into our midst, meets terrible forces of resistance. Again and again, so many flee the light, because their deeds are evil, that the sun of justice seems beclouded. Reflecting on all this, Rahner's general outlook is very sober.

It is important for us to explain this sobriety very carefully, because the practical attitude that one's view of grace and sin generates determines much of how one ventures into the world. We want "sobriety" to suggest neither a prejudice that human nature is vitiated by sin nor a grim-faced lack of joy. Rather, we want it to suggest that the Catholic Christian view of human nature urges us to be serious. There is a time to play, as well as a time to be serious, and it is a mark of maturity to discern which time has come. For the moment, let us concentrate on the time to be serious. It seems to suit the situation in our country and the Church as they head into the end of the twentieth century. In our country, the century's ninth decade had found much talk about a new cold war, nuclear arms, malnutrition, and a new registration of young men and women for military draft. In the Church a conservative backlash is well under way. These are calls to be sober, judicious, a careful discerner of signs of the times. These are times when nuclear devastation has started to take hold of many imaginations, when making peace has become the great moral imperative.

Perhaps three "situational" descriptions can make this matter of sobriety clearer. Consider, for instance, the situation of a person who specializes in peace studies. If he or she is working from an explicitly Christian viewpoint, it is likely to be either that of one of the traditionally pacifistic churches, such as the Mennonite, or of a fairly radical branch of a main-stream tradition, such as that of the Catholic Workers. Whatever the particular tradition, however, the Christian involved in peace studies finds the inertia of most public policy very discouraging. Concerning Latin America and the Middle East, politicians have shown little sign that they have learned anything from the failures in Vietnam and Iran. In Iran, for instance, the entire thrust of the United States government's initial reaction was to lay down a hard line. One heard virtually nothing about the abuses of the Shah's regime, virtually nothing about America's role in supporting it. There was no creative effort to plan a scenario that would allow the aggrieved Iranians a platform, no empathetic realization that they most desired a forum in which to present to the world their evidences of the Shah's wrongdoings. As a result, the situation stale-mated. Like kids in a schoolyard, each side sneered and jeered. By the time the mess was cleared up the Shi'ite Muslim clergy was in a position to unleash "holy war" wherever their craziness suggested.

The person working in peace studies will be hard put not to view Iran sadly. It clearly seems just another instance of deploying bankrupt, basi-cally dishonest policies. The fact is the United States did prop an inhu-mane regime in Iran, as it has propped inhumane regimes in many other countries. This fact did not, however, justify the illegal and cruel way that the Iranian students held Americans hostage, let alone the later excesses of Khomeini. It was not a wrong that justified another wrong. But it was such a basic ingredient in the snarled conflict that not to acknowledge it openly, not to provide for its obvious psychological force, was to choose a scenario condemned to failure from the outset. It was to choose illusion, dishonesty, and bad faith. Since this has happened in country after coun-try, writing a too solid portion of our nation's recent diplomatic history, it reveals a systematic wrongheadedness. There is a light "out there" in the facts of international history that American leaders have been fleeing. If the Bible still bears us practical insight, they have been fleeing such a light because their deeds have been evil. One can, indeed must, hope to convert the doers of evil deeds, the avoiders of truth's light, from their sinful ways, but when the sinful scenario has become operative policy such hope must be rather modest. Trying to bring a country such as ours from chauvinistic self-serving to a foreign policy consonant with God's truth is not a work for those of short stamina. It is a missionary trek bound to be a long haul.

A second situation that tempers one's Christian judgment to sobriety is that of minority groups such as American blacks. They have enough history in hand at the present to be as unoptimistic as people in peace studies. For close to twenty-five years, the American majority has had highly visible lessons in the breadth and depth of its racism. Even when one criticizes the stridency of some antiracist leaders, and acknowledges the complexity of some of the economics involved, a very sober estimate of the American will to change, will to do justice, must emerge. If black youth are presently the nation's most underemployed, with statistics in some areas reaching to better than fifty percent joblessness, there is no rosy future for a group who have had a dismal past. Black leaders therefore must fight heroically to keep rage and despair from taking away their peace or determination. Like people in peace studies, they have to remember that their battle will be a very long haul. They may decide that white America collectively has an unreachable conscience, and so content themselves with very pragmatic, politico-economic strategies. They may realize that they have to work as hard on black pride as on black economics, if they are not to lose the present generations to despair. But whatever their strategies or realizations, they must realistically expect only to make haste slowly. The white majority profits too much from the present arrangements for any but a deeply believing, saintly few to make sizeable changes readily. The American majority is neither deeply believing nor saintly, so any progress (and there has been some) is well worth treasuring.

We shall move into a third, smaller-scale situation momentarily, but before leaving these first two larger-scale situations we must note another reason for sobriety. It is difficult in the present climate of American opinion even to offer such critical analyses as these. In the eyes of some citizens, all criticism is unpatriotic. For sober theology, however, Americans are neither the best nor the brightest. We are just what our fruits show, and our fruits have been very mixed. It is not national pride, not falsely building the country up, that will set us free but truth-telling. It is not supposed tearing the country down that is our inner worm but lying and injustice.

Like large-scale situations, such as international conflicts, widespread racism, or widespread sexism, domestic difficulties also inculcate sobriety. Consider, for instance, the couple midway between happiness and divorce. In a representative script, they have been married eight years, have two children, and are in deep conflict. His great passion is his work, which more evenings than not keeps him out until eight or nine. Her energies are more dispersed, for she has the kids, the house, and a part-time job. She has the part-time job partly to keep her brain alive, partly because they need the money.

Unhappy with this state of affairs, the wife initiates a series of investigative hearings. Both researcher and prosecutor, she compiles briefs for a change. They ought to change their outlay of money, for they are getting deeper and deeper into debt. They ought to change their outlay of time, for they are growing farther and farther apart. Above all, they ought to change from the presently unjust distribution of housekeeping and child-rearing, for it is driving her crazy. Accused, the husband's first response is confusion. He knew that things had been rather hectic, but doesn't everyone in suburbia live that way?

The move beyond confusion, to action or nonaction, is where the couple come into crisis. As the husband decides to respond, so will their marriage go. Should he open himself to the light, accepting the validity of his wife's charges, their marriage can move to a new and deeper plane. Should he close himself to the light, refusing to discuss their problems, or to get counseling, or seriously to change his ways, their marriage is on the rocks. Look at the statistics in which marriages such as these now swim, and you will not be optimistic about the couple's prospects. Both parties, but especially the one who most offends justice, will have to be converted, if the marriage is to regain life or momentum, and conversion is a sobering matter.

Marital conversion usually goes hand in hand with mutual forgiveness. Trying to forget the shabby past, the partners pledge themselves to a new beginning. The effective solution to larger-scale situations, such as the racism and international standoff we described, equally entails conversion and forgiveness. That these terms are embarrassingly unusual for those contexts is a first sign of how disordered the situations are. Soberingly, most countries of the world have gotten into the rut of doing business irreligiously. They may prate about "Christian" or "Muslim" values, if these adjectives seem good propaganda, but they make sure that the serious ethical programs implied in the Bible or the Koran stay far from their boardrooms of power. Both the Bible and the Koran paint a God who renders harsh judgment on human injustice. Both envision a social ideal of almsgiving and compassion. The Bible probably is clearer on conversion and forgiveness, but each Koranic *surah* begins, "In the name of Allah, the compassionate, the merciful." All of this directly opposes the ordinary rules of the Middle Eastern game.

For Bernard Lonergan, the inability of human beings to sustain social progress is a primary revelation of our need for salvation. The injustice we hand down, generation after generation, shows how sin has become our social contagion. To reverse this state of affairs, the Christian God introduced a new order of redemption. He would redeem those enslaved by injustice with a new law of the cross. On the cross, Jesus suffered the expectable results for contesting an old regime of Satanic powers. He broke that regime, resurrecting to new possibilities, by suffering evil in love. The sober facts of the current human situation, as Christian theology comprehends them, lead to but one sure conclusion. We have not accepted Jesus' modeling of God's new law, have not been willing to suffer the price of genuine prosperity. Our situation is just as stark as that. Until we do effectively suffer evil in love, things will change very little.

FAITH, HOPE, LOVE

But surely suffering evil in love, living by the law of the cross, is an unrealistic solution? Surely a sober appraisal of the way out of our basic human dilemma cannot demand a superhuman generosity? At the heart of these questions, one glimpses the depths of the Catholic theology of grace. The power to suffer evil in love is nothing less than God's own life. No one less than God's child possesses such power. The *agape* of God which overcomes sin and death, the *agape* of God from which nothing can separate us—this is thoroughly divine. History finally, and wryly, reveals that to be human we have to be more than human. To overturn the contagious ruination of humanity into which each generation is thrown, there must be the incarnation of a divine love that recreates humanity from ruination's void.

In the previous sections, we spent sufficient time on the theme of grace as divinization to be able to say now that it is the ontological view that best meets the void of the problems of human sin. "Create in me a clean heart, O God, and put a new and right spirit within me," the Psalmist begged (51:10). Grace is God's ontological response to such a petition. It is the new creation that the old, ravaged order begs by its disorder. Here, however, we want to consider the "virtues" (powers) through which this new creation has traditionally been thought to work. Faith, hope, and love are the "theological" virtues because they most directly translate divine life into human strengths.

There is no completely adequate distinction of faith, hope, and love, for they interweave inextricably. Faith names the basic attitude of committing oneself to a mysterious God, hope names the attitude of living trustingly toward the future, and love names the warm creativity that is at core divine. Modern thought has tended to separate faith from knowledge, but that does violence to both biblical thought and any shrewd observation. Our commitments color more than a little of our knowledge. The basic options we make dictate a great deal of what we "see." A good example of this is the usually rather fruitless antagonism between doctrinaire atheism and doctrinaire theism. Where doctrinaire atheism sees in nature a terrible waste and disorder, doctrinaire theism argues that God is manifest in nature's overwhelming design. Where doctrinaire atheism assumes that "God" is a tool of exploitative upper classes, doctrinaire theism finds God to be the poor's one sure consolation. The data that the two sides use are supposedly the same. Each has equal access to evolutionary history, to economic history, to the sociology of Appalachia or Harlem. Yet they conclude at diametrically opposite evaluations—because they are primed to see goodness, or its lack.

Doctrinaire positions on just about anything tend to be unexperiential and uncritical. Where people discourse on God from experience, and try to make all their assertions gravely, they find little surety. Nature, for instance, is both ordered (otherwise we could not understand it) and prodigally wasteful (most species run to extinction). Human beings are both so exploitative and so surprisingly good that they keep God an ever indecisive inference. To live sanely in the midst of such a situation, one

has either to believe or be atheistic rather carefully. The existential difference between careful belief and careful atheism can be very slight. Accepting the finality of mystery, both open the heart and wait.

For Catholic Christianity, faith has too often been an unmysterious
matter of assenting to propositions. By and large, Protestant theology has
done better at rendering the solid gravity of biblical faith. There one finds
interpersonal commitment. There God is one's rock and salvation, one's
defense against fear. Like a friend walking with a friend, the biblical
person of faith trudges along with God. Thereby, mystery becomes familiar. If strange nights occur, when one has to wrestle with angels, or
strange demands occur, like Abraham's need to sacrifice his son, they are
exceptional testings. Ordinarily, life itself is faith's testing. Sufficient for
most days is the evil thereof. God is so suprasensible, and fellow human
beings can be so unattractive, that one only fulfills the twofold command
of loving God and neighbor by leaping beyond "evidence." Suffering is
so omnipresent, and the human heart is so deeply demanding, that assenting to propositions works little salvation.

Consider the situations we used above to establish a mood of sobriety.
To believe that God cares for situations such as the Iranian standoff, or
the racism that afflicts American blacks, or a shaky suburban marriage,
one has to come to grips with human waywardness and divine mystery
quite comprehensively. If we try to deal with such situations glibly,
whether in supposed faith or supposed unbelief, they come back to slash
us. God's "care" is sometimes as far from our expectations as the heavens
are above the earth. God's "will" is sometimes as contrary to our desires
as the will of an enemy would be. It is only at the bedrock, the level of
fundamental options, that faith has any stability. It is only when we come
in sight of a carte blanche, a blank check, that we are not likely to be swept
away. "Though he slay me, yet will I trust him," Job was made to say.
"Thy kingdom come, they will be done," Jesus wrote on his check. Moving from the mystery of life and goodness, faith finds a commission of
self, an abandon of self, that takes it across the mystery of death and evil.
Accepting its need for sense and love as its defining vocation, the religious self finds the strength to say that nonsense and hatred are not the
last word. Then, after living with such dispositions for a while, it finds
them experientially solid, known to be true because they have borne a
life's weight. They lead to ways of regarding the world, ways of regarding
fellow humans, that bring out the image of God.

Implied in this description is a pragmatic test: faith should make life
good, make people happy. Employing this test, Catholic novelists have
exposed many of faith's misuses. A line of literary critique runs from
Ireland to the United States, carrying the judgments of authors such as
James Joyce, Brian Moore, and Mary Gordon that Catholic faith easily can
rob people of their joy. *Final Payments*, [5] Mary Gordon's penetrating story
of a young woman trying to break the grip of her father's fiercely conserv-

ative Catholicism, sets the robbery thesis smack in the middle of feminist liberation. The heroine, Isabel Moore, spent the flower of her young adulthood caring for her invalid father. She was cut off from the normal maturation that her friends underwent, buoyed up only by the "status" her sacrifices gave her in the myth-minded circle of her Irish-Catholic neighborhood. But she herself never believed the pieties and world-hatings that fed the religion of the parish biddies. Nor did she accept the harsh, self-righteous, intellectualist faith of her professorial father. When she was set free into the world of her secularist peers by the death of her father, she started a dizzy roller coaster ride from snatching greedily at sexual pleasure to suffering fits of self-laceration. Her dilemma became classic: should she follow her hunger for pleasure, beauty, a happy life, or should she strive for the "real" satisfaction that comes from self-denial and a good reputation?

Gordon's intelligence and skill are such that each horn of the dilemma shows itself hollow. The "simple" life of pleasure and refinement does not stand up for long, for it leads to injuring others—in this case, by adultery. The apparently more simple life of self-sacrifice collapses equally: easily does it cover petty-mindedness, whining, pride, and stupidity. Before the reader's eyes, Isabel Moore acts out the profound battles involved in coming to a mature faith. For a mature faith is neither dehumanizing nor compatible with secular standards of "the good life." It says yes to the heart's longings for beauty and decent pleasure, no to the spirit's perverse ability to canonize inferiority and warp the heart's good longings. Ultimately, mature faith fights through to a God unco-opted by churchy religion, a love of neighbor unco-opted by "morality." It finds Christ's cross not where it chooses to declare the self a martyr but where daily life calls for integrity. It finds God's incarnation lovely—in sex, art, and friendship—without losing sight of the times when all mortal flesh must keep silent, all things passing are made relative. One can only achieve such a balance in the Spirit. Mature faith is a function of an intense human effort that keeps giving itself over to grace.

In our opinion, then, mature Catholic faith says yes to the heart's spontaneous desires. It affirms that we have a vocation to develop, create, and take decent pleasure. The only warning it puts before this affirmation is that we be honestly willing to see our vocation through. When it comes time to develop by refusing tawdry advancement or pleasure, will we take the next hard negative step? When it comes time to purify our creative talent by discipline, revision, greater honesty, will we make greater demands on ourselves? And when pleasure starts to get out of focus, to take us from more important things or to injure others, will we deny ourselves and let it go? These are test questions by which we can evaluate our faith's maturity. They concretize the Catholic view that human nature is not intrinsically depraved, while maintaining the sobriety about human waywardness that a hard look at human performance entails. With ourselves, as with other people, our first instinct should be cooperative. We should give our desires to enjoy the beach, or a good meal, or an attractive other person the benefit of the doubt. That way, we keep our desires from convoluting or festering inside. But we should also have the honesty and good humor to see how easily these desires try to take over the whole play. As we refuse to be foolish about others, to deny the facts when they abuse the benefit of the doubt, so we must refuse to be foolish about ourselves, not deny that we too easily lose balance.

Mingled with such a striving after mature, poised faith are strivings for a hope and a love that equally are gifts of the Spirit. We have to hope that some day we will grow mature, some day our desires will come to good fruition and balance. We have to love the selves we have been given, to show compassion toward our own weaknesses and encourage our own strengths. So too with the way we regard other people and nature. We have to hope that other people also will grow, and we have to help love free their good desires. If, for example, we know a colleague who is overly concerned about money, always complaining that she gets less than her fair share, the prompting of the Spirit in us is not the one that reads her attitude as a case of petit bourgeois envy. The woman *is* unattractively grasping, *does* burden you by her envy at others' success. But the Spirit inclines you to remember the signs of self-doubt she gives off, the evidences you have that something is difficult, her marital life, perhaps. What she does not need right now is another judgmental response that forces her to confront her demons ruthlessly. That is too much for her at the moment. Rather she needs a sort of tolerance and indirect help that will get her ready for such a ruthless confrontation in the future. She needs a minor-league "suffering evil in love" that will briefly interrupt her vicious circles.

You can imagine the larger-scale elaborations of hope and love that might bring antibodies to the international war zones or scenes of national injustice. Hope and love regularly are the medicine most needed. What does little to cure any of the cancers at work in such places is a legalistic or punishing hard line. Soberly, one has to propose generous, self-sacrificing moves that both honor the truth of the situation and advance it toward a greater justice. One has to hope that forgiveness and new beginnings are possible, to love the smallest sign of good will that any party shows. This is terribly difficult work, complicated in most cases because one has to sell it to one's allies as much as to one's enemies. It is the sort of positive, simple effort to live out Christian precepts that easily brings derision.

Those who deride the bearer of hope and love often do so in the name of realism. It is unrealistic, they say, to speak of forgiveness, or of doing business in the light of full disclosure. People will take advantage of you. They will consider you weak and ram your good will down your throat. Both analytically and historically, the deriders have a weak case. Analytically, it is clear that all possibility of human community, and therefore of significant prosperity, goes out the door when: (a) one has no mechanism for getting out of bitter antagonism; and (b) one cannot expect fair, honest dealing. Without forgiveness and honesty, interactions are warped from the outset. Historically, the wars and rumors of war that dominate the human story reveal a substructure of injuries unforgiven and trust continually destroyed. More positively, the few theoreticians of the human condition who have gained widespread respect—Plato, Confucius, Moses, Buddha, Aristotle, Jesus, Lao Tzu and their like—have all been champions of humane treatment. From recent times, the signal figure who brought faith, hope, and love to programmatic political success was Mohandas Gandhi. His commitment was to *satyagraha*—the force of truth. Shrewdly, Gandhi developed tactics of arbitration that encouraged all adversaries to submit their positions to the light. Martin Luther King, Jr. and Cesar Chavez are the American "politicians" who most explicitly have continued Gandhi's tradition. When the theological history of recent politics is written, they are likely to be the "statesmen" who prevail, the ones who leave some legacy worth emulating.

Realistically, then, Christian life commits one to considerable eccentricity and suffering. Realistically, human performance makes it imperative to *believe* that grace is stronger than sin. Soberly, one has to learn how to combine positive initiatives with frank postmortems—how to be open and encouraging without getting destroyed. If one knows what true "prosperity" entails, the temptations to cheat for passing advantage will grow less and less attractive. If one knows what sort of politics usually brings popular prestige, less and less will one aspire to high status. Realistically, openness to God and intimacy with friends are treasures far less corruptible. Realistically, they teach the lessons we most need. We need to know, solidly and unswervingly, that life is good enough to carry us through suffering. We need to know that God holds all time in her hand. We can only know these things if we experience the Spirit poured forth in our hearts. We can only know them if we venture to walk with a real, mysterious God in faith, hope, and love. When the mysterious God becomes not a figment of our wish-fulfillment but a daily assumption, a habit like eating and breathing, we shall begin to be realistic as the best products of the Catholic tradition have been.

SUMMARY

The Christian doctrine of God determines much in a "realistic" Christian outlook, but a partner to this outlook is the Christian doctrine of human nature. How do "grace" and "sin" concretely shape this humanity we carry? What are the primary denotations and overtones these significant words ought to carry? Grace primarily denotes something ontological— the divine being that God desires to share. More substantial than any behavioral implications is the love-life, the *agape* grace imparts. By contrast, sin is the lovelessness by which we fail the demands of our humanity. It is our closure to God, our refusal to respond. All too concretely, we see this closure at work internationally, in our national injustices, and in more restricted personal zones. But the Catholic view of human nature, of grace and sin in the concrete, saves the core of the human person from depravity. It is not the way of the Catholic tradition first to suspect and distrust.

On the other hand, Catholics have their own share in the Lutheran doctrine of *simul justus et peccator*—simultaneously both just and a sinner. Whoever does not distort the facts of human performance knows many *peccatores.* A certain sobriety therefore hangs over Catholic estimates of the human condition. It is not the way of this tradition to be optimistic, but rather to hope. For hope, like faith and love, is a precisely theological virtue. It is strength to anticipate a good future from God. The Spirit alone gives this strength, at the deep level where sin would discourage us, as the Spirit alone makes us continue to believe and love. Ultimately, then, the humanity we seek is a more than human venture. Ultimately we owe our selves, as our hopes, to the goodness of God.

STUDY QUESTIONS

1. What do we mean by "the carte blanche of deep faith"?
2. How does grace relate us to the "inside" of God?
3. Give an example of deep, serious sin and analyze this example in terms of lovelessness.
4. Why are peace studies likely to make one sober?
5. What would be a balanced, sober view of race-relations?
6. Explain the statement: "Faith names the basic attitude of committing oneself to a mysterious God."
7. Explain the statement: "Love names the warm creativity that is at core divine."

NOTES

1. See Eric Voegelin, *Order and History,* vol. 3 (Baton Rouge, La.: Louisiana State University Press, 1957).
2. See Paul Ricoeur, "The Logic of Jesus, the Logic of God," *Christianity and Crisis* 39:20 (December 24, 1979): 324–27.
3. For a profound view of sin and God's ways of restoring the "exchange" that sin breaks, see Rosemary Haughton, *The Passionate God* (New York: Paulist, 1981).
4. See Fernando Diaz-Plaja, *El Español y Los Siete Pecados Capitales* (Madrid: Alianza Editorial, 1966).
5. Mary Gordon, *Final Payments* (New York: Random House, 1978).

CHAPTER 6

The Christian Community

THE COMMUNITY OF JESUS

As we noted in our first chapter, the Catholic church currently presents an ambiguous appearance. On the one hand, it remains an institution of immense size and significance. On the other hand, many of its faithful, especially in Europe and the United States, question its vitality and relevance. In order to get a contemporary theology of the Church clearly in sight, we have to try to retrieve its original conception, the community that Jesus himself likely had in mind.

Jesus preached the Kingdom of God. The focus of his teaching and healing was the new reign of divine power he saw dawning. Realizing this, recent New Testament scholarship has stressed the eschatological character of Jesus' ministry. Though we cannot be certain just what Jesus had in mind, the best guess is that he expected the Kingdom to complete history. Whether or not Jesus linked this completion to his own death is uncertain, but some interpreters read his depression in the Garden, or his cry of abandon on the cross, as deep pain at the Kingdom's delay. At any rate, the proximity of the Kingdom accounts for Jesus' having made little provision for the continuance of his work. The strata of the New Testament that go back to the historical Jesus contain little that deals with a "church." After Jesus' death, when communities of believers started to work out the problems of continuing his mission, church issues became more pressing. It is from such different communities that many churchly interpretations of Jesus' teaching in the gospels derive. It is also such communities that furnish the context of Paul's epistles.[1] Thus, even though it was not a paramount concern of Jesus himself, the theology of the Church soon became an important New Testament interest.

Early Christians could derive the most important notions of what following Jesus entailed from Jesus' own preaching and example. For example, following Jesus clearly entailed living a life of love structured by the twofold commandment. The love of God and the love of neighbor as oneself were the basic "law" that Jesus had laid down. He did not develop this as a way to keep the community under control. He developed it as a brief statement about religious reality—about the core response that the goodness of God and the worth of our neighbors ought to call forth. To follow Jesus was to make his Father the prime treasure of one's life. It was to depend totally on this Father's goodness, to resolve totally to try to imitate this Father's love. Similarly, Jesus' example made it clear that he considered other men and women his brothers and sisters. They were members of God's family, objects of God's parental care. In the parable of the good Samaritan, Jesus showed that all fellow human beings, but especially those in need, are our "neighbors." In the parable of the prodigal son, he showed that God is willing to forgive even the ungrateful. With notions such as these, Jesus' followers had the essentials of the "constitutional law" that their good living together required.

In addition, they had other important directives. Jesus obviously had been a man of prayer. He had withdrawn from time to time into solitude; he had asked his Father to fill all his needs. Any group claiming to follow Jesus' way therefore would treasure prayer. Setting Jesus' example in the context of his Jewish faith, the group would ponder the scriptures and try to bring the events of recent times—above all Jesus' death and resurrection—into the story of salvation those scriptures recorded. Alerted by Jesus' example, then, the Church organized much of its prayer, scripture reading, and effort to expand the story of salvation into a ceremony that came to be known as "the breaking of the bread." That is, the church developed the habit of congregating for a simple meal in celebration of Jesus' death and resurrection. As the services of the Jewish synagogue had included a sermon or exposition of scripture, so the early Christians, most of whom were Jews, began to preach at their congregational celebrations. They also began to associate their worship with taking care of their poor, serving their needy. Thus, remembering Jesus, explaining their faith, and caring for the brothers and sisters dominated the early Church's gatherings. Gathering together, Jesus' followers found in the breaking of the bread the nourishment they needed to sustain a hardy faith.

All of this surely was quite informal. We know from Paul's letters that sometimes it was so informal it approached chaos. Various people would claim the floor and talk across one another in a babble of "inspired" utterances. Paul had to remind them that Christ's Spirit did not want disorder.[2] Speaking in tongues, to say nothing of swooning to unconsciousness, was not so important as a rational explanation of scripture or faith that helped one's fellow believers. Similarly, it was important that eucharistic groups maintain a genuine charity and a high moral tone. A genuine charity meant sharing their goods openhandedly and refusing to split into cliques. A high moral tone meant remembering that this meal dealt with the body and blood of the Lord, not with things of the "flesh." For the communities to whom Paul wrote, many aspects of faith were still only poorly grasped. They had a passionate conviction that something marvelously new had occurred in Jesus' death and resurrection, but they did not realize its full implications.

More than a lack of experience lay behind this state of affairs. The early epistles suggest that Paul, as much as Jesus, expected an early end to history. In the lifetime of many still living, the Lord would return to finish his work. The second coming or return *(parousia)* of the risen Jesus so dominated Paul's thought that his early letters pay little attention to secular affairs. Thus, he is more interested in what will happen to those who have died between the time of Christ's ascension and the Second Coming than he is in the long-range future of the Church. This situation changed after some years, but it helps to explain Paul's counsel that people stay in the state (married or single) they presently were in, his unconcern about slavery, and so forth. The time was short, the Lord would soon return. Questions of marriage, or slavery, or relations with the secular authorities seemed beside the point.

By the end of the Pauline period it was clear that the parousia had been delayed. Thus, the Epistle to the Romans took a longer, more historical view, and the Epistle to the Ephesians seems almost cosmic. For these epistles, the followers of Jesus, like Israel, had a mission to all the world. They were to proclaim what happened in Jesus, so that all people might know God's love. By the end of its first generation, then, the Church had begun to realize that it did not exist for itself. It existed to keep Christ's message and love before the world. Indeed, for the author of Ephesians the Church represents a great marital mystery. Those who believe in Christ share one life with him. If human beings have been made for God, the Church is where they realize their vocation.

The last paragraphs have drawn on Pauline theology. As Catholic scripture scholar Raymond Brown's recent book *The Community of the Beloved Disciple*[3] shows in rich detail, there were early churches organized around other theologies. A number of them apparently traced their roots to an eyewitness of Jesus, called the "beloved disciple." The original members of such circles may well have been Palestinian Jews, including some followers of John the Baptist, who accepted Jesus as the Messiah. Others, including Samaritans, joined them, and before long they developed a high Christology, according to which Jesus had existed with God before his birth from Mary. This brought them into fierce conflict with traditional Jews, who saw such a Christology as a blasphemous denial of monotheism. It also made the Johannine Christians open to Gentile converts.

A high Christology, conflict with the Jews, and "realized eschatology" (the final things already have happened in Jesus and the Spirit) are themes that distinguish the theology of the Gospel of John and the Johannine Epistles. Looking backward, then, we call the communities that held these beliefs "Johannine." At the stage of the epistles (ca. A.D. 100), the Johannine community had undergone schism, largely because some members had begun to downplay Jesus' humanity. Eventually, this latter group probably joined with Docetists—heretics whose theology frequently included a denial of Jesus' full humanity. Whereas before this internal conflict the Johannine Christians seem to have had only the loosest governing structures, after it they apparently accepted the hierarchical structures other churches were developing and merged with such other churches. They brought to the subsequent "Great Church" that all the orthodox communities comprised both their high Christology and their tradition of relying on the guidance of the Spirit.

The great doctrinal councils of the fourth and fifth centuries affirmed the high Christology of the Johannine tradition, and when the Johannine writings became part of the canonical New Testament their emphasis on the inner teaching of the Spirit became part of the great Church's treasury. This inner teaching could seem to be in conflict with the more formal governments of the non-Johannine churches, and ever since there has been a tension in the Catholic view of Church order. Because of its early controversies over doctrine, the Church realized that it had to have authoritative teachers who could decide whether an interpretation was faithful to Jesus' original vision. The vagueness of the criteria for orthodoxy in the Johannine writings suggests that the Johannine communities did not have such teachers, and that without them one was helpless against interpreters who claimed equally to represent tradition. By their problems, then, the Johannine churches showed the need for clearer structures of authority.

On the other hand, the structures mentioned in the rest of the New Testament are quite vague. Certainly they give no obvious design for later structures, whether of teaching or liturgical leadership. Thus, when Roman Catholics and Eastern Orthodox squabbled over questions of authority, neither side could settle the dispute by appealing to a clear New Testament picture. So too during the Reformation, when Catholics and Protestants squabbled over authority. Recent ecumenical discussion therefore has found the New Testament operating on a different level than subsequent controversies.[4] According to the scriptures, none of the "political" bases for the churches' squabbles and divisions is necessary or absolute. It may be that later developments had to come, and that some of them were better than others. None of the churches' forms of government, however, was clearly willed by God from the beginning.

John L. McKenzie is a respected Catholic biblical scholar who has been willing to read such New Testament evidence with an unblinking eye. In an early article on ministerial structures in the New Testament, he shows that the situation of the early churches was neither uniform nor highly developed.[5] Moreover, it seems that apostles—those who had seen the Lord—were not primarily church governors, that the churches described by Acts reached their decisions democratically, that we have no assurance that a definite officer led the community in prayer, and that there was no *magisterium*—no ministry of authoritative teaching such as that which later Roman Catholicism developed. On the other hand, there was a permanent diaconate (body of deacons), a married clergy, and a corps of female ministers. With an eye to present ecumenical discussion, McKenzie infers that the problem for Roman Catholicism is to explain how it could develop traditions that curtailed the original New Testament diversity and freedom.

The general response that Roman Catholicism has made to observations such as McKenzie's is that with experience the Church found it necessary to generate the offices and rules that it did. The rise of deviant teachings hastened the coming of the authoritative teacher. The milieu in which the ministry was to function made celibacy and excluding women advantageous. One can debate the wisdom of such historical decisions, and one can argue that conditions today require a change. But the general notion that doctrine and discipline have to develop, because later history raises new problems, is central to the Catholic understanding of the Church. The Church is not so chartered by the New Testament that it can never develop beyond the picture given there. The picture given there ought to be a primary source of direction, and anything that seriously compromises that picture, especially anything that compromises the love and freedom that the picture spotlights, ought nearly automatically to be vetoed. But under the Spirit the Church must have the power to develop. Otherwise, it can neither meet new challenges nor spell out the implications of its old faith.

Moreover, there is a significant sense in which the Church precedes scripture. The New Testament, after all, was the product of two generations' worth of Christian experience. Most of it came from the collective memories of individual churches, and all of it had to meet the "sense of the faithful." In other words, all of it had to win approval as being consonant with the living, oral tradition by which the churches had long done business. The Johannine literature, for instance, won approval only after a considerable time. The Apocalypse was judged orthodox later still. Through all this "judging," the churches relied on the Spirit. What they remembered having received from their forebears in faith, and what they found solid through their daily practice, ultimately depended on the Spirit's illumination. When Catholic theology defends doctrinal development and the place of living tradition, it ought primarily to mean this vital experience of the Spirit. Below the usefulness of such structural features as the episcopacy (government of the Church by bishops) and the magisterium, the Spirit keeps the Church faithful to Christ.

That is not to deny that the Spirit uses scripture as the basic mirror in which the Church discovers itself. The New Testament always retains a primary authority. Furthermore, the question of authority—of how power ought to be exercised in the Church—receives in the New Testament a very instructive answer. When it looks in this mirror, the Church discovers that all its power ought to be for service. Thus, Jesus says that he came not to be ministered unto but to minister. He says that those who wish to be great in his Kingdom must be the servants of all. Unforgettably, he girds himself with a servant's cloth and wipes the feet of his disciples. Station, power, office—according to the New Testament—are for service. It is by spending oneself for others in love that a Christian follows the Lord.

John L. McKenzie, again, has forced the Catholic community to confront this portion of its New Testament image. His recent book *The New Testament Without Illusion*[6] is an ironic study of the contrasts between the Church of early times and the Church of today. Without glorifying the archaic period, McKenzie shows that the Church has regularly forgotten its original power-base. In place of service and spiritual reliance, it has taken to the ways of the world. Thus, where Jesus made it clear that money is a spiritual menace, the Church has accumulated considerable wealth. Where Jesus made it clear that his followers ought not to lord it over others, as the "great men" of the world do, the Church has built gilded thrones. The Mercedes that leave the Vatican are all too like the Mercedes that leave other government headquarters. The bureaucratic administration of Church business is all too like the bureaucratic administration of other government business. By forgetting its early simplicity, poverty, and reason to be, the Church has lost much of its distinction. Thereby, it has often failed to be the community that Jesus sponsored.

WORD

For Karl Rahner, the community that Jesus founded is constituted by God's Word or self-revelation. Jesus, the divine Word incarnate, gathers a people to embody the revelation that he both brings and is. In Rahnerian jargon: "When the eschatological, reflex realization of God's self-communication revealed through Jesus Christ (the final climax of this communication) is explicitly embodied in an eschatologically definitive society, the result is what we call the Church. She both receives and announces this absolute revelation."[7] In our translation: When the definitive, once-and-for-all appreciation of what God has done in Jesus Christ, how God has offered human beings a share in the divine nature, takes social form, achieves an equally definitive communal expression, we have the "Church." For Christian faith, the Church is the community that God addresses and forms through the Word incarnate, Jesus Christ. This community has its being, its whole significance, from the salvation and grace that Jesus preached and brought about. It exists as the body of Christian salvation and grace, the assembly commissioned to spread the good news of what God has done in Jesus. So we might say that it has been spoken into being by the divine Word, and that in turn it exists to speak words of praise to God for the divine grace, words of heralding and invitation to other human beings that they too may hear of God's great love.

The words of the Church, then, are revelatory. When Christians come together, worship, listen to the scriptures, celebrate the sacraments, they remind themselves of the speech that God has made to them, the divine disclosures. So doing, they enter into a dialogue with God, in union with Christ their head and under the guidance of the Spirit, that expresses who they are, how they stand in the world. They (we) are the people that once sat in darkness and now has seen a great light. They (we) are simple folk —butchers, bakers, candlestick makers—who know, at least dimly: (1) that the God of creation has in Jesus shown that he wants to be our loving parent; and (2) that this faith-fact can be any human being's pearl of great price. So the Church, the Christian people, has words—explicit and implicit, express and tacit—of announcement, mission, and help for the world. They should be humble words, stressing God's gifts more than our human wisdom. They should be servant words, asking what help we may render. But unless we speak them, are busy at the tasks of announcing and serving Christ's gospel, we are not the Church that God founded by speaking forth the Word made flesh.

When the earliest Christians went forth to announce the gospel, they thought mainly of glad tidings. Something wonderful had happened and they wanted to tell the whole world. With time, however, they came to consider the Hebrew scriptures, in which they saw the person and work of Jesus prefigured, and then their own scriptures, what we now call the New Testament, to be special instances of the Church's Word. Both were the Church's Word because both were God's Word: important aspects of the self-disclosure that God had first made to Israel and then made in the Jewish prophet, messiah, healer, and revealer who was Jesus. In his historical study of the Christian Word, Frederick Crowe has stressed how quickly the early sense of the Christian message become a sense of God's Word. The time span probably was as brief as the generation from Paul to Luke. "The tentative conclusion that I have reached may be expressed as follows: Luke's theology, especially as revealed in his Acts of the

Apostles, represents a stage at which the Christian message is firmly established as the Word of God; Paul's theology represents the situation a generation earlier when the breakthrough to conceiving the message as Word of God has been made but not yet exploited, when the conception has not yet become so familiar as to be taken for granted in the thinking of the early believers."[8]

With time, the scriptural Word of God became an essential part of the Church's self-understanding. The Church could trace itself back to people like Paul and Luke, who had generated the New Testament, as it could trace itself back to Peter, James, John, and the other apostles who had physically seen the Lord. So the "book" that these early believers left was a precious record, something inspired by the Holy Spirit just as the Hebrew Bible or Old Testament had been. Moreover, the New Testament portrait of the Church stood as a constitution or blueprint, ever-available to remind the community what it had been in the beginning, how it was supposed to be when vision was fresh. Again and again, Christian groups studied the scriptures to reform their faith.[9]

On the other hand, the early vision was not the whole story. The Catholic view of the Church's relation to scripture has always stressed the fact that history moves on, the Church has had to develop. As Avery Dulles recently put it: "The essential reality of the Church is indeed a matter of revealed truth, for only through faith in God's Word do we understand the Church as expression and mediation of God's gift in Christ. We must continually go back to Scripture and to the ancient tradition in order to test and correct our vision of the Church. But the Church is a dynamic reality; it changes its manner of being and acting from place to place and age to age. It must be responsive to the demands of the times, for it has to signify and mediate God's grace to different groups of people, in accordance with their particular gifts, needs, and capacities."[10] The Word of God, we might summarize, is alive, as Hebrews 4:12 described it. It changes and grows with the Church, for it is a Word commissioning the Church, stirring the Christian community to better heralding, service, and worship.

SACRAMENT I

The Catholic understanding of the Church allows for no divorce between word and sacrament. Both flow from the revelation that the mysterious God has mercifully communicated to and through human flesh. Both are incarnational, entailed by the basic revelation God has made in Jesus the Word made flesh. Where "word" tends to denote speech, and to connote scripture, preaching, proclamation, and articulate reflection on the glad message, "sacrament" tends to denote ritualized acts, gestures, forms, and words that display the Christian message. Connotatively, it brings to mind baptismal water, eucharistic bread, the oil of holy anointing. Sacramentally, the community tries to materialize what it believes, what it hopes, what it loves. The water poured and words said at baptism express Christian faith in the divine power to forgive sin, communicate godly life, and incorporate new members into Christ's body. The story recalled and bread shared at the eucharist express Christian hope that God remains faithful to what happened in Jesus, that the community can become a family sharing one food. And so with the other sacramental actions. To the words of scripture and proclamation they add a ceremonial richness, a symbolic density, that would flesh out believers' love of God's love. They would be like common coins, put by steady participation in Church life into the minds and hearts of all the faithful, that they might transact the business of following Jesus beautifully.

The Church therefore is just as basically constituted by sacramentality as by the Word of God. Word and sacrament are but two aspects of a single revelation. The community of Christ stands in the world as a sign, a word, a sacrament of God's attitude toward the world. That is why it is so important for the Church to center itself in God's self-spending love. If the Church, the members of Christ, do not bring forth in the world the love and service that made Jesus so credible to his contemporaries, the gospel ceases to echo persuasively. Humanity does not have the full evidence of God's care that Jesus' Father intended. More minds are darkened, more hearts left bereft, than ought to be. To be sure, God works outside the established Church. The divine mercy has never abandoned any mind or heart. But God takes our character as people of flesh and blood so seriously that he has been willing to use, even stand behind, a fragile historical body like the Church. Indeed, for Catholic faith God has been willing to say, "Here is something authenticated by me. Here my love and salvation will never fail to be present."

These are statements of faith, of course, and they depend upon the Catholic notions of Church authority. The Church has the mission of making present in the world the revelation and grace of Jesus Christ. Therefore, the Church has the authority to serve revelation and grace in the enfleshed ways that Jesus himself served them. Taking bread and wine, dirt and spittle, Jesus communicated to whole people, not just minds, the love of God his Father. The stories about his healings, feeding of the multitudes, changing the water into wine, and the like show that from the beginning his followers thought of him as the bringer of salvation into every nook and cranny. Using his Jewish religious heritage, Jesus made so ordinary, unavoidable a matter as human eating and drinking a way to give himself to his friends and followers. His every intonation and gesture likely suggested that in this giving they could find the master-love of God, the key to their deepest personal and communal nourishment. Like the gestures and words of Jesus, the sacraments of the Christian community should bring healing and nourishment. Simple, strong, deep, and honest, they should tell people we are members of one another, tell the world God wants our health and prosperity, not our sickness, poverty, and war.

The master sacrament is the eucharist, and historically the eucharist has been the main-line or main-form of the Christian community's prayer. In Catholic interpretation, the eucharist remembers into the present the scriptural story of salvation, especially the climax of Jesus' sacrificial death and triumphant resurrection. Equally, the eucharist conveys the nourishing action of God that feeds our life of grace, our sharing in the divine nature. As we eat the bread and drink the wine, we must try to open to the presence of Christ they embody, let the creative power of the divine love fill earthly food with heavenly significance.

At the Catholic eucharist, the full human personality has been licensed to feed upon God's revelation. The liturgy has offered matter for the eye, the ear, the nose, the mouth, under the instinct that salvation is intrinsically holistic. Through the rhythms of the liturgical year, the Church has tried to capitalize on the quickening pace of fall, when summer luxury fades and time again becomes imperative. It has used the deep dark and quiet of the winter solstice as a backdrop for Christ's birth. The harsh times of full winter have become penitential, preparing for an Easter renovation in spring. Monastic settings have similarly capitalized on the rhythms of the day. Rising or retiring, monks and nuns have asked God's help, praised God's love, not just for themselves as individuals but for the whole Church, the whole humankind that is God's family.

Sacramentality therefore means concreteness, embodiedness, wholeness. It is faith using our strange position on the evolutionary map, our human peculiarity of sending meaning through material carriers. Thus, art and music rightly enter into Catholic worship. Special clothes and special utensils have a place. And throughout, the main intent is not to make something cultic or sacred, in the sense of something apart from ordinary life. That sometimes happens, but the main intent is to consecrate the ordinary, unveil the dazzling love of God present in all creatures, great and small.

SACRAMENT II

For Karl Rahner, the basic sacramentality of the Word made flesh and the Body of Christ uses the traditional Catholic system of seven sacraments as main channels.[11] These seven (which we may take as a number reaching out to wholeness) are acts in which the community expresses its faith that God's grace would quicken all of life, God's love would come to each significant situation. Thus, many of the seven official sacraments are geared to important moments in the life cycle. Baptism begins the life of faith. Anointing consecrates our ending. Confirmation begs the Spirit's strengthening for our mature witness to Christ. Matrimony seals the self-gift of two spouses with the blessing of the God who has loved to love through a body. When the community chooses new official ministers, orders anoints their call to service. When people want to relieve the burdens of sin, penance focuses the forgiveness of God upon the deepest recesses of their wrongdoing. And at the center of this wheel of occasional blessings and strengthenings, as the nub of all the Christian rites of passage and rhythms of renewal, stands the eucharist, the bread of life. There we believe Jesus present to fulfill the Johannine promise that those who come to him will never hunger, those who believe in him will never thirst. There the symbiosis or conviviality of the branches with the vine is repaired and renewed. The community can anticipate the messianic banquet that is the Synoptics' great image for heaven. It can again rivet itself to the passover from death to life that summarizes Pauline salvation.

The renewal of sacramental life is therefore the heartbeat of Catholic Christianity's ongoing reform. When the regular assemblies of a local church brim with beauty and comfort, challenge and nourishment, local Christians are in quite good shape. When the rites are flat and boring, routinized and barely prayed, the members grow wan and flabby. The fault is not with the traditional symbols. One could not ask for more basic, inexhaustible elements. The fault is with ourselves: our mystery-less milieu, our bureaucratic triviality and haste, our personal laziness and superficiality. When we give the symbols a chance, show them an attentive mind and heart, they can still erupt with the unique power of divine love, still turn whole personalities around. Then two or three gathered in Christ's name know that he is with them. Then the articles of faith about the living, resurrected Lord and the quickening, in-given Spirit flame with personal conviction. What is hard to bring off in a huge building filled with people who barely know one another can become almost easy in a little group of neighbors and friends. What once seemed foreign or archaic, words and ceremonies from a long-dead past, can again become a two-edged sword cutting to the joint of our misery, the marrow of our longing.

We could write scenarios for any of the official sacraments, or for several para-sacramental situations, that might concretize these possibilities. For reasons of space, we limit ourselves to two. First, consider the marriage ceremony, what it says about God's way of bringing life and maturation to most people. The two who are marrying pledge to become one flesh. At the microscopic level, where energies are nuclear, they pledge to work with might and main for the unity-midst-difference that all creation is in labor to accomplish. The early Greek philosophers who established most of the intellectual agenda of the West were fascinated by the problem of the one and the many. In germ, the man and woman who mature in marriage solve this most basic problem. Imperfectly but significantly, they walk around the intellectual and emotional hurdles, developing a commonality as strong as their differences, a community enhancing their separateness.

So Fred and Frieda, together fifty years, tell themselves, and any others who can read their strangely similar wrinkles, that it can happen: bread broken, joy shared, differences fused to creativity. Through good times and bad, high tides and ebb, faith, hope, and love can overweigh selfishness, stupidity, and sin. That now and then this happens, that occasionally two do become one and multiply in fruitfulness, quietly contradicts the world's apparent lovelessness. Fred and Frieda know that their sign depends on the great sign, the cross of Christ their strength. They know that their marriage is more a gift than a hard-won work, more a grace than a cause for boasting. Deep in their bodies, way down in their nerves, they sense the wisdom of a God foolish enough to want more than angels, delighted by loins and limbs.

Second, consider the sacrament of anointing.[12] To prepare mind and body for sickness and death, the Church anoints its suffering members, prays God's mercy and help. Remember, God, we are but dust, and unto dust we shall return. Look not upon our sins but upon the love you spent in our making, the price you paid in our saving. We have wanted to use your time well. Our better part has yearned to use mind and heart, soul and strength, body and imagination to your credit. But we are simply people. Our lives are short. We have never seen you. Be merciful to us, then, and take us by the hand. Consider the faith of your saints, the petitions of Abraham for Sodom. Hear the groans of your Spirit, her sighs too deep for words. Into your hands we commend our spirits. Now dismiss your servant in peace, letting us, his family and friends, hope that we, too, will end with the shine of your gladness, leave with your angels for the light so bright it had to be darkness.

MODELS OF THE CHURCH

Thus far, we have implicitly described the Church as a community, constituted by Word and Sacrament, that brings forth God's love. There are other models of the Church, however, and Avery Dulles has done ecumenical theology the service of outlining them clearly.[13] For instance, the traditional Catholic view of the Church stressed its institutional structure. From pope to laity, it was a "perfect society" pyramidal in shape. God had equipped the Church with the powers necessary to its task; the work of the Church's "officers" was to exercise those powers so that Christians found sanctification. Balancing this rather cold model was a view of the Church as a mystical communion. This view had sizeable support from scripture, especially from Paul's doctrine of the Mystical Body, and it stressed the Church's mystery. Sharing God's life, extending the Incarnation, Christians' deepest meaning was hidden with God in Christ. The grace that flowed from vine to branches was Christians' great treasure, a riches that would only be fully revealed on the last day. Prior to the last day, holy living was the main task.

In recent times a third model has gained prominence. It presents the

Church as the basic sacrament that makes God's grace manifest in the world. This is the Rahnerian view we developed above. It makes the community of Christians a sign of the world's inmost meaning. For instance, it suggests that Christian love is the best key to the significance of evolution and history. Fourth, however, theologians who are more political have pushed the Church in the direction of social service. For them the Church ought to be an avant-garde who minister to the poor, support causes that are just, pressure secular society to cleanse its conscience. Antiwar and antinuclear Christians often see the Church in this light. They speak of a commitment to human liberation, and they ring true biblically. The biblical God wants justice, as well as pure worship, effective love of our neighbors, as well as of herself.

A fifth model that Dulles describes focuses the Church on heralding the gospel. In this model preaching, proclamation, and missionizing are the key ecclesial tasks. This model, too, has New Testament warrant. For instance, the early Church clearly felt impelled to spread the story of Jesus to the ends of the earth. "Evangelization" is the word we hear for this activity today, and evangelical Christians often put "mainline" types to shame by their greater commitment to the Church's mission.

Dulles is careful to show that none of his models is exclusive. Each has its measure of truth, and the mystery of the Church is such that all of the models are necessary if a full ecclesiology is to emerge. There is an institutional side to the Church, inevitably, but it ought to serve the personal ends that Jesus had in mind. There is a profound mystical side, but it should not make the Church purely spiritual—so hidden that it ignores politics or economics. Sacramentality is intrinsic to the Church's life, but so too are preaching and public service, especially to the poor. The models therefore counsel an attitude of "both/and." The Church ought to be both a community of worship and a community of political impact.[14]

Let us develop these last two "oughts." If we correlate them with Jesus' twofold commandment, they make a case for a Church centered on radical contemplation and radical politics. In both instances, the word "radical" does not mean "violent" but "going to the root." By its obedience to the commandment to love God with whole mind, heart, soul, and strength, the Church ought to become a community of radical contemplation. Its liturgy and solitary prayer ought to love God precisely as God. God precisely as God is a living mystery of love more intimate than we are to ourselves. It is the "atmosphere" in which we live, move, and have our being. For the most part, good liturgical or private prayer simply directs faith in this "atmospheric" God so that faith becomes personal and passionate.

Giving the mystery a personal face, letting Jesus embody God's humanity, we can share with God all our concerns and hopes. To do this together, Christians of times past have found the regular, stylized prayers of the liturgy helpful. The only proviso is to pray these prayers gracefully, simply, as fresh and apt expressions of our own inner needs. Too much liturgical prayer loses real worship among external forms. Too little liturgical prayer is slow, spare, and poetic. Those who lead it, as those who share it, need to retrieve its *mystagogic* character. That was the Greek term for celebrating God's atmospheric nearness.

In the next section we shall deal with current ecumenical problems, but this aside on liturgical prayer prompts a personal recollection. We have been impressed by the initiation in prayer that regular attendance at Mass inculcates, for we have found in ecumenical situations that many Christian are uneasy with contemplation. That may not be true of Orthodox, who have a splendidly mystagogic liturgy, nor of many Anglicans and Lutherans. It does seem true of other Protestants. So much was this the case in one ecumenical gathering that the proposal to pray deeply together, using various traditions' liturgical forms, became divisive. The problem was not the legalities of intercommunion among members of groups officially still separated. For this group such legalities were quite minor. The problem was uneasiness in using any liturgical forms, including those of a eucharistic meal. Where common use of scripture was no problem, and retreat to private solitude left members free, common movement through traditional ceremonies caused difficulties. Our group did not have a good sense of how to let formulaic words focus our attention on the mysterious God. It did not know how to share words and feelings ringed by silence. As a result, it experienced Word and Sacrament as antitheses. One subgroup had grown up on pure preaching and could not celebrate sacraments easily. The other, largely Catholic, subgroup had to work to understand their difficulty.

Without an education in radical contemplation, then, the Church is not likely to worship its way toward unity. Without a sense of what it means, concretely, to be a group that constantly redefines itself by a common lifting of minds and hearts, the Church will continue to undervalue God's Spirit.

There is a parallel on the side of action. Without a commitment to radical politics the Church is not likely to fulfill the second great commandment, to love one's neighbor as oneself. It must have in the forefront of its self-modeling a sense that it stands in the polis, the city-state, as a champion of justice. Precisely what tactics this implies will always be a matter of prudence. We are not arguing for a specific set of programs. We are arguing that honesty and love are both the quintessence of good social life and the Church's public business. It takes little imagination or experience to realize that honesty and love are precisely what a vast number of public situations critically lack. Be it the local school board, the state's welfare program, or the nation's intelligence gathering, a depressing amount of public business occurs dishonestly, covertly, and with little love. "Hard ball" is the name of the political game, "realistically." "Realistically," politics is a jungle of power plays, a war of movers and shakers. Unless the Church stands over against this crippling philosophy, a vicious pragmatism will face little opposition.

Radical politics, politics that goes to the roots, deals with the conditions of human beings' social flourishing. We shall take a more leisurely look at this in the chapter on politics. Here the point is to suggest its implications for the theology of the Church. In our opinion, the Church has an obligation to use its accumulated wisdom, its economic resources, and its political contacts to promote all human beings' social flourishing. We must oppose the things that depress human beings, that deprive them of necessities and growth. Thus, rapacious land use, oppressive labor practices, wanton crime, bad housing, poor education, and inadequate medical care are all targets for Church concern. To its great credit, the Church frequently does champion those who suffer such abuses. We merely urge making this *diakonia,* this humane service, a deeper part of the Church's self-conception.

It ought to be clearer than it usually is that being a Christian, a Church member, entails forthright standing for honesty and love, forthright defense of justice. What "honesty," "love," and "justice" mean in particular cases has to be determined on the spot. Good Christians can differ in their evaluations. But the basic commitment to champion what is true, what is compassionate, what binds up wounds, is so central to following Jesus that Christian faith directly entails it. There can be no proper Christian faith where belief simply props the status quo. All Christian faith has to be prophetic and political, if it wants to affirm with Saint Irenaeus that "God's glory is human beings fully alive."

Radically contemplative and radically political, the Church ought finally to be a community of forgiveness and personal concern. Insofar as the deepest social problem we human beings face is the cycles of hatred that give us our wars and destructive competitions, the Church's prime sacramentality is its ability to reverse such cycles. Nowhere is its otherworldliness, its divinity, more evident than in its ministry of reconciliation. By the law of the cross, which Jesus embodied perfectly, the Church shows a way out of human antagonisms. Refusing to return hurt for hurt, Christians can help break the vicious cycles that give us our broken homes, our jungle politics, our international confrontations. This is terribly difficult work, and terribly important. Suffering evil in love, refusing to fuel the destructive flames, is clearly superhuman. We simply do not have the goodness, of ourselves, to love that well. Whenever it happens that people do endure evil without acting evilly in return, we can be sure that God's Spirit is active. In the depths of such purity, she has convinced someone that because God has been loving he or she should be loving in return.

That is the social, very practical, implication of the meditation on Jesus, the contemplation of Jesus' cross, which Christian faith has sponsored through the centuries. Such meditation has been one of humanity's last resorts against what the philosopher Hobbes saw when he said *"homo homini lupus"*—human beings are to one another as wolves. To be sure, there are dangers in meditations on Jesus, contemplations of Jesus' cross. All good things have dangers; these have led to "doormat-ism" or the expectation that life will be brutal. In our opinion, however, such dangers weigh less than the advantages that accrue when the Church keeps Jesus' suffering central. Jesus' suffering is God's answer to our human evil, as Jesus' resurrection is God's pledge the victory is won. Walking the way of the cross, suffering for what is right, Christians keep both God's answer and God's pledge shining. Without them, the world sinks toward total darkness.

We are well aware that this sort of talk, this focus on suffering evil in love, goes down hard. Even when it is clearly a counterpoint to good news and resurrectional joy, it costs more than any of us pays gladly. The price of great humanity seems impossible. We are not saints, and we resent the fact that a good world, a just society, now demands sainthood. Nonetheless, it is well for us to have the issues set clearly. The sooner we realize Christ's demands, our utter need of the Spirit, the sooner genuine faith comes in sight. There is so much ersatz, phony Christian faith that most of us are misled. As Kierkegaard saw in the case of nineteenth-century Denmark, "Christendom" has taken two-thirds of the gospel away. We grow up in a culture putatively "Christian"; we think we know what the gospel implies. In fact, our culture has watered the gospel down to bourgeois morality or patriotism. Suffering, forgiveness, the price of justice—they always break such "culture Christianity." Bourgeois morality or patriotism is too thin ice for real skating. Therefore, paradoxically enough, our deeper crises serve God's mercy. God will not abandon us to the superficial humanity that bourgeois morality or patriotism create. He will force us, through either creativity or suffering, to glimpse true human stature sometime.

The lesson for the Church might be to focus more directly on the ministry of reconciliation. As Bernard Cooke has shown in reflecting on the sacrament of penance,[15] the Church's ministry in this sacrament equates judgment with reconciliation. Only when people have been rejoined to one another and to God has sacramental justice been done. That would seem to argue for the broader and more creative use of the sacrament of penance. In ecumenical gatherings, for instance, penance could be coupled with eucharistic celebration, so that both Christians' common responsibility for their division and Christians' substantial unity were acted out ritually. With but a little imagination, the sacrament of penance could serve many domestic and neighborhood situations that cry out for healing, for reconciliation with both God and neighbor. In that case, "radical politics" would assume the humble form of tearing up rotten, misdirected roots and planting new seeds. As well, it would properly involve Christians in one another's social welfare.

For example, what does a couple on the verge of divorce for superficial reasons most need? What do their relatives and friends most have to risk? Could it not be putting a Christian accent on "I never promised you a rose garden," warmly being willing to share the pain? If we stand by alienated spouses, or alienated children, or alienated friends, stubbornly refusing to let Christian love become absent from their lives, we do work like Jesus. We often do it at cost, and we usually do it badly. But even to try to do it is to be the Church at its best. Even to try to absorb human pain is to conform to the mind of Christ.

If this is so, models that encourage the Church to legalism or impersonalism are simply bad. The work of reconciliation, as the work of radical contemplation and radical politics, has to proceed in freedom and love. Studies we have seen of the current revision of Canon Law suggest that Church leaders are still far from realizing this.[16] The new code remains impersonal, legalistic, a series of letters threatening to choke Christ's Spirit. It contrasts starkly with Jesus' way of dealing with people. With such misunderstanding near its top, the Church needs no enemies outside.

Once and for all, we have to realize that there is no Christian authority functioning impersonally. Any body or officer claiming to represent God has to deal with individuals concretely. Be it divorces, dispensations from religious vows, sins petty or sins great, the minister of Christ's love must know the heart with which he or she deals. (So too with local political conditions, local business practices, national policies of defense.) Where one cannot deal with actual people, one has recourse only to general principles, and general principles never brought anyone to penance or joy.

The most promising ecclesial development we've seen recently is the rise of what Latin Americans call *comunidades de base*. [17] These are groups of small scale, where members can know one another well. Often they gather at peril, persecuted by unjust civil regimes. Their focus is a study of scripture and a eucharistic sharing that rivet Christian faith onto present political circumstances. Regularly this spotlights Christ's cross. All try to listen to the Spirit from the heart. All try to muster the courage to walk Jesus' hard way, forgiving their enemies and persevering after justice. They are primed to bear one another's burdens. The joy of one is the joy of all. So, at least, do we idealize a community such as Ernesto Cardenal's Solentiname,[18] for such communities are the best model of current Church life we've seen.

CATHOLIC ECUMENISM

Early in the twentieth century Protestants began a movement toward the reunion of their disparate churches. Subsequently, Orthodox and Roman Catholics joined in. Since Vatican II, Catholics have had regular contact with Protestants and Orthodox. In bilateral theological commissions, especially, they have made good progress in removing age-old differences. Presently, Catholic-Orthodox dialogue is promising.[19] Other aspects of the ecumenical "movement" seem to have slumped. Nonetheless, any serious ecclesiology has to try to relate the splintered churches to the main Church. The bibliography offers several historical treatments. Our focus here will be positive suggestions.[20]

First, we assume that all Christians deeply desire reunion. There are signs that this is not the case, but we read the general ecclesiology of the Catholic tradition as a judgment that it should be. Scripturally, the classical text is John 17, where Jesus prays for his followers' unity. Traditionally, the first "mark" or "note" of the true church has been unity.[21] The psychology of sectarian identity explains much of the initial opposition to reunion. Many groups define themselves by contradistinction to others. Separatist practices develop lives of their own, and those in power oppose change. It is understandable, then, that churches are reluctant to make the sacrifices full reunion demands. Small churches, especially, fear that their identities as Baptists, Methodists, Lutherans, Mennonites will be lost. It is also sinful, if one takes division to be the Church's prime failure—the prime excuse for the world not to believe.

Second, we leave the specifics of other churches' sins to themselves and concentrate on our own. How do we Catholics manifest a sinful will to remain divided from other members of Christ? In part, we do this by suffering the psychodynamics just mentioned. Most American Catholics define themselves by distinction from Protestants. "We" have the Mass, the pope, an unmarried clergy, nuns, an international orientation, a strict sexual morality, and other such emblems. "They" do not. More sophisticated Catholics make qualifications (Anglicans, Lutherans, and Orthodox have the Mass, essentially; Baptists can have a strict sexual morality), but in the main a "we" and "they" mentality prevails. Indeed, much of the confusion among ordinary Catholics since Vatican II stems from the lessening of the clear-cut differences that used to set Catholics off from Protestants. With the Mass no longer in Latin, Friday no longer a day of abstinence, agitation for a married clergy, nuns in lay garb, the widespread practice of contraception, increased study of the Bible—with all these developments one needs a program to discern the Catholics from the other guys.

We sympathize with the loss that traditional Catholics feel today, but too much sympathy risks a desire to see the Church remain divided. Brian Moore's slim novel *Catholics* shows too much sympathy, but it is splendid on the human costs that change involves.[22] In this novel, traditional monks, called to obey radical changes of an imaginary Vatican IV, suffer a severe crisis of faith. The old ways have proven solid as a rock. The new ways (pivoted on a dialogue with Buddhists) are dubious indeed. In Moore's portrayal, unity is less valuable than the intensity possible when lines are rigid and doctrines are stark.

Catholics puts part of the standoff well. So do Walker Percy's *Love in the*

Ruins,[23] which mocks the spiritual wasteland we owe to the modern loss of faith, and the signers of what was known as the *Hartford Appeal.*[24] Across denominational lines, the signers called on the Church to repudiate American secularism (denial of a transcendent, otherworldly God). They had a good point, but they seemed to overlook a severe problem. The good point is that secularism denatures human beings and denatures Christian faith. If this world of space and time is all there is, Christians are of all people the most to be pitied. The severe problem is that many signers of the Hartford Appeal seemed to think in doctrinal or propositional terms, and so seemed to miss the real, existential battles.

If one believes that God desires all peoples' salvation, and has become available to all people as the gracious mystery holding their lives, then determinations of "faith" or "unfaith" must be more than **propositional**. However desirable it is to have clear enunciations of what Christians believe, it is more imperative to have keen intuitions of God's free presence. Many people who deny propositional presentations of God, Christ, considerable portions of traditional morality, and "transcendence" give rich evidence of being faithful to God's Spirit. If they are honest and loving, they "know" God. God is always more preconceptual than clearly grasped, always better evidenced by how one lives than by what one says. Those who do the truth come to God's light. Those who act lovingly manifest God's Spirit. Doctrines and names and uniforms are secondary. Primary is loving the divine mystery of life passionately and loving one's neighbors as oneself.

Let us take this back to ecumenism. Vatican II's *Decree on Ecumenism* (#11) speaks of a "hierarchy of truths." Some portions of Christian faith are more basic than others. Were we to concentrate on the basics and translate them into experiential terms, we might remove most obstacles to reunion. (We might also open Christianity to all people of good will.) Rahner has argued that Christianity has three cardinal mysteries: Trinity, Grace, and Incarnation. We have followed him in trying to render these three mysteries contemporary and experiential. Were theologians to concentrate on such fundamentals, and Church leaders to make them the touchstone of communion, they could cut through a dozen ecumenical roadblocks. For instance, Roman Catholics share the essence of life's meaning with anyone who, explicitly or implicitly, makes Jesus the decisive interpretation of how to live. Explicitly, all who confess Jesus to be Lord and Savior seem oriented to this interpretation. Implicitly, all who follow the twofold commandment, or suffer for justice, or accept death trustingly probably make an equivalent confession. At the least, a God as good as Jesus' Father interprets such generosity savingly.

Though Jesus surely is the center of Christianity,[25] we might develop analogous approaches to the two other cardinal mysteries. The effort in all three cases would be to cut to the bone of what really is necessary for intercommunion. (By "intercommunion" we mean both a general sharing of Church life and a specific sharing of the eucharist.) Behind this is the assumption that people finally summarize themselves in what recent moral theologians have called a "fundamental option"—a basic yes or no to God. Such an option or core act is never fully clear, but the effort to get to it greatly clarifies the nub of the ecumenical matter: Does one live as Jesus did?

We suspect many Christian theologians and church leaders lose a properly ruthless clarity because: (a) they have not appropriated the notion of a hierarchy of Christian truths; (b) they do not hear the call to unity as a divine imperative; and (c) they live in a sort of ghetto and so do not realize how trivial the outside world finds Christians' differences. In the horizon of the world religions, for instance, all Christians hold far more in common than they hold apart. Simply by bowing to Jesus, their orientations toward nature, society, self, and God are all distinctive. This commonality appears all the stronger against the background of a general culture that brackets belief in God. It is true that outsiders' observations on matters such as these have limited value, but many ordinary Christians share outsiders' impressions. People in many churches' pews feel that theologians and Church leaders diddle with nonessentials.

At the time of the separation of Eastern and Western Christianity (1054), a few doctrinal issues were important, but the major causes were differences of temperament, historical pressures, and disciplinary disagreements. At the time of the separation of Western Christianity into Protestant and Catholic camps, doctrinal matters loomed larger. The doctrinal differences between Orthodox and Catholics on the Trinity (does the Spirit proceed just from the Father or from the Son as well?) have diminished, but those on Church government remain. The Reformation disputes about salvation by faith alone, scripture alone being Christianity's norm, the primacy of private conscience, the status of lay people, and the like have withered away. In all these cases, theologians of both traditions have reached a solid reconciliation. Even more prickly issues, such as the place of Peter and the place of Mary,[26] have largely been smoothed. Papal infallibility remains a sore point, but there too progress is possible, for recent historical studies have shown how this dogma received legitimately diverse interpretations.[27] Globally speaking, then, the times are ripe for a new thrust toward unity. How might it come?

First, there would have to be great sensitivity to the questions of conscience that remain, and a way found to honor them. A powerful development of two convictions might succeed. One is God's will that Christians be one. The other is that there is a great difference between essentials and accidentals. Were essentials bare and profound enough, they could make almost all points of division accidental. For instance, among those who agree that Jesus is the decisive interpretation of human life, differences in understanding the eucharist seem accidental. Between transubstantiation and consubstantiation, or transubstantiation and symbolic interpretations, there need not be cause for division. All celebrate Jesus' decisiveness, which could suffice for communion. So too with papal primacy. It could be an accidental matter, requiring only an agreement that, historically and doctrinally, the Petrine ministry has been important.

The point to such an analysis is not to skip over hard questions. It is to find a way to keep hard (but relatively secondary) questions from keeping Christians apart. We ought by now to be sophisticated enough to make the Church a pluralistic community. Rahner sees the Church of the future as pluralistic,[28] and we see pluralism as an ecumenical gateway. Let the various traditions continue their distinctive ways, but let those distinctive ways not loom larger than their common faith in Jesus' decisiveness. Concretely, let them not keep Christians from sharing the same table, the same supper. The eucharist is the great sign of the Church's communion. Including scripture, it embodies God's Word. Were the churches to sacrifice their identities sufficiently to allow (better, to encourage) intercommunion, they would virtually destroy their division. That single agreement could suffice.

A venerable Christian maxim says, "In necessary things, unity; in doubtful things, liberty; in all things, charity." Would that this maxim ruled Catholic practice. Here its application to the ecumenical impasse need only be brief. First, only a few things in Christian faith are necessary. Though we would hold the twofold commandment and the three cardinal mysteries, all views reduce to the love necessary for salvation. Second, the doubtful things are correspondingly many. Only a little of "faith" or "order," to use the Protestant distinction, is at the top of the hierarchy of truths. Whether a church has an episcopal, presbyterial, or congregational authority, for instance, could be a matter of free choice, since it was such at the beginning. Third, exercising charity in all things means considering all other Christians friends, brothers and sisters, one's betters in parts of Christ's teaching or practice. If a pope treats non-Catholics lovingly, as John XXIII did, he removes two-thirds of their problems. If Baptists and Anglicans treat one another lovingly, they need not worship apart. As many of our economic problems lodge in the will, so do many of our ecumenical problems. The mind and imagination open a way, but the will holds back. Ecumenical prayer for reunion therefore ought to be mainly a begging for conversion: Create in us, O God, a new will, that we may be one, as You and Jesus are.

PARISH LIFE

The ecumenical Church is pressured nowadays to be about the business of stitching up the tears that have kept it from being the great sign of God's love in the world. The local, parochial, church is pressured similarly. But at the local level the tears tend to be smaller, more petty. The differences between Lutherans and Catholics, Catholics and Presbyterians, remain quite apparent, but the snarling secularism threatening them both, the aggressive "this-worldliness," makes many denominational Christians feel more like than unlike any other serious believers.

Secularism or "this-worldliness" is not always snarling, of course. It does some of its worst damage with a yawn, a jawbreaking "I couldn't care less." The opposite of a healthy religion is seldom a passionate hatred of God. More often it is a bone-deep indifference. Thus, many parishes now see their membership roles declining, or must wonder about the commitment of their majority. While the simplistic, Bible-thumping churches are sailing before a strong wind, the Christian mainstream is in the doldrums. For many Catholics, keeping the brain active seems incompatible with Sunday Mass. They find no need to go, because they find nothing arresting said. The old law of going as a bounden duty now convinces few. Only a new ability to unleash the Word, display the sacraments, seems likely to turn things around.

If this is so (and we quickly acknowledge that any quick sketch admits of many distinctions, needs many area by area qualifications), the times are more than ripe for a new look at the local churches.[29] For twenty-five years we have been speaking about nongeographic parishes, freer and more intimate communities. The time has come to do something with the Spirit who prompts such experiments. In this connection, one of the best books we have read recently is Edward Schillebeeckx's *God Is New Each Moment*.[30] In the background of many of its discussions is a notion of the local church as a "critical community." By this term Schillebeeckx seems to mean a place where gospel values really are put to the test, love of God and love of neighbor really are taken radically. Because of their radical thrust, critical communities can place the policies of both state and Church under serious scrutiny. In neither case is the critical intent simply negative or to make trouble. In both cases it is to free the prophetic power of the gospel, the urgent love of the sacraments. Celebrating these, the little groups find it natural to press for fuller justice, more humane government, better care of the poor, deeper commitment to peacemaking. "The Lord hears the cries of the poor," scripturally versed Christians have been saying for some time. The critical communities of European Catholicism, like the grassroots communities of Latin American Catholicism, are the little churches that are taking their cue from the needs of the poor.

Some of these theses Schillebeeckx frames in autobiographical settings. From his student days he had been interested in social issues, but after the Second Vatican Council, when progress seemed to grind to a halt, the question of how to help the Church respond to the great social problems of our day, the deep problems of peace and justice, became his most pressing agendum: "I looked around and saw various critical communities emerging in the Church. That was decisive for me. A marginal critical movement that was nonetheless spreading throughout the whole

Church. I wanted to go along with that movement and, as it were, super-vise it theologically, because I realized the future of the Church was in it. If the Church is ever to change at the top, I thought, it has to recognize that it is in fact becoming more and more a top without a base—the base, that is, people themselves, have gone their own way. It is only in this way that the top can change. And it will change!"[31]

To make this sort of change is not difficult in theory, although in practice it may be well-nigh impossible. All that has to change is our concepts of power and service. If ministry in the Church (on which topic Schillebeeckx has written a very powerful study)[32] were to become mainly a matter of communities choosing their natural leaders, and if the Church were to look upon itself as existing mainly to bring the good news of Christ to the world's most afflicted, then the walls that keep us from working and praying together, simply and joyfully, largely would crum-ble. There is nothing magical about building a good community. All it needs is normal brainpower, special honesty, and genuine love.

The brainpower is necessary to keep things in focus, properly target our prayer and work. The honesty must be more than what one finds in the world, where distrust has made community an endangered species. The love is God's life in us, the power of conversion. Ordinary people like ourselves can possess these simple requirements in quite adequate measure. Like the members of Paul's early churches,[33] we can come together in one another's homes, share our resources, and make a glad song to our God. Then, streaming out from our eucharistic fellowships, we can form small but powerful columns determined to keep such basic goods as economic justice, inexpensive health care, solid education, and progress toward peace at the top of our nation's and Church's agenda.

To be sure, all sorts of people who now profit from economic injustice, amazingly expensive health care, poorly supported public education, and dilatory progress toward disarmament and peace will oppose this or any other prophetic agenda. The little column of local protestors is sure to find money and venom targeted against it. At bottom, though, such a tiny parish will know it need not worry. When we can feel the breath of the Spirit, the calumnies of the world matter little. The goal of future Catho-lic pastoral policy, in our opinion, should be precisely to form critical communities in every nook and hamlet. Thereby, it would advance the day of the Lord, when the great ecumenical Church will be a network of free, prophetic churches.[34]

SUMMARY

The community that sponsors Christian realism is the Church, the assem-bly of Jesus' followers. Our first investigation was the Church's original shape, the community Jesus likely had in mind. Jesus' mind, as New Testament analysis uncovers it, focused on the Kingdom of God. After

Jesus' death and resurrection, his followers began to probe what he meant for the Kingdom. Slowly, they worked out a high Christology and an organization for service.

As it was developed, Church faith and service pivoted on Word and Sacrament. Rooted in scripture, geared toward proclamation, the Christian assembly has attempted to embody God's truth. By gathering to remember Jesus, and to celebrate their fellowship in his good news, Christians have fashioned graceful sacraments, above all the eucharist, which have provided saving help through the life cycle for millions.

Recent ecclesiology has spotlighted the different models by which the Church has understood itself or could understand itself today. They show institutional, mystical, sacramental, servant, and heralding sides of what is ultimately a mysterious assembling by grace. By radical contemplation and radical politics, those models might gain sharper focus. By closer interpersonal relations, the local church might be more gracious.

The bugaboo of current Church order is ecumenical division. A way around ecumenical division might be a greater stress on fundamentals, coupled with a stronger push toward sacramental intercommunion. A way to move the ecumenical Church toward its proper significance might be to recast parish life for the formation of critical Christian communities.

STUDY QUESTIONS

1. What part did Paul's expectation of the *parousia* likely play in his view of the Church?
2. What did the Johannine communities contribute to what later became Catholic ecclesiology?
3. What is the keynote of authentic Church authority?
4. Explain how the Church is founded on God's Word of revelation.
5. Why is the Church intrinsically sacramental?
6. How do Dulles' five models of the Church fit together?
7. Explain the psychology of ecumenical division.
8. What is the significance of Vatican II's notion of a "hierarchy of truths"?
9. What pros and cons do you see in the proposal that parochial life be slanted toward the formation of critical Christian communities?

NOTES

1. See Lucas Grollenberg, *Paul* (Philadelphia: Westminster, 1978).
2. See I Cor. 14:33.
3. Raymond E. Brown, *The Community of the Beloved Disciple* (New York: Paulist, 1979); idem, *The Epistles of John* (Garden City, N.Y.: Doubleday Anchor, 1982).
4. See the World Council of Churches, ed., *Baptism, Eucharist and Ministry* (Geneva: World Council of Churches, 1982).
5. See John L. McKenzie, "Ministerial Structures in the New Testament," in *The Plurality of Ministries,* ed. Walter Kasper and Hans Küng (New York: Herder and Herder, 1972), pp. 13–22.

6. John L. McKenzie, *The New Testament without Illusion* (Chicago: Thomas More, 1980).
7. Karl Rahner and Herbert Vorgrimler, *Dictionary of Theology*, 2d ed. (New York: Crossroad, 1981), pp. 448–49.
8. Frederick E. Crowe, *Theology of the Christian Word* (New York: Paulist, 1978), p. 23.
9. See Rahner and Vorgrimler, *Dictionary of Theology*, pp. 215–19.
10. Avery Dulles, *A Church to Believe In* (New York: Crossroad, 1983), pp. 1–2.
11. See Karl Rahner, *The Church and the Sacraments* (New York: Herder and Herder, 1963); also the fine new series edited by Monika Hellwig, *Message of the Sacraments* (Wilmington, Del.: Michael Glazier, 1982).
12. See James L. Empereur, *Prophetic Anointing* (Wilmington, Del.: Michael Glazier, 1982).
13. See Avery Dulles, *Models of the Church* (Garden City, N.Y.: Doubleday, 1974).
14. See John Carmody, "Eucharistic Worship, Radical Contemplation, and Radical Politics," *Occasional Papers*, no. 20 (Collegeville, Minn.: Institute for Ecumenical and Cultural Research, 1983).
15. See Bernard Cooke, *Ministry to Word and Sacraments* (Philadelphia: Fortress, 1976), pp. 405–521.
16. See Thomas J. Green, "Revision of Canon Law: Theological Implications," *Theological Studies*, 40:4 (December 1979): 593–679; William W. Bassett, "Canon Law and Reform: An Agenda for a New Beginning," in *Toward Vatican III*, eds., Hans Küng, Johannes Metz, David Tracy, (New York: Seabury, 1978), pp. 196–213.
17. See John Eagleson and Sergio Torres, eds., *The Challenge of Basic Christian Communities* (Maryknoll, N.Y.: Orbis, 1981).
18. Ernesto Cardenal, *The Gospel in Solentiname* (Maryknoll, N.Y.: Orbis, 1978).
19. See Edward Kilmartin, *Toward Reunion: The Orthodox and Roman Catholic Churches* (New York: Paulist, 1979).
20. See also John Carmody, *The Heart of the Christian Matter: An Ecumenical Approach* (Nashville: Abingdon, 1983).
21. See Rahner and Vorgrimler, *Dictionary of Theology*, pp. 74–75.
22. Brian Moore, *Catholics* (New York: Holt, Rinehart, and Winston, 1972).
23. Walker Percy, *Love in the Ruins* (New York: Avon, 1978).
24. Peter L. Berger and Richard John Neuhaus, eds., *Against the World for the World: The Hartford Appeal and the Future of American Religion* (New York: Seabury, 1976).
25. See Hans Küng, *On Being a Christian* (Garden City, N.Y.: Doubleday, 1976).
26. See Raymond E. Brown *et al.*, *Peter in the New Testament* (Minneapolis: Augsburg and New York: Paulist, 1973); *Mary in the New Testament* (Philadelphia: Fortress, 1978).
27. See John T. Ford, "Infallibility: Recent Studies," *Theological Studies*, 40:2 (June, 1979): 273–305.
28. See Karl Rahner, *The Shape of the Church to Come* (New York: Seabury, 1974).
29. On the theme of the local church, see the *Proceedings* of the Thirty-Sixth Annual Convention of the Catholic Theological Society of America (1981).
30. Edward Schillebeeckx, *God Is New Each Moment* (New York: Seabury, 1983).
31. *Ibid.*, p. 82.
32. Edward Schillebeeckx, *Ministry: Leadership in the Community of Jesus Christ* (New York: Crossroad, 1981).
33. See Wayne A. Meeks, *The First Urban Christians* (New Haven: Yale University Press, 1983).
34. On the new spirit needed for such an ecclesiology, we recommend Rosemary Haughton, *The Passionate God* (New York: Paulist, 1981).

CHAPTER 7

Spirituality

A CATHOLIC THEOLOGY OF STORY

The self is an irreducible reality, so any adequate theology pays careful attention to the self. This runs the danger of egocentricity, but most religions are quick to put up safeguards. For example, Buddhism teaches that the ego is an illusion, and Christianity teaches that the ego must die.[1] Moreover, the dangers of irrelevance are not less than the dangers of egocentricity, and without careful attention to the self, theology would seem quite irrelevant. For the self is the concrete subject that revelation addresses, the concrete object of Jesus' saving concern. We begin, therefore, with a recent spiritual interest that takes the self's history seriously.

Fusing recent literary criticism with developmental psychology, Catholics have lately joined the movement of American theologians toward "story."[2] Biblical theology, we have come to realize, often assumes a narrative mode. History, biography, and autobiography unfold as narratives. For this chapter on personal Christian living, autobiography seems relevant. Communities tell tales of their past, of where they came from and how they grew, but so do individual selves. We have always known this instinctively; the modern move "inside," towards subjectivity, has only made it clearer. For instance, modern literature has studied the self's dramas, through stunning probes of memory, imagination, and the subconscious. Marcel Proust and James Joyce show the wealth that such probing can retrieve. Psychoanalysis, whether Freudian or Jungian, has developed disciplined recall (anamnesis) and the analysis of dreams. Recent philosophy, both existentialist and phenomenological, has emphasized our temporality, which makes us "projects" and dramas. Even history has come to fuse the social and the individual. William Clebsch's recent book, *Christianity in European History*, [3] periodizes almost two thousand years according to representative Christian "types": a philosopher like Boethius, a prelate like Gregory. Lawrence Cunningham's *The Catholic Heritage* does a similar service for Catholicism. [4]

Catholic theologians such as John Dunne[5] and John Shea[6] have made stories bear concretely on Christian faith. Searching for God through personal space and time, they have brought "salvation history" to the individual life trajectory. They depend on schemas of the life cycle, such as Erik Erikson's, which theorize about the "typical" crises and strengths that childhood, adolescence, adulthood, and old age entail. Future theology of story likely will employ developmental studies directly focused on faith, such as James Fowler's.[7] However, whatever the theoretical scaffolding, the prime matter of a Catholic theology of story should be a three-way interaction among personal temporal experience, the model of Jesus, and divine mystery. Let us elucidate this three-way interaction.

Placed in space and time, having a body–and–spirit constitution that gives us a "world" and a march toward death, we human beings all develop unique narratives. We all are both tellers and tales. What we become, the "I" we each represent, is a mixture of things done to us and things we do. In the beginning, our parents did the procreative thing— gave us our genetic material. We grew in a protective womb, symbiotic with our mothers, and then suffered the traumas of gasping for breath, fighting off light, being separate. It took many months for this separateness to take hold, many months for us to realize our independence. In the terrible twos we pushed off negatively. Each "no" and "I won't" flexed our little egos. And so it went, through schooling, the first job, the first love affair. Each day brought its portion of experience, its packet of pressures and responses. If the guiding angels were good, we grew in an atmosphere of support. Our parents were loving, our neighborhood was safe. If mystery marked us for harder things, our home waters were brackish, our neighborhood was vicious. Either way, most of us kept struggling to develop, for that was our nature, our ever-changing fate. We needed growth as we needed food. Piaget and other observers of children make such demands almost ironclad.[8]

Typically, our scenarios have changed since "maturity." We have made choices about what we would study, where we would work, whom we would date. However conditioned, these choices were in part our own creations. For example, though a person could have studied medicine, she considered literature more fulfilling. Though she could have studied literature academically, she chose creative writing. For her it made literature more compelling. Though she entertained Bob, athletic and gabby, she responded to Jim, witty and quiet. So now she lives with Jim, shares parenthood with Jim, and wonders occasionally what "Mrs. Bob" is doing. In the morning, after the kids have dashed out to the school bus, she sets aside her coffee and turns to the next chapter. What happens to green frog and pink pig, now that they have escaped wicked weasel? An hour later, when it is clear she should not have listened to pig and put them in the mud puddle, she gazes at the blossoming cherry tree and daydreams. Would it have been better to go to grad school, be lecturing now on the brothers Grimm? Would it have been better to have skipped words and fancies altogether, to be dissecting green frogs rather than imagining them? "Two roads diverged in a yellow wood"—and she sits by a cherry tree. "Time, time, time, what have you done to me? What have I done with you?"

The Christian introvert muses about Jesus. What did time do to Jesus? What did Jesus do with time? We know so little of Jesus' story, in terms of hard fact, that imagination leaps too willingly. From the earliest apocrypha, Christians have embellished the child Jesus. Under Gnostic influence, they made him a tiny Hercules, scattering giants and bringing Satan low. For medievals, the child Jesus clung to Christopher, who carried him across the stream. But the core of Jesus' story, the firm reality reining fancy in, is his passion and death. Whatever his personal history, Jesus died on Calvary in witness to his God. Unto that end, he loved his Abba with whole mind, heart, soul, and strength. Unto that end, he loved his neighbors—his disciples, enemies, and us—as fellow children of God. The death that comes to all of us surely came to him early. He capped his thirty years with death's conscious embrace. Feeling his Father's hands, he commended his spirit. His death has become our principal lesson. We are to use time to end as Jesus did: to pass into God.

Paul spoke of our lives as being hidden with Christ in God. We are bound to find mysterious the Abba who seized Jesus. If God looms more imperatively at death, she has been with us from the beginning. No more than a nursing mother could the Spirit forget her charges. Various religious traditions have devised ideal stagings, sketching the way that the self might become more intimate with divine mystery. Hindus, for example, have spoken of four *ashramas* or life stations. In youth, one should study with a guru, be apprenticed to a master. Obedient, poor, chaste, one should study the tradition, the Vedas, and learn from the master's model what the tradition concretely intends. When the tradition has become second nature, one should return to the world. Marrying, engaging in business, taking civic roles, one should let early virtue uncloister. Sex and money, power and production—they will make early virtue mature. So will responsibility for a child, an elderly parent, or a family business.

By the time one's hair is gray and there are grandchildren, one has had enough of family and business life. After midlife, the spirit grows reflective. It wants time to sort things out, retreat from business. So the third classical stage was "forest dwelling." Leaving the world, one goes back to meditation. But whereas traditional truths first were long and wide, now they are very deep. Experience reveals the pervasiveness of desire. Long years make *karma,* the Hindu notion of moral cause and effect, persuasive. If forest dwelling achieves the breakthrough it seeks, there comes the fourth stage of enlightenment. At one with the universal Atman, the Spirit that is the world's soul, the realized Hindu ends as a wandering *sannyasin,* a sage stripped and free. The whole world is his oyster; he teaches with a begging bowl. The message is: All life is instinct with God. Atman abides in every person and corner. Wisdom is union with Atman. The story can have a very happy ending.

Christian notions of the life cycle, the ideal faith-story, took a somewhat different direction. Because Jesus' life was a battleground of sin and love, Christian biography began with the cleansing of sin and ended with union through love. The purgative "way" was a path for beginners. Those who became serious about faith, who wanted to work at sanctity, took up asceticism. They disciplined the body through fasting, work, and penance. They disciplined the mind through meditation, study, and obedience. The goal was to throw off old, selfish habits, to put on the "mind" of Christ. The goal was immersion in the tradition, filling up on the biblical scenes.

In a few years, the generous could expect a transition. Habituated to external discipline and virtue, their next tasks were more interior. In prayer, they usually grew tired of meditation. Reflecting on traditional "truths," probing biblical scenes, making firm resolutions—it all seemed more and more arid. From the depths, the Spirit asked something simpler. "Abide, gaze, attend," she said. In a word, "contemplate." Where meditation was reasoned and analytical, contemplation was affective and collected. Where meditation stressed the mind, contemplation stressed the heart. For the transition sought "illumination." One wanted to "know" in a deep, interpersonal way. With Jesus, one wanted not head to head but heart to heart. Thus, the illuminative way tended to move down into darkness. Paradoxically, it overshadowed the mind, put thought in the shade. For slowly, one was "understanding" that God is no thing. Slowly the mystery, the living too-fullness, was coming home.

Illumination had an energy to pervade one's whole life. Spouse, children, friends—they all became more complex, and so only within reach by great simplicity. The spouse who was beyond analysis one learned by embracing. The kids flying everywhere stayed the apples of one's eye. Where an old friend had first been like-minded, now he or she was a fellow pilgrim. Moving together, friends communicated by silence as much as speech. They relied on one another unquestioningly, felt fully broken in. Now and then, light broke through the cloud, to show how marvelous these simplicities were.

The climax of the Christian story was the unitive way. More and more, mystery was the traveling companion. The God of Moses, with us as he would, became a present reality. If he chose, this was strictly mystical, strictly a thing undergone. Grasping the soul, God espoused it experientially. Delighted, the soul wanted more and more to decrease, that God be all in all. Delighted, the body felt tears of joy, overflowing gratitude for brother sun and sister moon. Ignatius's tears, Francis's joy, Teresa's nuptials proclaim the unitive message. John Berchmans, one of the Jesuit "boy" saints, put unitive living humbly. He was playing billiards, the biographers say, when someone asked what he would do if he knew he were to die the next hour. "Keep playing billiards," he said. Whatever was honest, decent, permitted could carry God's presence. Whatever the purified spirit felt could be God's inspiration. All things were clean to the clean. Only evil minds would find them evil. The grace of union largely burned away concupiscence, wrongful desire, making nature supple and transparent.

When we excavate from such traditional Christian piety nuggets still relevant today, we find the centrality of God's mystery. Time unfolds from a Beginning to a Beyond. Our stories, with all their circumstantial specificity, are tales with a single moral. We all have to learn to love life in face of death. On the way, we all have to learn how living and dying are paradoxical. The seed that falls in the ground burgeons in the spring. By dying Jesus became Lord. The "good life," full of foam and gusto, may be a species of dying. The penthouse pad can imprison the spirit. So, illumination reflects from union toward purgation. All the Christian ways cross the cross. Yet Christian storytellers delight in resurrecting myth and symbol. They make us all hope to grow round and full. Then, we would be light as little children. Then, time could take us outside.

PRAYER

The Catholic notion of the three "ways" could have fit all Church members, but few laity appropriated it. For common folk, prayer and moral fidelity staked out an apparently more pedestrian way. Prayer was usually vocal: Our Father, Hail Mary, the Rosary. The moral fidelity was to the commandments, as the catechism detailed them. But under such apparent simplicity, many grew spiritually wise. Tutored by the Spirit, they turned their prayers to loving conversation with God, their morality to self-sacrifice. By the simplest of wisdom regimes—bare pondering of their experience—they achieved a balance between this-worldliness and otherworldliness, the now of grace and glory's not-yet.

Unpretentiously, such people sometimes realized the pith of the Catholic matter. No matter how their experiences went, where their lives took them, it could turn to religious profit. Were they to achieve financial success, they could praise God for his bounties. Were they to suffer hard times, they could learn deeper detachment. Even their sins could work thanksgiving, as the Easter vigil sang: O happy fault, which merited so great and such a Redeemer. What anthropologist Robert Redfield called "the little tradition", the people's folk ways, also wrote divine comedies. Many simple people, uneducated in express theology, let God purge them, enlighten them, fill more and more of their days. Living with a traditional Catholic family in Madrid, we saw this centuries-old pattern continuing. The widowed grandmother, wrinkled and all in black, spent her time in two occupations. She cooked the family's meals, and she prayed. If cooking took six hours each day, praying took several more.

We do not say cooking and praying exhaust sanctity. Blaise Pascal, the brilliant seventeenth-century scientist, shows how traditional faith's journey can be many-sided. But we do find personal Catholicism implying serious prayer, on both historical and theological grounds. Historically, all professional religionists have been obligated to regular prayer, and all pious laity have been commended to it. Theologically, prayer is probably the most distinctively religious act. That was comparativist Friedrich Heiler's opinion, and theological analysis confirms it. Lifting heart and mind to God, one directly limits the "world." Whether at a public liturgy or a private *prie-dieu*, the person who tries to pray enters the spiritual struggle. From Antony in the desert to the abbot of Moore's *Catholics*, serious prayer has meant testing one's convictions. Persevering prayer puts both God and self to the test. If nothing "happens" at prayer, no light or help appears, what can "God" mean? If nothing happens at prayer, how can the self claim faith? Expressly or not, many Catholics know these questions. That may be why many avoid serious prayer.

It is true that work can be prayerful. "To work is to pray" is a venerable monastic motto. It is also true that contemplative prayer builds on natural dispositions. It comes more easily to old people than young, to introverts than extroverts. But there is solid testimony from humanistic psychology that maturity entails both interiority and exteriority, as there is solid testimony that it entails both "masculine" and "feminine" traits. More compellingly, there is solid testimony from Christian experience that contemplation can enhance almost all personalities. If they find a proper form, almost all who believe can profit from quiet, imagination, centering, and peace.[9] For that reason, contemplation is more than faith's testing. Through the centuries, it has also been faith's nurture.

But what is contemplation? How do we mean it here? First, it is not meditation. Meditation, in Christian parlance, is the **discursive** mental work we mentioned above. (Eastern "meditation," as in Hinduism or Buddhism, is usually not discursive, so there is a Western-Eastern terminological difference.) As we mentioned above, contemplation often follows meditation, when the spirit grows weary with thinking. Second, contemplation may work in vocal prayer, or it may avoid express words. The simple faithful we tried to sketch above often prayed the Rosary throughout their lives. For many, however, the words were not the prime focus. Through the words, they sent affections to God. The words held their imaginations, kept them from daydreams or distractions. Or the words served slow pondering: Our *Father*—that God should be parental! Full of *grace*—that a teenage girl should bear God! Smoothed by long usage, the words slipped by while the heart held loving conversation. Repeated vocal prayers did not grow wearisome, were not just empty clatter, because communion flowed beneath them. They could be empty clatter, as Rosaries at wakes or sing-song litanies showed, but they did not have to be. In the deeply religious, they were slow, loving, contemplative.

Third, contemplation could employ the senses and imagination. Loyola's *Spiritual Exercises* offers a clear method. Take a scene from the gospel—Jesus being baptized by John. Contemplate this scene, by applying each of your senses. See the water of the river Jordan. Note the steep hill behind. Watch Jesus kneel down before the Baptist. Mark his humility, his grace. Then hear what he and John tell one another. Listen to the changing of the guard. Was either of them shouting? Did the heavenly voice startle both? Then sniff the air, smell the water, catch the organic rushes. Feel the dirt of the shore, the texture of John's girdle, the tangle of Jesus' hair. Savor with Jesus the baptismal water. Taste his wet, flowing robe. In every way, imagine yourself a contemporary, a witness to that happening. With little thought, few ideas, let your senses do the praying. Let them help you *be* there—poised, receptive, watchful, admiring. You are doing what thousands before you have done. You are gazing on the Lord—as illiterate peasants did in Chartres, following the stained-glass stories; as street sweepers did in Saint Peter's, before the "Pieta."

However, the heart of contemplative prayer has been its dark nights or clouds of unknowing. Dark nights recall John of the Cross. His classical writings on mysticism describe a cleansing of the senses that mediates between the purgative and illuminative ways, and a cleansing of the spirit that mediates between the illuminative and unitive ways. In both cases, the Spirit labors to teach us how God is God. During the dark night of the senses, she weans us from imagination, thought, and feelings. Though the stress that contemplation places on love assumes that warmth and peace often come, the Spirit qualifies our enjoyment. In early spiritual experience, we need the support of consolation—bright ideas, good feelings, peak experiences. God gives these helps, but not so that we confuse them with divinity. Against our tendency to wrap ourselves snugly in consolation, the Spirit teaches us that consolation is God's *gift*. Against our tendency to be upset during "desolation" (the absence of consolation), she teaches us that patient fidelity purifies.

Thus, a primary "illumination" is the relativity of emotion. Emotion is a way to sense God, an instrument of the Spirit, but it is not divinity. God's love is totally fulfilling, but to experience God's love totally, we have to put human selfishness aside. The depths of self-abnegation come in the dark night of the spirit. There the Spirit works our detachment not just from good feelings but from much "faith," "hope," and "love." Insofar as these theological virtues have not penetrated to our core, and so shone as utterly God's doing, we tend to lean on them, rather than purely on God. As good feelings can screen the self from God, so can imperfect virtue. Those whom God purifies profoundly, in the antechamber to the nuptial suite, are burned of all self-reliance. In John of the Cross' experience, they often feel abandoned. But the spirit keeps a flame of love living, so that one day their embers reblaze. Then union is regular and amazing. Then they are free as a bird. The slightest attachment to things ungodly can keep the soul fettered, so the night of the spirit would burn all attachment away.

There is a profound wisdom in John's contemplative program, as in his complementary program of asceticism. The terminology of both programs, though, is rather forbidding. "Dark nights" or "the ascent of Mount Carmel" may seem only for heroes. That is not so, but it shows the Church's wisdom in encouraging other terminologies. One that recently has returned to favor stems from an anonymous fourteenth-century English classic, *The Cloud of Unknowing*. William Johnston and Basil Pennington are two current writers who have used the *Cloud* to good effect.[10] Essentially, the *Cloud* describes the overshadowing of the mind that occurs when prayer becomes serious. Those drawn to an interior simplicity find that thoughts no longer satisfy. Their tendency is to become discouraged, and so to give up on prayer. A wise spiritual director will show them how their uneasiness may be changed to progress.

God wants a being-to-being relationship. Only that is deep enough to satisfy. To achieve that, God makes us dissatisfied with superficial relationships. Coming into our consciousness, the divine mystery wraps us in opaqueness. We cannot think God as such, because God as such is infinite, immense, too "thick." But we can entertain God as such, can attend and love. The *Cloud* advises just such attention. If it helps, we may take a simple word, such as "love" or "God," and use it to beat against the cloud. That way, we have an arrow to direct our attention. But whether we use an arrow or not, our whole effort ought to be to quiet down, to rest in the center. There God encourages a simple being-with. The author of the *Cloud* is so convinced of the surpassing value of this being-with that he fights off all competitors. There is nothing we can do for our own salvation, or for the good of others, that compares with this direct communion. For the author of the *Cloud,* this direct communion justifies contemplative living experientially.

If we set traditional teaching such as that of John of the Cross and the author of the *Cloud* in a contemporary framework such as Rahner's, it becomes more testimony about divine mystery and grace. Rahner works from the slightly different Ignatian tradition, but his analyses of the times of "consolation,"[11] his going behind *The Spiritual Exercises,* takes other schools into account. We are so made that transparent communion with God is the core of our desire. Only God as God can meet the thrust of our minds and hearts, but God as God is too pure for our sin. So the Spirit loves us to a certain "adequacy," making us less impure. Contemplation is nothing more than that. Working, praying, making love, witnessing politically, we are called by the Spirit to open. When we open, God as God can both invade us and use us. When we open, our work, prayer, making love, and witnessing politically can be sacramental. "Opening," of course, is more than a bit of sleepy attention. Fully mature, it is total generosity. But even we who don't reach total generosity, who are not nominees for canonization, can let time and the Spirit erode our false defenses. Even such as we can learn wisdom by suffering the Spirit.

The overwhelming value of contemplative prayer, then, is its foundation in bedrock essentials. If God is, and is *God,* then everything is theological. God is so encompassing that nothing is real apart from God. We can only see any entity or relation truthfully by estimating its Godwardness. For personal living, this means a happy condemnation to mystery. In the horizon of Christian grace, all stories would unfold a wonderful climax. If we would, we could hear invitations to a marriage. If we would, we could commune with the All. Were that to happen, every spot would be lovely. Were that to happen, the Father would be meat and drink. Jesus lived out from the Father. Contemplation can help us do the same.[12]

MARRIAGE AND FAMILY LIFE

In dialectical method, the juxtaposition or conflict of a thesis and its antithesis is supposed to bring synthetic light. That comes to mind here, because following contemplation with family life will seem to many antithetical. Traditionally, vowed religious were the Catholic Church's contemplatives. They had the leisure for instruction, asceticism, and lengthy prayer. Married people did well to make a morning offering, a noon Angelus, and an evening examination of conscience. "Now I lay me down to sleep, exhausted and distracted," the parent of six usually said. Thus, a first question for a contemporary Catholic theology of marriage and family life might be: Is contemplation possible? Testimony from many quarters shows it is. For instance, *The Wind Is Rising,* produced by the Quixote Center, contains several essays by married people that deal with serious prayer.[13] When they are convinced of its value, even harried parents can make time for quiet talk with God. Seizing some free time, when the kids are away or asleep, they can focus all the whirl toward the cloud.

We begin with this conviction because marriage cannot be a solidly Christian vocation unless it has access to faith's deepest roots.[14] Faith's deepest roots are God's love. God's love can come in many ways, but contemplation is prominent among them. Therefore, our theology of marriage will make it emerge compatible with contemplation. The "one flesh" two spouses hope for will be as exciting an adventure, as rich a potentiality, as the other Christian vocations. As much as these, it will mean commending one's spirit into God's care. We suspect few marriage counselors urge couples to share contemplation, but that just judges most counselors. Anyone who knows contemplation's power to repair a care-worn soul will urge it enthusiastically. For the constant reclarification marriage needs, and the constant forgiveness, contemplation is a marvelous remedy.

Below we consider marital eros, and its link with *agape* (God's love). For the moment, though, let us stress family life. In the traditional theology of marriage, it was primary. Two persons came together that their love might issue children. Begetting children and raising them was marriage's prime reason-to-be. Separating the stress on biology, let us appropriate that view's wisdom. Children do externalize spouses' love. Their begetting and raising does weave cords of common concern. Anne Morrow Lindbergh's *Gift from the Sea* gave the past generation poetic lessons in such themes. Sensitive to time, she saw it fashioning marriage like:

an oyster, with small shells clinging to its humped back. Sprawling and uneven, it has the irregularity of something growing. It looks rather like the house of a big family, pushing out one addition after another to hold its teeming life—here a sleeping porch for children, and there is a veranda for the play-pen; here a garage for the extra car and there is a shed for the bicycles.[15]

No matter that Lindbergh's images came from the upper class. Her basic insight obtained for all: Time shared is bonds woven. The great weavers of bonds are children.

Stereotypically, women have championed this wisdom. Like the old *wicca* (wise woman), they have kept close ties with nature. Nature is growing, including, organic. So would most traditional women have marriage be. Counter to men's absorption with work has been women's traditional absorption with children. Obviously, these assignments are up for grabs today. So, the Christian theology of marriage has to make more of parenting for men, and of work for women, than it did in the past. We shall take up women's work at the end of this chapter. Men's parenting is apt right here.

In our view, parenting ideally involves both spouses, with their particular amounts of reason and emotion. If a father actually is more sober, let the tasks of sobriety be his. But if he actually is more tender-minded, then let the tasks of tender-mindedness be his. William James divided personalities into tender- and tough-minded. We think a child needs, or at least profits from, a man who is rational and emotional and a woman who is the same. Apart from tasks biologically determined, such as nursing or giving birth, fatherhood and motherhood are mainly parenthood. Parenthood supervises sex-specific initiations, for we continue to have men's

women's groups, but its main tasks are not sex-specific: giving physi-
___ ___d emotional support, inculcating tradition, and guiding offspring to
freedom.

Most theologians do not attend much to children, and that is a loss.
Were they to attend seriously, they might realize how much imagination
good catechesis demands.[16] The traditional catechisms, with their definitions and memory drills, were the work of underachievers. There is far
more we might accomplish, had we the playfulness. For instance, there
are wide extensions for the theology of story. Children all love stories,
all respond to "once upon a time." Elie Wiesel has preserved for contemporary Jews the Hasidic genius with stories. Would that some disciple of
Rahner had grown up in a Hasidic circle. Then fairy tales that exorcise
children's fears, rhymes that help them love language, might radiate from
a Christian center. Then we might plunge to the psyche to baptize Oedi-
pus and Electra. Theology can only gain by involving itself with creative
imagination, and who better to keep it interesting than children? "Once
upon a time," children know, is both now and never. It bears upon here
and now, but it comes from Narnia, utopia, a place of free play. If little
ones make up the Kingdom, the Kingdom is a place of free play. The
implication parents should hear is that free play in the family assimilates
the family to the Kingdom.

All our duties are lighter when we recess regularly for free play. To be
sure, there is a time for fact, and strict history. All time is not for free play.
However, in an age of executive parents, fact needs little protection. It
is creative intuition, healthy imagination, that the national endowments
must guard. It is shared play, and the joy it nurtures, that many kids most
need. By entering their play and education, we can do a great deal for
their faith. We can show it is a happy sharing, with a Church of many good
times.

The extensions to conjugal love are important. Previously, we sketched
the low points of Catholic anti-eroticism. Sexual play is something few
Christians have handled well. For instance, few have known how to let
love be sensuous. Few have applauded the male-female duel. Most
theologians have allegorized the hints of God's passion—the places in
Hosea and the song of Solomon. Therefore, most bedrooms have turned
out the lights.

Eros goes out to the beautiful and the fulfilling. That is obvious in sex,
but true also in study and art. Are disorders in sexual eros more profound
than those in study and art? Is that why we have fixated there? If we
compare evils, our fixation has been a serious mistake. Indeed, our fixation has meant not letting people realize, from their own experience, how
demanding erotic love becomes. To stand on its edge, and see more than
one's own fulfillment, takes one toward agape. Many couples attain this,
but few without much labor. The sadness Aristotle found after coition
shows that sexual eros is no full religion. No finite good satisfies for long,

not even our intensest union. Only when intense union moves in a horizon of unrestricted love, open to God's more can it finally not be frustrating. To ask it to be the whole, or even the prime, is to taste the ashes of idolatry.

We put the matter of sexual union elliptically, that fine matters stay fine. The base line, though, is urging marital eros on. As Montessori kids explore and explore, so should married couples. Kindling their imaginations, turning their wits, let them try all decent options. If God is a consuming fire, Plato was right to call eros a god. We have shown how a god can be an idol. Let us now show how it can be a sacrament. In other words, let us bring conjugal eros to the sanctuary, as we have brought eating and drinking. Plunging the paschal candle into the baptismal water, let us celebrate Christ's union with the Church.

RELIGIOUS AND SINGLE LIFE

In this section, "religious life" means consecration to God through public vows of poverty, chastity, and obedience. Thus, it means monks, nuns, brothers, and many priests. Through Church history, they have been an inestimable resource.

Their beginnings go back to the desert, where zealous Christians early sought relief from the world. More positively, they sought total absorption with God. From the Edict of Milan (313), which set Christians free from Roman persecution, religious life prospered. Community living became the rule, in both the East and the West, for experience showed that total absorption with God was not for the untutored.

It was for the poor. Taking Jesus' beatitudes and counsels seriously, early monks and nuns lived with few material things. They wanted to be free for prayer, service, or pilgrimage. Similarly, they wanted to be free of family burdens, and to fix all their eros on God. So they made Jesus' counsel of chastity the matter of a second vow. Obedience capped their dedication, for it reached deep into the will. To follow the will of another, who stood for God and the common good, was deep asceticism.

Insofar as these three vows go against worldly instincts, they spotlight the witness of religious' *being*. By what they are, or what they try to become, religious symbolize the eschaton. The eschaton is God's free consummation of human history. It takes us outside the world. By their existential style, religious ought to witness that God surpasses the world, that the eschaton is heavenly. They ought *ontologically* to be a sort of scandal. Other, different, possessed of Jesus' peculiar values, religious ought to confound a horizon limited to money, pleasure, and individual freedom. If the beholder's eyes see only those, religious are bound to be offensive.

That is something of the tradition of religious being. Complementing it, as action complements essence, have been religious' works. Their services, in schools, hospitals, missionary outposts and more, have been a second witness. Mother Teresa of Calcutta, now recognized worldwide through the Nobel Prize, is the daughter of a centuries-old line. Vincent de Paul, Louise de Marillac, and countless others preceded her in embracing the poor wholeheartedly. It is Mother Teresa's charisma to have embraced the most abject poor in an age of rampant luxury. The nations of the North, who can afford noble prizes, find her utterly unearthly. The nations of the South, who scarcely share the earth with the North, find her one of their own. One need not embrace Mother Teresa's conservative theology to applaud her saintliness. She continues religious' venerable tradition of showing the average person biographic possibilities he or she probably never glimpsed.

In the contemporary context, religious face a cluster of serious problems. Since Vatican II, almost all groups have been preoccupied with "renewal." They have lost a significant fraction of their membership, and have felt somewhat adrift. That may be changing now, as though they have turned a corner. The authors of one recent sociologically based study, *Shaping the Coming Age of Religious Life,* [17] thought recent times represent a shift in the conception of religious life as drastic as that of great changes in the past. We suspect they are right. If the Vatican II ecclesiology of "the People of God" takes hold,[18] so that lay Christians no longer consider themselves second-class, religious life will have to be chosen for its intrinsic merits. That will probably diminish the number of religious, but deepen and clarify their vocation. The gift of religious vocation, especially that of virginity, may be rarer than past ages assumed. Nonetheless, when it brings people to maturity and freedom for service, it is a most powerful index of God. Out of deep contemplation and supportive community lives, religious can put the heavenly Jerusalem on Main Street. All but the purely contemplative among them want this. We pray that Church authorities grant them the freedom to attempt it.

Historically, single Catholics have received worse than short shrift. Neither "special" like religious, nor "normal" like married folk, they have easily seemed eccentric. "Bachelor" and "old maid," for instance, have not been positive terms. There are signs that this is changing. Single Christians still grope for a theology of their vocation, but perhaps with less sense of inferiority. They draw ambiguous support from the common culture, where singles' economic clout and recreational needs have won considerable attention, and from the liberation of both women and gays. However, sexuality remains a pressing issue, for our moral theology doesn't quite know what to advise. From the past it receives the stern verdict that all intercourse outside of marriage is grievously sinful. From the present it receives joshings that continence went out with the ark. The individual has always had to make the final decision, but he or she must find a middle road today midst swirls of constant confusion.

As the needle returns to the well-worn groove, so does this return us to eros. The close ties between sex and love, body and spirit, argue that traditional morality had much wisdom. The generous evidences of repression that traditional morality caused argue that things need to be more flexible now. In the absence of sufficient precisely contemporary experience, singles' sexual activity demands especially prudent discernment. When an attraction arises, honest prayer will be a giant help. Things *are* different because of cultural changes. Our travel, variety of work roles, awareness of psychological forces, and controls on fertility make us somewhat nontraditional. Until the full implications of this change become clear, we have to go case by case.

A great advantage of being single is the freedom it can offer. Those who want to serve in a variety of situations, or who feel drawn to works especially absorbing, may find singleness God's provision. Dag Hammarskjöld of the United Nations comes to mind. Slowly, he found that his work fit his (hard-won) faith and was a preoccupying vocation. Less dramatically, there comes to mind an aunt who spent forty years at the same hospital. She trained there as a student nurse and died there near retirement. For decades she lived in a single room, breakfasting for seven cents a day. She was Santa Claus to several families, a good friend to dozens outside. If the opportunity arose, she would travel on the shortest notice. If the opportunity did not arise, she was content with the usual rounds. In time she took over the outpatient department, serving the poor from teeth to toes. With little incongruity, she would go from Lenten devotions to a clinic on venereal disease. Her main resource, though, was early morning Mass. Having nursed and buried her own mother, she moved into the nurses' home. From there it was but a skip to the chapel, and before long she was hearing Mass daily before dawn. Though she died rather young, there was a sense of fulfillment. Her solitude had not been loneliness, for she had generated a wealth of good deeds.

Passing from one vocation to another, especially through divorce or widowhood, throws many traditional Catholics into a state they had not expected. Whatever the duration, it is something come from God. Christian providence justifies that conviction, but something more recent could enhance it. That is the understanding, again implicit in the ecclesiology of Vatican II,[19] that all the Christian vocations are more alike than different. Whether one is married, a religious, or single, one is first a member of Christ. Catholics are a long way from fully realizing this, as those who have left one state for another too often learn. One who leaves home for religious life can still suffer incomprehension. One who leaves religious life to marry can still find bitterness. The person, especially the woman, who is newly single, is a social irregularity. If divorced, she is almost a triple threat. This is a sad commentary on our faith. To find, for instance, that friends from religious life consider a common habit more important than a common faith is saddening, even angering. However right it is that religious shore one another up, a blindness to deeper things suggests idolatry. Analogues from other vocations suggest the same. Below our legitimate vocational differences, we ought to be neither Jew nor Gentile, slave nor free, male nor female, married, religious, nor single. We ought to be brothers and sisters in Christ.

WORK, PLAY, AND ECOLOGY

Work cuts across all the Christian vocations. Married people work, inside and outside the home, to keep the family going. Religious work in fields and classrooms. Single people staff offices, factories, schools, and hospitals. If Freud's statement about human health is true concerning love, it is equally true concerning work. Unless they find their work satisfying, most people do not write happy stories. Thus, the Genesis association of work with the sin of Adam and Eve does not mean we should help labor be painful. Rather, we often most clearly reflect God by interacting with materials, natural or human, creatively. By making, doing, serving, we redeem most of our time. Contemplation is a doing, as well as an undergoing, but here "work" will mean action. What light do Christian convictions shed on active work? What do they counsel for this great portion of our spirituality?

Though he is no friend of Marx, Eric Voegelin has given the author of *Das Kapital* his due regarding work.[20] Marx was the first significant labor theoretician, the first to show work's economic and philosophical depths. As is common knowledge, his view was rather grim. The average laborer in industrial England was little better than chattel. It took that most advanced country decades to pass laws limiting laborers' hours. In the late eighteenth and early nineteenth centuries, 14- to 15-hour work days were common. So, from simple observation, Marx saw that most people experienced work as alienation. It stood between them and nature, them and society, them and their selves.[21] Whereas the preindustrial artisan often had a satisfying craft, the factory worker did mindless tasks mid absolutely wretched working conditions. Mindlessness and damaging conditions continue in the United States today. The assembly line is a straight recipe for boredom; the conditions in the mills, steel or textile, remain hazardous. What keeps us from changing such obvious inhumaneness? Why does so much work continue to cause alienation?

Much of the answer is greed. As a society, we place greater value on profit than on work-fulfillment. Therefore Christians, as well as Marxists, have summonses to lay at the unbridled capitalist's door. When he forced his hearers to choose between God and mammon, Jesus strongly limited capitalism. Despite certain Christian groups' close identification with capitalist drive and prosperity, limiting it remains the first Christian instinct. Fortunately, the brunt of recent Catholic social doctrine has emphasized this theme eloquently. From Leo XIII to John Paul II, the popes have qualified the rights of capitalism. In other creative theology, the verdict is even starker. Latin American theologians, for instance, see North American and European capitalism as the root of their people's poverty. Looking at Chile, they even see it alongside their people's politics: ITT and the CIA were instrumental in Allende's downfall.

More personally and positively, economists such as the Catholic E. F. Schumacher have proposed an excellent alternative. Schumacher's posthumous book *Good Work* repeats themes from his early one *Small Is Beautiful*, including those of its essay "Buddhist Economics."[22] In that essay, a main point is simplicity. Too much Western work goes toward producing complicated nonessentials. By contrast, the Buddhist ethic that Schumacher learned about in Burma emphasized spareness and the worker's welfare. For example, clothing was to be functional and simple. True Buddhists would rather produce uncut cloth that can be draped elegantly than a peacock variety of fashionable clothes. The uncut cloth cost little, in time as well as money, and did not feed vanity. More generally, what happened to the worker, and to the recipient of the work, was more important than what happened to the bank account. If either worker or recipient suffered diminishment (alienation), the work had gone wrong somehow. For work ought to occasion spiritual growth. It ought to supply fundamental needs, advance the worker's self-expression, and encourage cooperation. Any other, negative, result would make work irrational, inhuman.

Studs Terkel's interviews with working people show that much Western work is indeed inhuman.[23] From waitress to mechanic, his interviewees are frustrated. Women suffer special frustrations, as do minorities. Sexism, rampant in our work culture, lays vicious hands on the clerical pool. Indeed, women suffer discrimination by every objective index. In pay, power, or promotion, they come up short. Things are changing slowly, but with great resistance. When it colludes with profit and power, sexism makes a diabolical trinity.

Thus a full equalization of women in the work force is potent, theologically. If they stay free of male biases, women managers might redeem much business. For humane administration, as humane work overall, focuses first on people. Women's current biological-cultural inheritance tends to make a personal focus instinctive. It is the rare woman who is not sensitive interpersonally. It is the rare woman who, if not manipulated by male pressures, would not rather cooperate than compete. Were Catholics to join feminist labor theory to Christian instinct like Schumacher's we could be as critical as Marxists, and far more constructive.

The Scott Bader Commonwealth, with which Schumacher was associated, tried to make work a fair sharing. It insisted on work groups of small scale, so that workers could know one another, and on an equitable distribution of profits. Schumacher lamented that a seven to one salary ratio, top to bottom, was the best that Scott Bader could accomplish, but if you compare salaries of the head of ITT and a lowly clerk, you might call Scott Bader a paradise. At ITT the ratio would be about seventy to one.

Of course, salary ratios, and even working conditions, are not the whole story. Christian labor reform means doing all we can to make work a form of self-expression and service. Refusing to produce junk, insisting on quality, focusing on basic needs, we ought to work in the image of our parental God, who labors always for our growth and healing.

A hinge between work and play is poetry, the old-fashioned *poesis*. Yesterday *poesis* meant "making"—crafting, fashioning, creating. Today it is little different: Good poets craft words to diamond hardness by disciplined imagination. Imagination has to well up from the unconscious, and then fit itself to forms or patterns. The free, finally uncontrollable welling-up is a species of play. The fitting to forms and patterns is more onerous, a species of work. So the poet is both player and worker, both *homo ludens* and *homo faber*. When you find your own *poesis,* you find half your own reflection of God. Wisdom played before God, and then entered the form of creation.

It is hard to balance play and discipline in the study, even harder when the poet runs into business. In the study, one must trick free fancy to make new suggestions—to reach back to childhood, wonder "what if the farmer's daughter. . . ." The tricks of discipline are less subtle, but equally important. Whoever said genius is ninety percent hard work knew whereof she spoke. Having set fancy free, one has to corral it and then set it to plowing. There is no substitute for regular plowing, if one wants either productivity or an uncramped style. Where a method actor would discuss a scene for two hours, Laurence Olivier would walk through it ten times. It is by doing that a creation plays out its potentials, by baking that dough becomes bread. So creative art, however humble, means lessons in freedom and discipline. Play stands on the side of freedom, work on the side of discipline, but they serve a common purpose. The happy worker loves labor for its creativity, plays with discipline to advance the self.

There is little play when creativity runs into business. Too often, those who bankroll art devour the revenues. As a rule, those who create receive ten percent, those who produce ninety. Even when profit keeps its hands off creativity itself (which is far from always), its "reality" sours the play. Many artists keep a close eye on the ledger. But those who give our culture its fresh vision often have a childlike vulnerability. The play portion of their creativity, the fancy they develop, makes them confused by money and profits. What have money and profits to do with making something beautiful? What do they know of the spirit or the muse?[24]

Exercise is an area where the body can share in play. True, the body can share in play through sport or song or dance. But exercise is more democratic, demands fewer special skills. Also, it has venerable connections with religion, especially in the East.

If you run, swim, do aerobic dance, you can discipline your body to play. Once you're in shape, so your muscles don't protest, you can begin to go beyond the physical. Of course, the physical always remains, but there is a further spiritual potential. You can feel a groove, a circuit, a "way." When it comes, you start to run integrally. Your body does not fight your mind. Your spirit trains all your senses, recording the impact of your feet, the wind at your cheek, the purr of your pulmonary engines. And it plays these recordings to the God of creation, who made matter for such communion.[25] So doing, it recalls Native American themes.

Amerindians, of course, were more "ecological" than their white antagonists. Though some of our lore about them is unfortunately romantic, it is true that they honored nature. The plant to be cut, the deer to be shot, merited an explanation. In the hard cycle of lives, where one survived off the other, hunting kept a poignant sadness. Similarly, farming kept a touching gentleness, for it dealt with a pregnant mother. To tread heavily on the earth in the days of spring was to injure a living matron.[26] When we consider the American earth today, we do well to remember that history. The strip-miner's myth has ousted the myth of the matronly earth, and what has taken her place? Along Love Canal, beside Niagara Falls, people grew leaden from chemical pollution. There was no life where their children played, no water still nontoxic. Farther west, the story just changes its scene, but sings of acid rain.

Though its own practice cautions against great expectations, Eastern religion might be an ecological ally. The Logos and Wisdom that emerged as the Tao (Way) made nature China's prime divinity. Return to nature, the Taoist sage Lao Tzu said, if you wish to find your own essence. The uncarved block is the better self; the Tao moves patiently like water. The Taoist sage Chuang Tzu taught the same naturalism but he put it more pungently. It is better to drag your tail in the mud, to be contented like the turtle. If you drag your tail to court, you are more than likely to lose it. As a Zen Buddhist finds nature to be harmonious, so does a Chuangtzuian Taoist. In any logic worth its salt, that would make for an ecological religion.[27] Contemporary Japan shows that scarcity of logic is not peculiarly Western—its smog may soon ruin its rock gardens.

For Catholic theologians, ecological reform will be hard, if our population continues to be urban. Without a firm footing in the land, we shall have to work through pollution's toll on humans. Jesus cannot be pantocrator, Lord of all, if the *all* is rotten and polluted. The air we breathe, the food we eat, the water we swim must be purer. If that means a steady-state economy, an advance toward Ernest Callenbach's "Ecotopia,"[28] so be it. By its fruits, the economics of "bigger is better" shows itself suspect. So does the theology of "nature is a slave, a pawn of our good pleasure." Future Catholic spirituality has to work harder to make us love nature as a set of fellow creatures with clear and holy rights.

SUMMARY

Where the previous chapter dealt with ecclesial aspects of Christianity, this chapter began with the Christian self. At the outset, we looked at the current theological interest in story. We all have a tale to tell, and its substance is our self. History, biography, and autobiography converge on such telling, as does biblical narrative. For the individual, religious traditions have staged the life cycle with both ceremonies and received wisdom. The Hindu schema of four *ashramas* was a powerful influence on India. In the West, Christians spoke of three successive "ways." A major index of those ways' development was the sort of prayer each urged. The shift from purgative to illuminative living, for instance, often correlated with a move from meditation to contemplation. "Contemplation" has had various connotations in Christian history, and it is useful to explain them. The profoundest has been the mystics' effort to know God as God.

Some would argue that contemplation in the mystics' sense is bound to be elitist. Others, stressing the common foundation that all Christian vocations have in baptism and grace, would not withhold it from any who find it attractive. For all people, married or single, religious or lay, God does the contemplative calling. So prayer is a way that the vocations share, but there are other ways that they differ. For instance, by their vows religious oppose the "world," and by their service they confound it. Single persons' service can do the same, though singles now need a clearer theology of vocation. Married couples try to grow to one flesh, and to raise the next generation. For the latter task they need imaginative help, which could return us to the theology of story. Finally, all Christians contend with eros and agape, work, play, and nature. Any future Catholic spirituality therefore will have to be holistic.

STUDY QUESTIONS

1. In what sense are we each a teller and a tale?
2. Explain the traditional three stages of Christian spiritual development.
3. Why is prayer a prime test of faith?
4. How valid do you find the argument from *The Cloud of Unknowing* that being with God is the most valuable thing any person can do?
5. Discuss the biblical symbol of marriage as making two one flesh.
6. What is the ontological scandal that religious life ought to be?
7. What seem to you the key tasks of the spiritual life of a single Catholic?
8. Why should Christian spirituality concern itself with work?
9. How should a Christian spirituality coordinate work and play?
10. Why should ecology be on the next generation's spiritual agenda?

NOTES

1. See Denise Lardner Carmody and John Carmody, *Religion: The Great Questions* (New York: Seabury, 1983).
2. See, for example, John Shea, *Stories of God* (Chicago: Thomas More, 1978); idem, *Stories of Faith* (Chicago: Thomas More, 1980); Thomas Cooper and John Navone, *Tellers of the Word* (New York: LeJacq, 1981).
3. William A. Clebsch, *Christianity in European History* (New York: Oxford, 1979).
4. Lawrence S. Cunningham, *The Catholic Heritage* (New York: Crossroad, 1983).
5. John S. Dunne, *A Search for God in Time and Memory* (New York: Macmillan, 1969).
6. See, for example, Shea, *Stories of God.*
7. See James W. Fowler, *Stages of Faith* (San Francisco: Harper & Row, 1981).
8. See Robert Kegan, *The Evolving Self* (Cambridge, Mass.: Harvard University Press, 1982).
9. See Roger Corless, *The Art of Christian Alchemy* (New York: Paulist, 1981).
10. See William Johnston, ed., *The Cloud of Unknowing* (Garden City, N.Y.: Doubleday, 1973); Basil Pennington, *Daily We Touch Him* (Garden City, N.Y.: Doubleday, 1977).
11. See Karl Rahner, *The Dynamic Element in the Church* (New York: Herder and Herder, 1964).
12. See Harvey Egan, *What Are They Saying About Mysticism?* (Ramsey, N.J.: Paulist, 1982).
13. William Callahan and Francine Cardman, eds., *The Wind Is Rising* Hyattsville, Md.: Quixote Center, 1978).
14. See Walter Kasper, *Theology of Christian Marriage* (New York: Crossroad, 1983); Denise Lardner Carmody and John Tully Carmody, *Becoming One Flesh* (Nashville: The Upper Room, 1984).
15. Anne Morrow Lindbergh, *Gift from the Sea* (New York: Vintage, 1955), p. 80.
16. See Thomas H. Groome, *Christian Religious Education* (San Francisco: Harper & Row, 1980).
17. Lawrence Cada *et al., Shaping the Coming Age of Religious Life* (New York: Seabury, 1979).
18. See Richard P. McBrien, *Catholicism,* vol. 2 (Minneapolis: Winston, 1980), pp. 593–95.
19. See Pope John Paul II, *Sources of Renewal: The Implementation of Vatican II* (San Francisco: Harper & Row, 1980), p. 112.
20. Eric Voegelin, *From Enlightenment to Revolution* (Durham, N.C.: Duke University Press, 1975).
21. See Robert L. Heilbroner, *Marxism: For and Against* (New York: W. W. Norton, 1980).
22. E. F. Schumacher, *Good Work* (New York: Harper & Row, 1979); idem, *Small Is Beautiful* (New York: Harper & Row, 1973).
23. See Studs Terkel, *Working* (New York: Pantheon Books, 1974).
24. See Ann Tyler, *Celestial Navigation* (New York: Alfred A. Knopf, 1974).
25. See John Carmody, *Holistic Spirituality* (Ramsey, N.J.: Paulist, 1983), pp. 76–85.
26. See Joseph Epes Brown, *The Spiritual Legacy of the American Indian* (New York: Crossroad, 1982); Sam D. Gill, *Native American Traditions: Sources and Interpretations* (Belmont, Calif.: Wadsworth, 1983).
27. See John Carmody, *Ecology and Religion* (Ramsey, N.J.: Paulist, 1983).
28. Ernest Callenbach, *Ecotopia* (New York: Bantam, 1977).

CHAPTER 8

Politics

TRADITIONAL CATHOLIC SOCIAL TEACHINGS

Social justice has been on Pope John Paul II's mind from the beginning of his pontificate. In part, this interest reflects his pastoral experience in Poland, where a Communist regime forces Catholics to reflect on the sociopolitical features of their faith very carefully. In part, it also reflects his need to respond to movements in Europe and Latin America that insist on the gospel's political impact. So long as John Paul II influences Catholic theology, then, the social dimension of traditional faith will likely be front and center.

In treating the materials of this chapter, we depart somewhat from a Rahnerian outline of current Catholic theology. Although Rahner has long stressed the historical character of human existence and long admitted its social side, politics and liberation have not loomed large on his horizon. That has provoked a sizeable reaction from some of his disciples, as we shall see below. He has responded to their criticism quite favorably, allowing that Christian visions such as his own do have to develop a theology of politics, and even signing protest statements, such as that which a group of German theologians issued on the eve (Fall 1978) of the Latin American bishops' meeting at Puebla to oppose manipulations by the Right.

The reason systematic theologians such as Rahner did not pay much attention to social issues in the past was the tract division of the theology they inherited. If one worked in dogmatics or systematics, one paid little attention to biblical studies or moral theology, and vice versa. This division has now broken down. Nonetheless, it shaped theologians of Rahner's generation, making social justice the province of moralists. The moralists had considerable material on which to concentrate, for from Pope Leo XIII on the papacy became interested in questions of labor, justice, and international order. The stimulus to this interest was historical: Europe was in the throes of various social changes. The upheavals of 1848, the year of Marx's *Communist Manifesto,* brought home to conservatives that the established order was in crisis, and by 1891 Pope Leo, himself temperamentally quite conservative, had realized that social justice bears heavily on Catholic faith. Since his *Rerum Novarum* of that year, papal theology has distinguished itself through a series of increasingly more visionary social statements.

David Hollenbach's recent *Claims in Conflict*[1] focuses on the central issue organizing the series of papal pronouncements: the dignity of the human person. On the way to a creative dialogue with non-Catholic theories of human rights, Hollenbach provides a concise history of the recent Catholic tradition. For Leo XIII the watchword was, "Man precedes the State." In other words, political and legal institutions are good or evil by the standard of what they do to human beings. They exist for human beings, not vice versa. On the other hand, Leo opposed democratic theories of the state. Arguing from **natural law** tradition, which sees rights and duties as built into human nature by God, he opposed the notion that political power and moral values are the product of humans' free choice. Rather, there is an objective order that balances human voluntarism and moral restraint. Reading this position in the context of its times, one can see an effort to hold a middle ground between tyrannies of either the Right or the Left.

Rerum Novarum also took aim at economic abuses. By 1891 industrialism had shown the abuses to which it was liable, and many people had grown aware of workers' oppression. Leo argued, in defense of workers, that systems that stripped them of their dignity, for instance, by paying wages that failed to allow them a decent living, stood condemned as the offspring of greed. The next innovator in Catholic social teaching, Pius XI, worked in a historical context dominated by three contemporary developments: the Great Depression, the consolidation of the Russian Revolution of 1917 into a functional Communist regime, and the rise of fascism in Italy and Germany. His encyclical *Quadragesimo Anno,* issued in commemoration of the fortieth anniversary of *Rerum Novarum,* combined a reaffirmation of the dignity of the human person with a keen look at the economics of depression. Its principal protest was directed against vast disparities in human wealth, and it championed the proletariat. Although Pius rejected a Marxist-Leninist framework, in which the proletariat were counseled to class warfare, he condemned the capitalist tendency to reduce people to merely their economic functions. The implications of the "Body of Christ" demanded that the worker be more than an interchangeable part of a huge machine. Out of this same conviction Pius opposed National Socialism. *Mit Brennender Sorge* (1937) rejected Nazism because it subordinated human beings to the state, the Aryan race, and Germany's ongoing structures of power.

Deeply influenced by World War II, Pius XII made the central traditional tenet, the dignity of the human person, more explicit still. Developing natural law theory, which had the danger of seeming rather extrinsic and wooden, he taught that all forms of social life are essentially moral relationships. From that teaching it follows that decent social life—decent politics, economics, and culture—is impossible without conceiving of the state as a community of morally responsible citizens. That might have sounded utopian, had Pius not issued a balancing call for legal and institutional structures that could give such a community a firm shape. Moreover, Pius XII went into some detail on the specific rights that human dignity entails. His Christmas address of 1942, for instance, spoke of rights to maintain and develop one's bodily, intellectual, moral, and religious dimensions; the right to exercise religion through worship and charitable works; the right to marry and procreate; the right to work; the right freely to choose one's state in life (e.g., the right to answer a religious vocation); the right to use material goods; the right to exist, have a good name, and develop one's own culture and national character; and the right to have international treaties observed and natural law respected.

The next leap forward in Catholic social teaching came with John XXIII, whose relatively brief pontificate not only begot the influential encyclicals *Mater et Magistra* (1961) and *Pacem in Terris* (1963), but also provided an international gathering, the Second Vatican Council, that could imprint the principles of those encyclicals on Catholic leaders' consciousness. The Johannine encyclicals sailed the human rights channel full speed ahead. Indeed, John responded to the growing strength of the Italian Communist Party by admitting that Communist teaching could have "elements that are positive and deserving of approval." His encyclicals were more sophisticated than his predecessors' in other ways, too, acknowledging the complexity of both national and international social relationships. In fact, *Pacem in Terris* was a watershed in Catholic social teaching, because it systematically applied the fundamental criterion, the welfare of the human person, to the various zones of social relationships. From this humanistic center, civil, political, social, and economic rights form a web. Human beings are so intrinsically social that this web constitutes much of their well-being.

During the Second Vatican Council the bishops assembled gave considerable attention to social justice. Two documents were special fruits of such attention, that on the Church in the modern world and that on religious liberty. In situating the Church in the modern world, the Council more clearly came to grips with the historical aspects of social situations than previous Catholic teaching had. Whereas the scholastic framework of the previous teaching had a tendency, from its roots in classicist thought, to abstract from temporality and change, the conciliar document faced change squarely. All specific situations in which justice is to be achieved both suffer the impress of the past and partake of current consciousness. Realizing this, contemporary human beings are tempted to relativism. The bishops wanted to avoid relativism, but they also wanted to sympathize with the confusions and difficulties that rapid change brings. Concrete social morality often will be a matter of prudence and discernment. For instance, anyone trying to achieve justice through the political apparatus of a pluralistic Western society will face compromise every day. Anyone pondering the ethical implications of rapidly moving areas like biological or chemical research will have to think creatively.

The Council's statement on religious liberty both explained the implications of the current fluid situation for Catholic social doctrine and removed a blemish of the past tradition. The implications of social change boiled down to a vote for development. Catholic social teaching should change and grow. It has to recognize the empirical truths of new situations and advance its core convictions to illumine them. The blemish on past Catholic human rights doctrine was its restriction of religious liberty. Though that doctrine had nuance, outsiders had grounds for their impression that when Catholics were a minority in a given population, they spoke out loudly for the right to worship, educate their children in parochial schools, and proselytize. When they were a majority, they wanted the special rights of an established religion and, consequently, a curtailment of the competition. For instance, in Spain the rights of Protestants were distinctly inferior to those of Catholics. In many eras of European history, the Church had seriously abused the civil and religious rights of Jews. The conciliar document made it clear that all human beings have the right to form their religious consciences freely and express them publicly. Americans were especially proud of this doctrinal development, for their experience in a pluralistic situation, as argued elegantly by the Jesuit John Courtney Murray, was the strongest force provoking such change. Murray had come under a cloud in the 1940s and was prohibited from teaching on church-state relations. The conciliar decree on religious liberty was his great vindication.

During the pontificate of Paul VI Third World peoples received special attention. In *Populorum Progressio* (1967) and *Octagesima Adveniens* (1971), Paul brought the historicity of social institutions to bear on the problem of underdevelopment. *Populorum Progressio* is subtle, sophisticated, and tentative, as the complexity of its problems demands. Development ought to occur on all levels, economic and spiritual, and it ought to take into account the worldwide community of nations. Thus, Christian conscience constrains rich nations to limit economic expansion that would, willy-nilly, depress or abuse poor nations. God gives the goods of the earth for all the earth's people. In many cases, the name of poorer people's justice will be development toward economic parity. *Octagesima Adveniens,* written to commemorate the eightieth anniversary of *Rerum Novarum,* acknowledges the conflicts that developmental justice can encounter. In that regard, it offers a limited approval of Marxist and socialist tools of analysis, distinguishing them from their **ideological** or philosophical foundations. A stimulus to such approval was the Marxist-Christian dialogue that flourished in Europe in the 1960s.

The 1971 international Synod of Bishops affirmed many of the principles in Pope Paul's encyclicals, as well as their global horizon. Also, it offered a new version of the old criterion of the human person's dignity. When a society marginalizes a significant number of people, injustice clearly prevails. Removing marginalization, or increasing participation, therefore, offers a great tool, both theoretical and practical, for advancing social justice.

The recent popes' social teachings have a new spokesman in John Paul II, as his encyclicals and addresses have shown from the beginning. More compelling even than cogent social theory such as that of John Paul II, though, has been the example of individuals and agencies that have put Catholic faith in the oneness of the human family into practice. Mother Teresa of Calcutta has deservedly received great attention for her self-sacrifice on behalf of India's most wretched poor, but she has been preceded over the centuries by hundreds of nurses and missionaries similarly dedicated. In the United States the relief agencies of many Catholic dioceses have distinguished themselves by their labors on behalf of the indigent, most recently on behalf of Vietnamese refugees. Indeed, the international character of Roman Catholicism makes its charities an effective reminder that we human billions share a single, small and fragile planet.[2] And whatever is done for starving Africans, Asians, or other Third World people is an act pregnant with faith, for, as **Rahner** has shown, in the final analysis, love of neighbor and love of God are one.[3]

It remains, then, only to tally the strengths and weaknesses of the recent popes' social doctrine. In our estimation, the strengths of the recent "gospel of peace and justice," as Joseph Gremillion has named Catholic social teaching since John XXIII,[4] include the following: a worldwide viewpoint; independence of local political or economic party interests; and a consequent ability to criticize socialistic and capitalistic abuses equally. The Catholic social justice tradition has kept the concrete life of individual human beings front and center, and often it has endeavored to speak a generalist language, translating its convictions for nonbelievers and basing them on the humanity that all people share.

Among weaknesses or lacks that remain we reckon, in agreement with

Hollenbach, that Catholic social teaching could do more to suggest concrete ways of arbitrating social conflict. Hollenbach suggests three strategic priorities: The needs of the poor take priority over the wants of the rich; the freedom of the dominated takes priority over the liberty of the powerful; the participation of marginalized groups takes priority over the preservation of an order which excludes them. Were these strategic priorities to win acceptance, the justice that a Christian expects from arbitration would be close at hand.

Two further weaknesses are the tradition's slighting of ecological issues, and its silence about its own failings in justice. The slighting of ecology shows in Gremillion's "Overview": the references are passing, abstract, and woefully inadequate to the abuses. Of the 138 pages, only 2.5 deal with "Environment and Human Settlements." This indicates the low rank that ecology has had in even the most recent Catholic social teaching and it also suggests the cause: Catholic social thought has considered nature only in relation to humans' use of it.

The Church leadership's relative silence about its own failings in justice is a matter of ordinary human weakness, but also of insensitivity. The truism that any group's idealism is discredited by its contradictory practice has special acuteness when that idealism supposedly expresses divine revelation. Thus employers who closely represent the Church (e.g., heads of Catholic schools and hospitals) and oppose collective bargaining or the formation of unions; Church leaders who refuse to reverse the marginalization of women; and the lack of due process in proceedings against "suspect" theologians all vitiate the lofty social preaching. They and other blind spots cause more than the cynical to wonder whether the Church's eloquence isn't a rather cheap voice *ad extra*—a rather easy preaching to the nations rather than the self.

POLITICAL THEOLOGY: EUROPE AND NORTH AMERICA

Largely from contact with Marxists, European theologians outside the Roman center have tried to open the Catholic tradition to radical social criticism. Frequently this opening has been rather cerebral, entailing (especially in Germany) heady discussions of hermeneutics (principles of interpretation), the sociology of knowledge, the utopian functions of imagination, and so forth. At its center, though, has been a commendable concern to accept the manifest truths in a Marxist critique of class antagonisms, ideologies, and false consciousness. For instance, it seems a fact, hidden only from ostriches, that one's position in a society shapes one's perceptions of that society's economics and politics. Thus, those who profit from the status quo tend to preserve it, and even to overlook its injustices. By contrast, those whom a status quo oppresses are primed to see injustice everywhere.

Similarly, it takes no great historical or contemporary exposure to admit truth in the Marxist claim that religion can prop false consciences and an unjust status quo. When religion is unreflective, or closely coincides with nationalism, it is slow to translate God's call into doing the truth in love. That slowness is partly understandable, as all human weakness is, and partly the irrational, ugly tardiness we call sin. Colluding with the wealthy and the power bearers, religionists, Catholic Christians among them, have in some situations become tools of oppression. Admitting this, denying that it is a legitimate implication of the gospel, and showing parallel abuses in Marxist regimes has advanced European Catholics into "political" theology. Many have accepted the Marxist challenge of making faith alleviate suffering and overturn systemic abuses. With at least implicit reliance on a theory of universal grace, such theologians praise truth and goodness wherever they find them, caring more for the game than the players' uniforms.

Perhaps the most prominent European Catholic political theologian has been J. B. Metz, and his relationship to Rahner is interesting. He was Rahner's student, edited *Hearers of the Word* (Rahner's clearest anthropology), and remains a close friend. Yet "Baptist," as Rahner calls him, led the criticism of transcendental Thomism such as Rahner's, on the grounds that it neglected the importance of sociopolitical factors. Transcendental Thomism's strength lay in its analyses of individual consciousness. It was in good measure bringing Aquinas into dialogue with Kant and Hegel. But it did not move on from Hegel to Marx—to social factors and *praxis* (action, practice). The Frankfurt School of socio-philosophical analysis was a major influence on thinkers like Metz who felt these inadequacies. That school's often convoluted analyses of social consciousness and ideology provided Catholic political theologians with sources of articulation. Rahner himself engaged in dialogues with Marxists, and admitted the need for a political broadening, but this movement seems to have occurred too late for him personally. He was so formed by reworking individual Christian consciousness in the context of Kant, Hegel, and Heidegger that the political dimension has remained an addendum. In his pupil Metz, however, it has become an effective focus of brotherly love.

Metz is not the clearest of theoreticians, and European Catholic political theology remains less than a lucid force. A link between it and North American political thought, though, is the work of some students of Bernard Lonergan. Matthew Lamb and Fred Lawrence, for instance, have been influenced both by European political hermeneutics and Lonergan's transcendental method. Their papers from the *Lonergan Workshop* show the rich potential of this dual influence.[5] Lonergan's strengths include a clear cognitional theory, to ground the analysis of "horizons" in which political theology delights, and a strong empirical bent. While both he and his followers criticize empiricism (the view that only sensibly verifiable facts matter), they retain an Anglo-American temper and want close contact with experience. That has meant considerable work in economics, philosophy of science, and other disciplines. In effect, the Lonergan school calls for wholesale interdisciplinary collaboration, and Lonergan's methodological depth provides good suggestions for how such collaboration might proceed.[6] The result could be a more profound political science and theology, rooted in a religious analysis of human consciousness.

The theoretically-minded wing of North American political theology therefore tends to read Marxist analyses with some critical distance. Insofar as those analyses often occur in an ideological framework, with less than lucid objectivity, they suggest the deficiencies of Marxist atheism. As a secularist's horizon can be pernicious, closing off God and the Spirit's farther reaches, so can a Marxist atheist's. By both experience and analysis, many Catholic thinkers in North America find human consciousness, especially human judgment and love, implying more. This finding may not appear especially political, but in fact it soon tends to be. For to answer questions of justice, the common good, the proper distribution of material resources, and the like, one must say what human beings are made for.

European partners to the Marxist-Christian dialogue quickly realized this, so they concentrated on hope. Extending analyses of human time, such as Heidegger's, they became fascinated with the future. Insofar as both Marxists and biblically sensitive Christians consider the future open, they share a central conviction.[7] Add their common instinct to imagine the future as a realm of greater justice, and they are at least cousins. When they further agree that we cannot sacrifice the present to the future, cannot be unjust today to secure justice tomorrow, they are brothers and sisters. For having an open future and a conscience set on justice now is a deep act of faith. It makes life's mystery such that honesty and love are the paths to a better tomorrow.

Some North American thinkers have also been drawn to sociology. When sociology is not a weak-minded mongering of the obvious (what Eric Severeid called "slow journalism"), it can give political theology considerable help. In the tradition of Max Weber and Emile Durkheim, North Americans such as Peter Berger and Robert Bellah have done stimulating studies of religious consciousness. Bellah adds a socialist political sympathy, Berger one more conservative, but either way, the stage on which they move has been sufficiently ecumenical to entice numerous Catholics. For instance, Avery Dulles joined Berger in the Hartford Appeal. The younger Jesuit sociologist John Coleman studied with Bellah and does political theology somewhat in his style.[8]

Two publishing ventures by North American Catholics manifest other directions that political theology has taken here. Orbis Books has done yeoman service in introducing Americans to Third World theologies. From Maryknollers' missionary contacts, Orbis has almost single-handedly translated the bulk of recent key Latin American, African, and Asian theologians. Their works reflect the break with colonialism that many Third World peoples have recently accomplished, as well as their continuing struggles with Northern economic imperialism. Ecclesiologically, they imply missionary questions such as how to export the gospel without exporting Western culture, as well as the host of moral and infra-church political questions that the "Third Church," based in the Southern Hemisphere, provokes.

The second publishing venture is a joint project involving the Jesuits' Woodstock Theological Center in Washington, D.C., and Paulist Press. Working with government officials, and drawing on interdisciplinary expertise, Woodstock has produced several works on justice and public policy that have an air of realism—of being in close touch with how government actually operates and what constraints actually obtain. Sometimes their oblique asides are as interesting as their explicit analyses. For instance, in introducing a volume on personal values in public policy, Maryland Senator Charles McC. Mathias tells how he was finally moved to support congressional representation for the people of the District of Columbia by a sense that it simply was right. That this consideration apparently was far down on his instinctive list, and even farther down on his colleagues', speaks volumes he may not have intended.[9]

Political theology takes a less studious form among the many North American groups who go at it pragmatically. They often combine activism with a strong liturgical, contemplative, or community life, and frequently they target their efforts concretely. For example, Catholic Workers have long tried to render service to the urban poor. Establishing houses in the inner city, they have run soup kitchens, centers for discussion, and networks of neighborhood support. Drawing on Hispanic Catholicism, Cesar Chavez and leaders of the United Farm Workers have tried to bring justice to the fields where migrant workers toil. Other groups have been ad hoc collections of Christians in opposition—to the war in Vietnam, the denial of civil rights to blacks and women, the oppression of gays, or nuclear development. (Among the last one finds some of the strongest Catholic ecological awareness.) We shall consider black and feminist liberation theologies in the next sections. Here the summarizing point might be recent shifts in consciousness that have divided Catholics politically.

On one side are those who read the signs of the times as a call to across-the-board opposition. They interpret racism, sexism, environmental pollution, and militarism as an interconnected network. The common denominator is blinding self-service. Because it is profitable and advantageous, large groups of North Americans support systems that discriminate against minorities and women, continue to ravage the land, and keep the arms race building. The base form of this profit is financial: The status quo makes these people a comfortable living. Therefore, the gospel's message of peace and justice must be joined to the gospel's poverty. It is those who give up notions of the good financial life that are most likely to become radically Christian.

On the other side are many who doubt the Church's competence to enter political battles and so want religion to be more private. Reacting to the turmoil of the sixties, they turned the volume down in the seventies. The wise among them know that there are risks of being co-opted, and the more impressive among them work at structural change. But many feel little kinship with radical Christians and relegate them to a past that failed. For instance, that Daniel and Philip Berrigan now inhabit the margins is for many the proof of their ineffectiveness. Unfortunately, what commitment to social justice *is* effective is a question many conservatives do not welcome. On the other hand, a noticeable number of Catholics would agree with exiled Russian novelist Aleksandr Solzhenitsyn's critique of Marxist-Leninism, including its rather militaristic approach to liberation. In their view, Christ came to slay evil, and our times represent a great warfare between darkness and light.[10]

BLACK LIBERATION THEOLOGY

Among radical Catholics black theology continues to be a strong influence. Among conservatives it often conflicts with neighborhood interests. The fine documentary history of black theology recently edited by Gayraud Wilmore and James Cone shows what has happened since the heyday of Martin Luther King, Jr.[11] It also shows how marginal black Catholics have been: Catholic statements comprise about 5 of the history's 625 pages—less than 1.5 percent. They include a judgment that an articulate black Catholic vanguard is presently emerging, but that seems largely a pious hope. The smallness of the black Catholic population, and the mainline character of most Catholic institutions, suggest that black Catholic theology is not likely to make radical impacts.

Consequently, it is the diffusive impact of Protestant and secularist black thought that has been, and probably will continue to be, the prime black political influence on Catholic theology. After pursuing civil rights, and then starting to realize the extent of structural racism, black theology has fanned out in several further directions. It has supported black power, criticized white religion as racist, shown some openness to dialogue with white theology seeking radical justice, reflected on the black church, confronted its own problems regarding women, and most recently allied itself with Third World thought, especially that of Africans. Such a change in a fifteen-year period shows that black theology has been more than vital. What appear to be its current politico-theological perceptions?

Though black theologians naturally differ, they tend to agree that racism is a systemic evil, close to the bone of both white culture and white religion. From that they move in diverse directions, some separatist and some ecumenically pragmatic. Separatists prefer to be left alone, to control their own destinies. Ecumenical pragmatists work with anyone who can help them improve blacks' conditions. Another set of movements is theoretical. There are black theologians influenced by Marxist analyses, and others who are drawn to the Bible. The latter often read scripture as a text of liberation, and often have close ties to the black church. They point out that, historically, the black church has been one of the few places of black power, and one of the few places of black hope.[12] Admitting that such hope could turn other worldly, they argue that it usually retained an acute sense of the present. Whether heard in a rural town or an urban ghetto, the biblical passage revealed the enemy. Black theologians of Marxist orientation underscore the economics of oppression, and also the psychology. They shout against pie in the sky religion, so they help the biblicists make a case for the primacy of praxis.

Related to the primacy of praxis, or action, is the primacy of the black community. For those held together by the Church, the Church is palpably social. Despite the problems such sociability can bring, which parallel the problems of the intense Jewish village,[13] the togetherness of the black church, its suffering shared, can make white church experience seem anemic. We know a white woman whose time in an interracial church in Harlem left her unfit for white churches. When she was sick her community rallied round, and when she got better they all partied. Such genuine concern flowed out that for her "the church" has to be an intense fellowship. To show up on Sunday as a duty, hear a pale message and share a pale smile, is no Christianity she considers worth pursuing.

If ecumenical contacts we've had are representative, this small episode suggests another problem blacks have with white Christianity. In addition to the racism it frequently carries, white Christianity can seem to have little soul. At issue in such an impression is more than a clash between two neutral cultures. Insofar as Christianity entails being a people, and living for love, "soul" is not something indifferent. Rather, feeling and doing, singing and expressing, are of the essence. There is a warmth black religion knows, a warmth it develops if given half a chance, that most white churches have not fostered. When one ties this warmth to shared suffering, one has a pristine Christian cell. Whether they are conscious of it or not, many small black groups resemble nothing so much as first-century Christian churches.

Reflecting on black experience for a symposium on "Dilemmas of Pluralism: The Case of Religion in Modernity," Vincent Harding has advanced this shared suffering into an **epistemological** distinctiveness.[14] From their experiences of downtroddenness, American blacks probably have the best understanding of Jesus' message available in our land. Just as Latin American theologians stress the importance of identifying with the poor, so black theologians of Harding's persuasion stress Jesus' solidarity with black poverty and discrimination. It was the poor to whom Jesus preached good news. It was the poor whom Jesus beatified. It is the poor, consequently, who are best positioned to understand many fundamental portions of Christianity. Primary among these is God's association with justice. If "divinity" means anything midst oppression and suffering, it means the redress of a present order that should not be. It should not be that some people throw away more food in a day than other people see in a week. It should not be that malnutrition virtually programs some children for failure by the time they are five. And, above all, it should not be that the skin one wears can determine one's destiny. Any God worth considering has to be the opposite, the enemy, of such evils.

Because they think "God" has deflected many of their people from working on this-worldly change, some black thinkers castigate religion. Most black theologians, though, deal rather gently with even their people's superstitions. While they want religion to work social change, to be concerned for bodies as much as souls, they know the despair that is always close in the ghetto. This intuitive knowledge is confirmed by psychiatric studies: When internalized, racial inferiority often breaks out in destructive rage. How much crime, internecine prison violence, and infra-black cruelty this explains is hard to say, above all for white outsiders. What all signs indicate, however, is that many blacks have found religion a psychic necessity.

If the choice is between possible illusion, by taking biblical myths as literally as if they were snapshots, and hopelessness, clearly possible illusion is preferable. The black mother of epic stereotype, long-suffering and a fervent believer, concretizes this creative response to impossible conditions. The resiliency that Harvard psychiatrist Robert Coles found in the ghetto would have been impossible without her amazing grace.[15] The male side of the coin is a more terrible tangle. Deprived of many of the symbols of male achievement, especially the basic one of a decent job, black males have faced overwhelming crises. The figures on unemployment for black youths today (often almost 50 percent) draw the base line. What future do those figures allow, and what do they say of American justice? Anyone hearing Catholic social teaching, or just unmuffled conscience, knows where the grapes of wrath are stored.

There are analogous descriptions and inferences embedded in the experience of Chicanos and Asian-Americans. The former have a hard time getting Hispanic bishops, the latter are so minor a Catholic number that they are close to invisible theologically. Perhaps their most visible group has been the Vietnamese refugees. Some dioceses, especially in the Midwest, have been quite Christian to them.

To other such marginal peoples, as to the theological community generally, black theology reports on the effects of slavery. If American theological history had room for only a single symbol of our sin, beyond doubt it would be slavery. That may change in the future, if our playing with nuclear fire brings the unthinkable, but to the present black experience epitomizes how the New World has gone wrong. Presuming to some special title, some errand in the wilderness or manifest destiny, European emigrants to the New World showed incredible ambitions. Of course, there also were many noble truths, and many simple human foibles. But there were core blindnesses with roots in the will that made the pale face wolfish.

Though it would be convenient to turn aside and discourse on the Protestant ethic, or the bastardization of Calvinism that capitalism has wrought, the focus of this book suggests that Catholics attend to themselves and their own doctrine. The Spanish and French who threw Catholicism into the race for the New World did not greatly distinguish themselves from their Protestant competition. When the bishops of Latin America met at Puebla, they recognized the native Indians as the most abject of their continent's poor. When the upwardly mobile Catholics reached the boardrooms of power in the United States, they did not change discriminatory policies dramatically. No, the gospel of radical justice separates the "sheep" from the "goats" across denominational lines.

FEMINIST LIBERATION THEOLOGY

Black theology focuses on poverty and racism. Looking to God for relief, it reads the gospel as a social liberation. Feminist theology focuses on sexism. It reads the history of culture, non-Christian and Christian alike, as a long tale of women's bondage. In fact, since the rise of history, society after society has been patriarchal, in a negative sense. Women have not been equal to men in opportunity, dignity, or power. What equality they had in matriarchal times, during mesolithic agriculture and worship of a great Mother Goddess, is lost to recorded memory. East and West, women historically have been subject—to fathers, then husbands, then sons. For a woman not to marry and produce sons was for her to live wretchedly on society's margins.

It is true that the rise of what we now consider the world religions somewhat improved women's lot, but that is a relative judgment.[16] The Buddha raised women's station in India (though aboriginal India may have treated women better than the India of his time), and the option of going to a Buddhist nunnery was a significant liberation. Nonetheless, women never received equal access to Buddhist power or honor. In East Asia the Tao had a feminine modality, but the prevailing Confucian mores can only be called **misogynistic.** Judaism arose from very patriarchal beginnings, in which a woman was legally property. Talmudic Judaism made some provision for women's rights, but the morning prayer of the pious Jew still thanks God each day for not having made him female. Muhammad improved Arab women's lot significantly in such areas as marriage, divorce, and inheritance. However, the Koran clearly subordinates women to men, and the tradition that followed regularly took the more subjugating reading.

Jesus' rather evenhanded treatment of women and men therefore stands out from the usual practice of world religions. While it might be excessive to call him a feminist, since he did not explicitly reject contemporary Jewish patriarchy, he did implicitly overturn much prejudice. For a rabbi to consort freely with women was unthinkable in Jesus' time, as the disciples' reaction to his dialogue with the Samaritan woman (John 4) suggests. Unthinkable too was Jesus' view of marriage, in which the same stringency applied to both sexes. That astonished the disciples, as the Master's association with prostitutes astonished the Pharisees. The Son of Man, then, was Lord not just of the Sabbath. He also was Lord of the prevailing sexual mores: free to have friends, work cures, recognize faith regardless of gender. Pauline Christianity preserved some of this freedom, when it saw "in Christ" neither male nor female. Unfortunately, it also carried over strains of Jewish misogynism, especially when we count in the Pastoral epistles. For them woman was the first to fall, a sex weaker and not wholly clean. By the time the New Testament canon was closed, the freedom and leadership that women had had in many of the early communities had been lost to a "love patriarchalism."[17]

The fathers of the church, East and West, found asceticism and feminism incompatible. As was true for Buddhist monks, celibacy wrote woman off as a temptress. Tertullian, Jerome, Augustine, and Chrysostom all furnish misogynistic quotations.[18] Augustine's own experiences with concubinage and Manicheanism seem to have rendered him unfit to appropriate Paul's egalitarianism. Augustine's equation of intercourse with the transmission of original sin was a disaster for women, as was his opinion that sexual pleasure has no end other than procreation. Chrysostom wrote fulminations against women that can only be called disgusting. At least on bad days, women were for him storehouses of phlegm and spittle. That Chrysostom became a great authority in Eastern Christianity, Russian as well as Greek, did little to alleviate Orthodox women's oppression. In the West, where Augustine was the dominant figure until the later Middle Ages, women also fared badly. Medieval town law spoke of the husband's right to smash his wife's face in, should she oppose his sovereign will. Aquinas did little for women, since he accepted the Aristotelian biology that made woman a misbegotten male, and the Reformers' return to the Bible meant a return to pristine patriarchy. A few of the left-wing Reformation churches gave women equality,[19] but the overall story, Protestant and Catholic alike, was, by today's standards, one of rampant sexism.

We have rehearsed this history because contemporary feminists have made it a running start for their liberation analyses. They note the biblical influences, the Gnostic influences (Gnostic opposition to matter and the body often focused on women), and promising roads that orthodoxy rejected. They also note the Fathers' venom, the dark phenomenon of witch-hunting, Luther's offhand view that woman ought to "bear herself out," and the many current faces of Christian sexism. Among the Catholic feminists prominent in this work stand Rosemary Ruether, Elisabeth Schüssler-Fiorenza, and Mary Daly. Schüssler-Fiorenza is a New Testament scholar who has retrieved roles and authorities that women had in early Christianity and that male scholarship has overlooked. At the beginnings, Church order was not so rigid as it later became, and Paul's letters suggest that women led local churches. Similarly, the role of women such as Mary Magdalene shows how apostleship could have been nonsexist. Some feminists consider Schüssler-Fiorenza a reformer rather than a radical, but her self-description is "woman-identified."

Another "reformist" who bristles at the title is Rosemary Radford Ruether. Her original field was patristics, but she has broadened her historical studies to other temporal periods. Ruether combines considerable learning with a bent for radical politics, so her feminism is part of an organic socialistic vision. Ecological, communitarian, egalitarian, Christian, and free, her "church" would be very exciting. It would bite sizeable chunks from the established version, but each bit would be backed by good reasons. Ruether is too sophisticated historically, and too aware psychoanalytically, for establishmentarians to dismiss her easily. Indeed, her concern for justice and political commitment could teach them many of the lessons they most need.

In the beginning of her career Mary Daly was a Catholic theologian, but she has since renounced any Christian allegiance. The progression evident in her books—*The Church and the Second Sex, Beyond God the Father,* and *Gyn/Ecology*—[20] is from reformist Christianity to militant feminism. We saw the beginnings of this change at Boston College in the late 1960s. Daly was denied tenure there, unjustly, and political rallies forced the administration to reverse its decision. Such treatment exemplified the thesis of her first book: Women are less than second-class citizens in Catholic history. Building on her studies of Tillich, Daly's second book tried to remove sexism from God. The sharpest angle in Catholic theology's bias, she astutely realized, is the maleness it has attributed to God. No matter that the high theologians admitted that God is beyond sex, the popular tradition took "Father" seriously. Moving to a God who is active being, a verb more than a noun, she suggested, might cut out theology's apparent sanction of patriarchy. In retrospect, however, this theological suggestion was but a way station.

Gyn/Ecology is a full-scale rehearsal of patriarchal religion's horrors. In chapters on Chinese foot-binding, Hindu widow-burning, African genital mutilation, Christian witch-destroying, and current gynecological practices, Daly shows how women have suffered. The language of the analytic portion of her text is highly self-conscious and punning. She is reflective enough to realize that the history she is telling suggests a new philosophy. So she would have women become "spinners," "witches," and "crones," retrieving those words' original possibilities. It is an impressive semantic exercise. Added to her empirical case studies of male savagery, it makes the work a milestone.

Unfortunately, these positive reviews are not the whole story. By its middle, *Gyn/Ecology* is more than excessive. By its end, it is too bitter to be borne. Of course, what one person is willing to bear may seem to another relatively light. Immersed in a tale of horrors, Daly probably thought no rhetoric too shrill. But there is a point beyond which righteous wrath throws the preacher off balance. In theory that point is where one stops loving unrestrictedly. After that there are people one need not regard, people outside one's pale. They do not have humanity like one's own, so they can be treated as another species. Erik Erikson describes this phenomenon as "pseudospeciation." Denying biology and common sense, it helped Greeks to consider foreigners *barbaroi*, Gentiles to pillory Jews, whites to treat blacks as primates.

The pseudospeciation in Daly's case is a reverse sexism. Men have so swollen in her imagination that they incarnate the enemy. This **misanthropy**, for all its historical title, runs aground on common sense. Men are almost half the race; infant boys are not responsible for the past; many women are happily heterosexual; despite all its problems, marriage still works quite often. No nicking the edges destroys the core accuracy of these observations. To shut oneself up in a misanthropic coven is to opt for a lot of illusion.

Daly's case shows how militant feminists have gone searching for a new religion. Actually, they have gone searching for an old religion, one that claims roots in pre-patriarchal times. This religion is nature-oriented and life-affirming. It entails a witchcraft, but one wholly positive.[21] Ritualizing its convictions, new witches celebrate old mysteries close to the Mother. The Mother is Earth and Life, the mystery to which we all owe our being. Menstruation, intercourse, birth, and nursing are phenomena richly symbolic of her. Most covens work democratically, some admit males, and probably all are trying consciously to redress the unhealthiness that an excessively male, aggressive, phallic culture and religion have wrought.

Insofar as such witchcraft departs from Christ, rejecting his solutions to death and sin, we put qualifications on its acceptance. Nonetheless, it offers Christian liberation thought a great deal that is positive, especially through its emphasis on ecology. The liberation theologies we have seen, and the Latin American one we shall look at next, all neglect this ecological dimension. It is no accident that they all also have recognized women's oppressions only tardily. Thus, a specifically feminist liberation school, sensitive to women's position in all churches and cultures, is both a large need and a strong benefit.

Finally, specifically Catholic foci of feminist liberation theology have been priestly ordination and abortion. The closure of the priesthood to women epitomizes how the Catholic church has denied women equal access to authority and service. Almost unanimously, feminists consider it a symbol of deep sexism. Abortion is more contested, for few Catholic feminists support abortion. Most sympathize with women who, usually under great pressure, feel that they must have an abortion, and many distinguish their religious ideal from politico-legal realities and vote prudentially for women's free choice. But the Catholic sense that from its earliest beginnings human life is sacred keeps most who have grown up in this tradition opposed to easy abortion. No Catholic feminists, however, are happy that their church gives so much occasion for thinking that Catholicism is misogynistic. All consider Catholic sexism a serious sin that smothers their tradition's best instincts.

POLITICAL THEOLOGY: LATIN AMERICA

The most logical link between this section and the preceding one forces us to begin with some criticisms. Insofar as the final document of the Latin American bishops' Puebla meeting,[22] whose topic was evangelization, represents liberation theology's official impact to date, feminists have little to cheer. The document does treat women's situation in both Latin American life and Christian evangelization (Nos. 834–849), and does note how they often suffer double oppression. Generally, "women have been pushed to the margins of society as the result of cultural atavisms—male predominance, unequal wages, deficient education, etc." The result is their "almost total absence from political, economic, and social life." Specifically, there are the evils of women's sexual exploitation, through growing eroticism, pornography, and prostitution; there are also the economic evils of poor wages, noncompliance with laws designed for women's protection, abusive conditions for domestic employees, and so forth. Finally, the document has a sentence on the Catholic church's failings: "In the church itself there sometimes has been an underevaluation of women and minimal participation by them in pastoral initiatives."

Following this enumeration of negatives, the document asserts women's theological equality and dignity, using examples from scripture, above all that of Mary. Applying this to the present, the bishops speak of women making "a real contribution to the church's mission," but the next sentence shows their limited horizon: "The possibility of entrusting nonordained ministries to women will open up new ways for them to participate in the church's life and mission." In other words, males will continue to hoard the power pieces. Jon Sobrino, an El Salvadorian theologian whose work on liberation Christology has made him very prominent, has written an illuminating commentary on the Puebla document that finds its center to be a firm identification with the poor.[23] However, Sobrino says virtually nothing about the special poverty a majority of Latin Americans suffer because of their sex. It is left to Robert McAfee Brown, commenting on the significance of Puebla for North American Protestants, to make the hard observation that *machismo* has affected even the most progressive Latin American theologians.[24] Bluntly, it has blinded them to women's inferior status in their culture and theology.

A second shortcoming of the Puebla document, again also applicable to Sobrino's commentary, is its neglect of ecological considerations. This criticism has little special edge, however, for among liberation theologians only feminists are consistently ecological. Others seem so concerned with social questions that things not directly bearing on the sufferings of the poor receive only scant attention. A last disappointment of Puebla is its weak ecumenism.

Failings such as these three mean that liberation theology must not seize all the Catholic attention. As David Tracy has shown, a fully adequate contemporary theology must pivot between the canonical Christian texts and the full range of human experience.[25] If a theology slights half the race, makes little of Christians' need to overcome their divisions, and does not see nature's current dilemma, it is not the full understanding of faith that we presently need.

We make these criticisms harshly, because the rest of our report on Latin American liberation theology is so positive. There is no other portion of the Catholic theological world that approaches Latin America's political depth and passion. Latin American liberation theology has taken Europe's interest in Marx, joined it to the realities of the ghettos of the poor, and forged a powerful insistence on liberational praxis. Since Gustavo Gutierrez's pioneering work, *A Theology of Liberation,*[26] Latin America has led the illumination of Christian praxis. Biblical critics, such as José Miranda, have probed scripture's insistence on justice. Sobrino's Christology shows the primary of *following* Jesus,[27] and other thinkers, Protestant as well as Catholic, have illumined sin, grace, and the rest. A good introduction to all this is Robert McAfee Brown's *Theology in a New Key.*[28]

What, then, does praxis imply? First, it has a theoretical implication. The Latin Americans are instinctively theoretical, due to both their own literary tradition and their ties to European philosophy. Thus, one finds many discussions of hermeneutics and ideology. The upshot of these discussions is usually the primacy of action over thought. North Americans know much of this from their own pragmatic tradition. William James, John Dewey, and C. S. Peirce all championed the primacy of doing. In simple terms, the argument is that only full engagement in a situation allows the full truth to emerge. True, we interact with situations, environments, and people just by thinking about them. We interact most richly, however, when we take our convictions to the trenches and find out how they feel, whether they work, what we will suffer for them. It is the difference between contemplating an appendectomy and undergoing it. The pain imagined and the pain actually felt differ instructively. So do imaginary poverty and the grinding reality, an imaginary imitation of Christ and carrying the cross step by step.

Second, praxis means letting realities speak, not doing theology *a priori* (from the head down). The Puebla document shows that this thesis has not been fully accepted by the Latin American church. The document's doctrinal portions are quite *a priori* and fit its pastoral portions badly. Latin American theology has a special need to struggle with this problem, for the *a priori* comes naturally to the romance language mind. (In English-speaking countries, empiricism and common law tradition militate against it.) Still, all theologies need to question constantly whether they are elucidating basic faith—are clarifying lives Christians actually are living. Few theologies have gazed so unblinking as those from Latin America.

For, third, the praxis of Christian faith in Latin America each day encounters massive evil. Not only is there staggering poverty. Perhaps worse, there is an economic injustice, caused considerably by Northern conglomerates, that grows decade by decade. An illustration is Brazil, touted as Latin America's industrial giant. Between 1960 and 1970, the top 5 percent of Brazilian income earners increased their share of the national wealth from 27.4 to 36.3 percent. During that same period the share of the bottom 80 percent decreased from 45.5 to 36.8 percent. Things have not improved dramatically since 1970. When the top 5 percent of a country earn almost as much as the bottom eighty, justice cries out for revolution.

Brazilian leaders realize this, of course, as do leaders of other Latin American countries with similar economies. Consequently, they have developed a brutal regime, based on police surveillance and torture. "National Security" is the buzzword such Latin American regimes employ, as a blanket justification for their repressions. Because most of the opposition analyzes the politico-economic situation with Marxist tools, and aims at restoring the country to "the people," the dictators use "National Security" as vigilance against Communist revolutionaries. When the Somoza regime fell in Nicaragua, American television sent back mini-lessons on the rise and fall of a small National Security operation. Somoza and his family had shamelessly padded their own pockets. Yet they claimed to be protecting "the people" from teenage "revolutionaries" who wanted basic food and shelter. Northern interests had long propped Somoza, as they have long propped similar dictators.[29] When he started to fall American officials beat a hasty retreat, trying not to get splattered with his failure. That they already had years of blood on their hands seemed altogether secondary. This sorry history continues today with the American presence in Central America.

When commentators looked for women's presence at the Latin American bishops' Conference at Puebla, they found one especially poignant clustering. Wives, mothers, and sisters who had had family members "disappear" joined to ask the conference's help. That people who oppose Latin American regimes "disappear," sometimes turning up weeks later mutilated, sometimes never resurfacing at all, is part of the southern landscape. Like the increasingly polluted cities, it is a constant psychic pressure. On the whole, Church leaders have faced such pervasive evils courageously. Again and again, priests, nuns, dedicated laity, and bishops have spoken out strongly. It is another measure of the dictators' corruption that these appeals have not dented their operations. In countries massively Catholic and traditional, Christian leaders are imprisoned, tortured, and slain as enemies of the state. If the ancient notion, that the blood of the martyrs is the seed of faith, remains valid, Latin America has the brightest of paradoxical futures. Its martyrs now number into the thousands, and there is no sign when it will stop.

That the Puebla document should, despite strong reservations from the episcopal Right, have emerged championing Latin America's poor is another sign of liberation theology's power. The light it carries, the good it encourages, the justice it makes plain are simply too godly to thwart. The link it forges between Jesus and the suffering is like the medievals' "golden chain." In the poor, love of God and love of neighbor take flesh brutalized. By identifying with the dispossessed, Latin Americans have recovered the Suffering Servant of the gospel. Like the legendary Veronica, who gave Jesus a cloth to wipe his face and received back an indelible portrait, they contemplate a haunting visage. The eyes are sad, the cheeks are hollow, but the chin is firmly set. As El Greco's painting of Veronica's cloth shows, the Christ is a suffering victor.

Identifying with the suffering Christ, as the poor give him his mystical body, has moved Latin Americans to pedagogical and ecclesiastical innovations. Pedagogically, Paulo Freire and others have focused on raising consciousness.[30] This is familiar from women's groups, but its Latin American form is theological. Through greater political and economic awareness, Latin Americans lay the foundation of a new illuminative way. To understand the theology of injustice, they join it to Christ's sufferings. The ecclesiastical context for this pedagogy is their *comunidades de base*— "grass-roots" gatherings, such as Ernesto Cardenal's in Solentiname, in which members analyze together their experiences and the gospel. Together, raising consciousness and forming grass-roots communities offer the rest of the Christian world a stimulating model.

Though most do not realize it, other Christians, especially Northern Catholics, have a great stake in Latin American theology. For following Jesus, faith's politics, and God's identification with the poor, this theology is unmatched. As Catholic economist Barbara Ward's recent *Progress for a Small Planet* shows, the economics of Latin America are replicated throughout the Southern Hemisphere. As Robert McAfee Brown's commentary on the Puebla document adds, President Carter continued America's involvement in Latin American political theology, by ordering the CIA to put "activist" priests and nuns under surveillance ("lest he be confronted with another Iran-type situation"). Through the politics of the Reagan administration, we Americans have continued to be in the Southern struggle right up to our bad conscience. In Iran we winked at torture for economic profit. In Latin America we still do the same. The bottom line of liberation theology is that economic profit is a dirty word. It has brought structural violence, *violencia blanca,* to millions. That most liberation theologians consider counterviolence a last resort shows their deep Christianity. Suffering injustice with imaginative love, they try to slay the beast that oppresses them with the sword of the gospel.

PEACEMAKING

The beast that oppresses the whole world in these last decades of the twentieth century is the specter of nuclear war. Few responses to this potential evil have galvanized more comment and reaction than the Pastoral Letter of the American Catholic bishops, "The Challenge of Peace," that appeared in the late Spring of 1983. The letter has four principal parts: I Religious Perspectives and Principles Regarding Peace in the Modern World; II Problems and Principles; III Proposals and Policies to Promote Peace; and IV The Pastoral Challenge and Response:

The first part, on religious perspectives and principles, deals with "Peace and the Kingdom" (biblical perspectives), "Kingdom and History," and "Moral Choices for the Kingdom." Among the biblical perspectives brought forth are the Old Testament's hopes for peace: "Furthermore, in the midst of their unfilled longing, God's people [Israel] clung tenaciously to hope in the promise of an eschatological time when, in the fullness of salvation, peace and justice would embrace and all creation would be secure from harm."[31] At the end of its survey of New Testament themes, the Pastoral Letter concludes: "Because we have been gifted with God's peace in the risen Christ, we are called to our own peace and to the making of peace in our world. As disciples and as children of God it is our task to seek for ways in which to make the forgiveness, justice and mercy, and love of God visible in a world where violence and enmity are all too often the norm."[32] After providing a balanced view of the tension between the Kingdom (or eschatological dimension of faith) and ongoing history, the first part concludes with a lengthy survey of the traditional Catholic criteria for a just war. Recently a new movement, more preoccupied with nonviolence, has come to share the moral stage with this traditional just war theory, and the bishops see the new outlook as complementing the old.

All the more so is this the case when we specify that the newness of the current situation entails the lethal power of nuclear weapons. In Part II the Pastoral Letter notes the large body of papal literature that recently has been urging a curtailment of the arms race. Then, reflecting in their own name, the bishops put the crux of the dilemma clearly: "We see with increasing clarity the political folly of a system which threatens mutual suicide, the psychological damage this does to ordinary people, especially the young, the economic distortions of priorities—billions readily spent for destructive instruments while pitched battles are waged daily in our legislatures over much smaller amounts for the homeless, the hungry and the helpless here and abroad. But it is much less clear how we translate a no to nuclear war into the personal and public choices which can move us in a new direction, toward a national policy and an international system which more adequately reflect the values and vision of the kingdom of God."[33]

Next, the Pastoral ruminates on the paradoxes of the currently prevailing strategy of deterence: May a nation threaten what it may never do? May it possess what it may never use? The bishops see their own role as helping to bring people to the point where they will resist the resort to nuclear war as an instrument of national policy. Since prevention is the only cure, the bishops want to encourage prevention. And here the core of their perception seems to be: "We believe it is necessary for the sake of prevention to build a barrier against the concept of nuclear war as a viable strategy for defense. There should be a clear public resistance to the rhetoric of 'winnable' nuclear wars, or unrealistic expectations of 'surviving' nuclear exchanges and strategies of 'protracted nuclear war.' "[34]

Concerning the actual use of nuclear weapons, the bishops condemn targeting population centers, initiating nuclear war, and any easy assumption that (a retaliatory) nuclear war could remain limited. After a full reflection on the whole convoluted notion of deterrence, the bishops make three specific evaluations: (1) proposals (e.g., that we plan for repeated nuclear strikes) that go beyond deterrence as a way to prevent the use of nuclear weapons by others are unacceptable; (2) we must not seek nuclear superiority ("sufficiency to deter" is the limit); and (3) deterrence should be a step on the way to a progressive disarmament. As means to improve the current (threatening) situation they recommend agreements to halt the development of nuclear weapons systems, bilateral deep cuts in nuclear arsenals, a comprehensive test ban treaty, the removal of short-range nuclear weapons, the removal of nuclear weapons from places where they might easily be overrun in the early stages of a war, and strengthening safeguards that would prevent the unauthorized use of nuclear arms. The concluding sentiments of Part II include the telltale line: "Nevertheless, there must be no misunderstanding of our profound skepticism about the moral acceptability of any use of nuclear weapons."[35]

The bishops' positive proposals to promote peace include accelerating work for arms control, minimizing the risk of any war, getting clear the connections between nuclear and conventional defenses, clarifying the role of a civil defense, developing nonviolent means for resolving conflicts, and honoring the mutual rights of the state to require military service and individual citizens to register their conscientious objections. Beyond these, the bishops raise their sights to a new world order that would better honor the unity of all nations and lessen the presently antagonistic relationship between the superpowers. In line with such a new world order, a better politics would better provide for the real interdependence of all people in today's world.

Part IV, dealing with internal church matters, focuses on the role of committed Christians as communities of conscience, the educational programs needed to develop consciences sensitive to the enormity of today's problems of war and peace, the way that peacemaking links with a reverence for all life (including the lives of the unborn), and the need for penance and prayer. The bishops then address a special word to each of several categories of people whose relations to peacemaking have peculiar overtones: clergy, educators, parents, youth, people in military service, people in the defense industries, people in the news media, and finally all Catholics in their roles as citizens. The base line of the general Conclusion of the Pastoral Letter is that good ends (peace) cannot justify immoral means (weapons that kill indiscriminately and threaten whole societies). As John Paul II has said, we need a moral about-face that will say no to the whole matter of threatening to make nuclear war. In the bishops' view, "There *is* a substitute for war. There is negotiation under the supervision of a global body realistically fashioned to do its job."[36]

In the wake of the bishops' Pastoral, all sorts of commentaries arose.[37] On the whole, readers agreed that the issue is of paramount, probably unique importance, and a majority thought that the bishops' public statement was a positive contribution to a necessary debate. Where conservatives tended to question the bishops' competence to discuss the political and military aspects of the issues, liberals tended to be greatly encouraged. It remains to be seen what overall effect the Pastoral will have, either on American governmental policy or American religious life, and whether the considerable consultation of different experts and laity that preceded its publication will become the bishops' standard operating procedure in other areas. But the mere fact of the Pastoral's strong statement was an announcement that the American Catholic Church is now a moral force to be reckoned with.

ECOLOGY

Ecology has not stood high on the theological and moral agenda of the Roman Catholic Church, but perhaps the ecological implications of the nuclear arms buildup will soon bring more Catholics to an awareness of ecology. Nuclear war clearly threatens the basic ecosystems of the whole earth, and thereby it looms as an assault on God's entire creation. There are few types of arrogance more overwhelming than the insult to the Creator that nuclear war would entail, so we may hope that Catholic theologians soon will begin to include in their analyses of military and economic matters human beings' responsibility to preserve and respect creation.

At the present time, however, it is a largely Protestant contingent of scholars who have focused on ecological issues.[38] Many of them, such as John Cobb and Joseph Sittler, have drawn on the process thought of Alfred North Whitehead, which offers a good framework for appreciating the interconnectedness of all creatures. Among Catholics, numerous contemplatives have spoken out for the values of living simply and in harmony with the land, but the mainstream of the Church still seems to move in **anthropocentric** tracks. This is probably true of the Protestant and Evangelical majorities as well, so ecological issues now pose the ecumenical task of raising consciousness all around.

As a brief contribution to such a consciousness-raising, let us sketch the argument that we have developed at greater length in a book entitled *Ecology and Religion.* [39] The overall argument has two parts: "The Recent Dialogue Between Ecology and Religion," and "Toward a New Christian Theology of Nature." Part one first takes up issues from natural science, offering a definition of ecology (the study of the interrelations among various biosystems) and detailing some of the lurid statistics on the current state of the waters, the air, the land, and the animals. Clearly enough, our current Western technological lifestyle is a threat to the well-being of the whole planet (even apart from the question of nuclear war).

Chapter two deals with technological and economic issues. These break down into such topics as energy-generation (e.g., the pros and cons of nuclear power), the use of nonrenewable and renewable resources, the development of what E. F. Schumacher has called an intermediate or appropriate technology, and the debate between economists who favor a steady-state model of interaction with the earth and those who push for continual expansion. Chapter three advances the argument into the political and ethical arenas. World hunger, population control, the rights of nature, policies for future generations, and the place of aesthetics come under consideration. All make an impact on our view of nature and so all raise questions about the assumption we Westerners have made that nature, the physical world, exists mainly for our own free use. In this context Bernard Häring, one of the few Catholic moralists who has seen the significance of ecological issues, has put matters well: "A chastened, sober anthropocentrism implies a consciousness of our belonging to the whole. In a certain sense we can say, 'We are members of one another,' also in view of the sub-human reality."[40]

Chapter four, dealing with religious issues, spotlights some of the conversions that the ecological crisis seems to be asking of us. For example, all of the negative data suggest that our consumerist lifestyle is killing nature. Only a conscious choice for spare, simplified lifestyles can open the way to a beautiful year 2100. Certain themes of feminist theology, and such traditional Catholic theological themes as sacramentality and reverence for life, pitch in to support such a conversion. But the precisely religious factors in the current ecological crisis must not be underestimated. Until the West begins to see nature as more sacred, nature will continue to be threatened by a great deal of greed and selfishness.

Part two evolves from these reflections and begins to sketch a positive Christian response. To do so, it employs Bernard Lonergan's notion of the different, interlocking "functional specialities" that a cooperative, ecological theology would employ. First, there are foundational considerations. These include such matters as the value-changes that come with Christian conversion: a sense of grace, of the gratuity and sacramentality of nature, of our sins against nature and our powers for nature's redemption. Chapter six then turns to the biblical doctrines of nature. While neither the main portions of the Hebrew Bible (the Law, the Prophets, and the Writings), nor the main portions of the New Testament (the Pauline, Synoptic, and Johannine Writings) detail an adequate appreciation of nature, both testaments have many useful strains (stewardship, appreciation of God's presence in nature, etc.) that we might exploit positively today. The same is true of the later history of Christian reflection, from the apologists and early church fathers through the medievals and reformers to our contemporary theologians. Although they have hardly been candidates for membership in the Sierra Club, most have stressed that creation is God's free gift.

When we try to put these historical elements into systematic order, the core consideration seems to be nature's status as a creature, a free making of God. In the traditional Christian view of creation, God has to be present to everything that has being and life. Thus there is a presence of God in nature that solicits our profound respect. It is a less personal presence than what we find in human beings, but the closer we come to God the more likely we are to appreciate the divine beauty and strength manifested in the seas, the mountains, the deserts. Chapter nine, dealing with the ethical implications of such systematic reflections, focuses on such matters as our duty to preserve nature (since we did not create it, we have no right to destroy it); our need to provide for future generations of human beings; the tacit demand of the earth that we not exceed its carrying capacity (the maximum use it can handle); population control; technological reforms; and the simplification of our lifestyles. The concluding chapter tries to mold the foregoing reflections into a spirituality that would stress the interrelatedness of all creatures, the place of a naturalist prayer, the development of nonviolent attitudes, and the importance of reconciliation, hope, and witness. The result, we hope, will be a raising of consciousness that might help all Christians, but especially Roman Catholics, begin to repair the damage we have been doing to God's and our world.

BUSINESS ETHICS

When one contemplates faith holistically, nuclear war and economics, ecology and theology, become interlocking concerns. The production of nuclear weapons is a very lucrative business; the way that we think about God shapes much of the way that we regard nature. In a highly technological society, especially, a great deal of culture, education, and politics revolves around the business of developing natural resources and providing human services. We ought to criticize such business carefully. Otherwise we shall wake up to find that we have realized philosopher Karl Jasper's image of modernity: a great machine that no one is running.

In this section we focus briefly on the great dynamo of American culture: business. Is the main obligation of being an American citizen contributing to the Gross National Product? Is a good notion of being a Christian making money that might trickle down to the less fortunate? Perhaps surprisingly, the Christian community is quite divided in its answers to these questions. Affirmative answers are far more numerous than we find comfortable.

For example, the leading fundamentalist preacher Jerry Falwell links biblical faith to the free enterprise system: "The free enterprise system is clearly outlined in the Book of Proverbs in the Bible. Jesus Christ made it clear that the work ethic was a part of His plan for man. Ownership of property is biblical. Competition in business is biblical. Ambitious and successful business management is clearly outlined as a part of God's plan for His people."[41] Michael Novak, a social analyst with Catholic roots, makes human beings the great benefactors of nature and nature itself the prime polluter: "It is as though creation was left in an unfinished state, as though human beings were called forth to be co-creators and to discover values in what nature itself wasted, polluted, destroyed, and abandoned recklessly: things awaited human beings for a recognition of their value and the invention of ways to make them things of value. To put this point the other way, there is a not-niceness in nature. The pollution of one thing by another, the destructiveness wrought by one part of nature upon another part of nature, was not first brought about by human intervention, and it was not first brought about by industrialization. Nature was raw and cruel to nature long before human beings intervened. It may be doubted whether human beings have ever done one-tenth of the polluting to nature that nature has done to itself. There is infinitely more methane gas—poisonous in one respect, and damaging to the environment—generated by the swamps of Florida and other parts of the United States than by all the automobile pollution of all places on this planet. In our superhuman efforts to be nice and to feel guilty, we try to take all the credit for pollution, improperly."⁴²

Fortunately, Fallwell and Novak do not persuade many leading Catholic theologians. On the other side of the ledger stand entries from radical critics of the Western, high technological style such as Ivan Illich, who thinks that the professionalization of the Western economy and its various services is highly depersonalizing: "The price of progress, says Illich, has been loss of autonomy. As area after area of human life becomes professionalized, individuals lose the ability to take charge of their own lives. The focus of individual well-being has been transferred to forces that lie outside the self. What masquerades as human progress has been a prescription for human powerlessness. Scitovsky had preached liberation from debilitating affluence in the form of addicting comforts. Illich calls for liberation from disabling dependence on domineering professionals."⁴³

High among the domineering professionals that now greatly shape American business life and culture are the lawyers. Thomas Shaffer, a former dean of the Law School at Notre Dame, has noted several shortcomings in the current American conception of legal practice: "My law practice was among the rich. I noticed in that world that lawyers tend to become like their clients. Wexler noticed no similar danger when one practices among the poor. Lawyers for the rich become like the rich; lawyers for the poor become like lawyers. That is backwards, in both cases. Christians are called to become poor, not rich; to become humble of spirit, not like lawyers. But—and this is Wexler's point, and it is true of the point Jesus makes in the Sermon on the Mount about becoming poor—humility in a professional culture means the humility of suffering servanthood. It means the service of a servant in doing what we do as professionals. . . . The adversary ethic is the most cherished and the most vulnerable of the consequences of our profession seeing itself as a guild specializing in justice. The adversary ethic announces that justice is zealous loyalty to the interests of one's client. It seems unable to entertain an ideal of professional service involving faithfulness rather than loyalty —one difference being that faithfulness aims at goodness rather than the realization of interests."⁴⁴

Clearly, then, legal ethics in particular and business ethics in general, since they involve value judgments about both our economic system and our professional attitudes, are complicated matters. As Shaffer's remarkable reference to the Sermon on the Mount indicates, however, there are basic guidelines from the gospel and Christian tradition that can greatly simplify our problems. In our view, these include the notion that the needs of the poor take precedence over the wants of the rich. Supplying basic services takes precedence over supplying luxuries and trivia. A style of servanthood is preferable to a style of domineering or manipulation through esoteric knowledge. Economic justice and ecological preservation are curbs on personal profit-making and nature's exploitation. If people cannot maintain honesty and integrity in their jobs, they had better consider a change of career. If their work contributes more to creating social problems than to solving them, their work will be their hanging judge.

Business has no exemption from the general Christian laws governing the use of our time. We cannot serve God and mammon. We cannot denature the Christ of Phillipians 2:5-11, who emptied himself. As Robert Lekachman has argued well, greed is not enough.[45] Only an economics operating as if people mattered, a business in the service of human beings rather than stock portfolios, merits a Christian support.

SUMMARY

Although Catholic ethics has always had a social dimension, that dimension has come to the fore in the last ninety years. Perhaps its best known form is the stream of papal encyclicals begun by Leo XIII in 1891. We use a recent study of their central focus, the dignity of the human person, to present traditional Catholic teaching on social justice.

Through more individualistic ventures, theologians on the Continent and in the Americas have pointedly turned "social" into "political." The European stimulus in this direction has been dialogue with Marxist theory. North American political theology also has had a theoretical interest, but the liberation movements of blacks and women probably have been more influential. Racism and sexism are pervasive social flaws that show injustice's deep biases. From their experiences of injustice, both blacks and women have gained special insight into the scriptural thesis that God sides with the poor.

It is Latin American liberation theology, however, that has formed the most influential Catholic school. The document issued by the Latin American Bishops' Conference from its meeting at Puebla, Mexico, in 1979 is a compromise piece, but it clearly sounds a call for liberation. That call means a firm identification with the poor. It also means naming the evil-doers who have made South America a land of dictators and repressors. In the blood of many martyrs, liberation theologians see a paradoxical hope. If Latin Americans are willing to die for the truths their grass-roots church experiences and consciousness-raising reveal, there is hope for the rest of the Catholic world. The economic and political oppressions that afflict Latin American have mirror images all over the Southern Hemisphere, and behind most of them stand capitalist influences from the Northern Hemisphere. So the Latin American struggle is our own.

Recently our own political struggle in the United States has drawn the Catholic bishops deeply into the public debate about nuclear arms. The bishops' 1983 Pastoral Letter, "The Challenge of Peace," combines a sophisticated awareness of the complexity of the issues with a strong doubt that nuclear war is ever a moral option. In such related ethical areas as ecology and business life, Catholic thinkers are also expressing strong doubts that the current ways most Americans evaluate their options would please the biblical Christ.

STUDY QUESTIONS

1. How distinctive is the central issue (the dignity of the human person) in the recent popes' pronouncements on social issues?
2. Evaluate Hollenbach's three strategic priorities.
3. Why should Catholic theologians be concerned to bring their views into dialogue with Marxists?
4. How central a symbol of American religious history is black slavery?
5. What are the strengths and weaknesses in the argument that the closure of priestly ordination to women makes the Roman Catholic church sexist?
6. Why does Latin American theology lay so much stress on praxis?
7. Evaluate the recommendations that the Catholic bishops make in "The Challenge of Peace" for reducing the current threat of nuclear arms.
8. Discuss the bishops' substitute for war.
9. In what sense has the religious root of the ecological crisis been anthropocentrism?
10. Discuss the impersonal presence of God in nature.
11. Evaluate Michael Novak's view of the "not-niceness in nature."
12. Discuss Thomas Shaffer's views of the legal profession.

NOTES

1. David Hollenbach, *Claims in Conflict* (New York: Paulist, 1979).
2. See Barbara Ward, *Progress for a Small Planet* (New York: Norton, 1979).
3. Karl Rahner, *Theological Investigations,* vol. 6 (Baltimore: Helicon, 1969), p. 231–49.
4. Joseph Gremillion, *The Gospel of Peace and Justice* Maryknoll, N.Y.: Orbis, 1976).
5. See Fred Lawrence, ed., *Lonergan Workshop,* vol. 1. (Missoula, Mont.: Scholars Press, 1978).
6. See Bernard Lonergan, *Method in Theology* (New York: Herder and Herder, 1972).
7. See José Miranda, *Marx and the Bible* (Maryknoll, N.Y.: Orbis, 1974).
8. See John A. Coleman, *An American Strategic Theology* (New York: Paulist, 1982).
9. See John C. Haughey, ed., *Personal Values in Public Policy* (New York: Paulist, 1979).
10. See Aleksander I. Solzhenitsyn, *The Mortal Danger* (New York: Harper & Row, 1980).
11. James Cone and Gayraud Wilmore, eds., *Black Theology: A Documentary History 1966–79* (Maryknoll, N.Y.: Orbis, 1979).
12. See J. Deotis Roberts, *Roots of a Black Future* (Philadelphia: Westminster, 1980).
13. See Elizabeth Herzog and Mark Zborowsky, *Life Is with People* (New York: Schocken, 1962).
14. Vincent Harding, "Out of the Cauldron of Struggle," *Soundings* 61:3 (Fall 1978): 339–54.

15. See Robert Coles, *The Children of Crisis* (Boston: Little, Brown, 1964).
16. See Denise Lardner Carmody, *Women and World Religions* (Nashville: Abingdon, 1979).
17. See Elisabeth Schüssler-Fiorenza, *In Memory of Her* (New York: Crossroad, 1983).
18. See Rosemary Radford Ruether, ed., *Religion and Sexism* (New York: Simon and Schuster, 1974).
19. See Rosemary Radford Ruether and Eleanor McLaughlin, eds., *Women of Spirit* (New York: Simon and Schuster, 1979).
20. Mary Daly, *The Church and the Second Sex*, 2d ed. (New York: Harper & Row, 1975); idem, *Beyond God the Father* (New York: Harper & Row, 1973); idem *Gyn/Ecology* (Boston: Beacon, 1979).
21. See Starhawk (Miriam Simos), *The Spiral Dance* (New York: Harper & Row, 1979).
22. See John Eagleson and Philip Scharper, eds., *Puebla and Beyond* (Maryknoll, N.Y.: Orbis, 1979).
23. Ibid., pp. 289–309.
24. Ibid., pp. 330–46.
25. See David Tracy, *Blessed Rage for Order* (New York: Seabury, 1975).
26. Gustavo Gutierrez, *A Theology of Liberation* (Maryknoll, N.Y.: Orbis, 1971).
27. See Jon Sobrino, *Christology at the Crossroads* (Maryknoll, N.Y.: Orbis, 1978).
28. Robert McAfee Brown, *Theology in a New Key* (Philadelphia: Westminster, 1978).
29. See Penny Lernoux, *Cry of the People* (Garden City, N.Y.: Doubleday, 1980).
30. Paulo Freire, *Pedagogy of the Oppressed* (New York: Seabury, 1974).
31. National Conference of Catholic Bishops, "The Challenge of Peace: God's Promise and Our Response," *The National Catholic Reporter*, 19:33 (June 17, 1983), 9.
32. Ibid., p. 10.
33. Ibid., p. 15.
34. Ibid.
35. Ibid., p. 19.
36. Ibid., p. 27.
37. See, for example, "Forum," *The National Catholic Reporter*, 20:16 (February 10, 1984): 9–19.
38. See, for example, Paul Abrecht and Roger L. Shinn, eds., *Faith and Science in an Unjust World*, 2 vol. (Philadelphia: Fortress, 1981).
39. John Carmody, *Ecology and Religion: Toward a New Christian Theology of Nature* (Ramsey, N.J.: Paulist, 1983).
40. Bernard Häring, *Free and Faithful in Christ*, vol. 3 (New York: Crossroad, 1981), pp. 15–16.
41. Jerry Falwell, *Listen America* (Garden City, N.Y.: Doubleday, 1980), p. 13.
42. Michael Novak, "Seven Theological Facets," in *Capitalism and Socialism: A Theological Inquiry*, ed. Michael Novak (Washington, D.C.: American Enterprise Institute for Public Policy Research, 1979), pp. 118–19.
43. Edward Stevens, *Business Ethics* (New York: Paulist, 1979), p. 210. See Ivan Illich, *Toward a History of Needs* (New York: Pantheon, 1978); Tibor Scitovsky, *The Joyless Economy* (New York: Oxford University Press, 1971).
44. Thomas L. Shaffer, *On Being a Christian and a Lawyer* (Provo, Utah: Brigham Young University Press, 1981), pp. 160, 163. See Steven Wexler, "Practicing Law for Poor People," *Yale Law Journal* 79 (1970): 1049.
45. Robert Lekachman, *Greed Is Not Enough* (New York: Pantheon, 1982).

Conclusion

PERSONAL THEOLOGIZING

Contemporary Catholic theology has accepted the changeable, historical character of the Christian tradition, and with that acceptance has come pluralism. In academic theology, Catholics now write from a variety of viewpoints. With an acceptance of modernity's turn to the subject has come a stress on authenticity. Increasingly, Catholic theologians are loathe to put forward doctrines that they cannot fully accredit personally. For instance, current psychology makes theologians find traditional Christology problematic. Schillebeeckx, Küng, and others are in trouble with Rome for their reservations about the adequacy of the classical theological formulas for today's world, and the resolution of their troubles will say much about the authenticity of future Catholic theology.[1]

History and authenticity have led Bernard Lonergan to stress interdisciplinary collaboration. To handle the reams of new information and viewpoints, theologians must specialize; to keep theology from fragmenting, they must make their specialties communicate.[2] A more personal way to handle diversity is to grasp firmly God's mystery, as Karl Rahner has done. The fact of mystery is something that even the most rigorous criticism cannot erode. Finally, the political facts of life have forced current theology to examine faith's praxis. What action flows from this thinking? More fundamentally, what action flows into this thinking? If liberation theology becomes part of future Catholicism's landscape, praxis will loom large.

We have summarized these recent shifts because they have analogies in personal theologizing. Insofar as faith guides a person's life, new theological approaches have personal implications. We shall indicate some of these implications momentarily, but first let us justify the notion of personal or amateur theologizing itself. The notion is that every Christian ought to love seeking her faith's understanding. "Amateur" implies a work of love, and the tradition relates amateur theology to the Spirit. When faith manifests the Spirit, we notice a love of authentic religion. That is, the Spirit fosters a love of understanding God, of getting a better hold on Jesus, of seeing the twofold command more clearly. She is behind the savor we find when pondering scriptural passage or discussing grace.

At first this can seem pious, even affected. Before long, however, it is sober and unobjectionable. For we humans do need to consider our lives under this aspect of eternity. The wisdom that psychologist Erik Erikson puts at the end of the life cycle beckons us earlier. Many feel it in adolescence, when a teacher or a book first stimulates their minds. They see what education could be, and they suffer ever after. The love of wisdom may seem muted in middle age, but it reasserts itself regularly. When money troubles arise, or children are contrary, or parents die, we are rocked back to ponder. The same happens when we suffer backbiting on the job or learn that another marriage has shattered. Indeed, by the time the children have left the nest they may find us sententious—all too ready to philosophize. The theologian would have us be ready to theologize—to brighten the eye of our faith. Aristotle thought a person needed fifty years before he could discourse on ethics well. The Spirit seems to think fifty years ought to make one ripe for the mystery of God.

By the fact that we have faith, intelligence, and time, we are ripe for at least amateur theology. If we have accepted Jesus' extraordinary humanity, we have staked out the first mile of a Christian way. If that way is to go farther, we have to develop what we first accepted. The tacit crisis in many Christians' faith is its underdevelopment. They have done little with theology since they left catechism class, and they wonder why their faith seems childish. Granted, they ought to get adult fare in the Sunday sermon or the diocesan newspaper. But often they do not, so their religious childishness is their own problem. They are individuals with capable minds and free wills. Why can they not take responsibility for developing their faith, as they take responsibility for developing their financial security? The summer schools overflow with good theology workshops. The periodical rack groans. The problem, then, is not a lack of fare but a lack of appetite.

Still, it is not hard to sharpen appetite. Even uneasiness can be an aperitif. Just as most workers feel underemployed, so people generally feel underchallenged and bored. This reflects their poor education. If they knew their minds and hearts, they could find in a week's experience material for a lifetime of study. Amateur theology can be the process of turning ordinary experience into material for deep study. Assuming faith in Jesus, it tries to regard the world as a child of grace. In other words, the amateur theologian explicitly compares her experiences with those of Jesus, testing Jesus' proposition that God shares our time lovingly. The process itself is open-ended. One can delve into Jesus or human experience for years and never glimpse the end. Therefore, the light must come more from the doing than from the ending. Simply making Jesus and one's present time dialectical, conversational, usually produces a flame.

It also draws a hermeneutic circle. Taking Jesus as God's human form, amateur theology probes both good times and bad. Consider, for instance, school times. When we actually are learning, we never question the value of school. Learning has a rightness that is self-justifying. Thus, one grows in mastering accounting. Both the mathematics and the business it involves develop intelligence. There are further questions, such as where to use one's accounting knowledge, but even if we answer them badly our knowledge itself is good. To understand is to use time well.

Similarly, to fail to understand is to seem to use time badly. This may be deceptive, since significant understanding can demand an incubation period of confusion, but let us assume that it is not. Let us assume that given materials for study are unintelligible. Because of poor teaching or sloppy texts, many students run into this situation. In our case, it occurred with canon law. Though the teacher and the text offered principles, they fell into no coherent order. This was utterly frustrating, and we found relief only through what Lonergan calls an "inverse insight." One day we realized that there was nothing to understand. Canon law had no coherent system, no explanatory connection to ontology, theology, or political science. The only thing to do was to memorize it. That was painful, but at least we were no longer seeking something unattainable.

From a good learning experience the amateur theologian can better appreciate what it means that God is light in whom there is no darkness at all (John 1:5). From a bad learning experience she can learn that unintelligibility is not mystery. Canon law, for instance, would only be mysterious if it held a fullness of understanding one could intuit at a higher level.

So far, our examples have been speculative, but practical examples can serve equally well. A good personal relationship carries overtones of communion. If things go well with a friend or lover, we grow a full set of affective ties. They illumine the scriptural conviction that human beings should not be alone, give weight to the scriptural adage that a brother helped by a brother is like a strong city. If the passion is profound, they may even bring to mind "love is strong as death." Of course, a good personal relationship will bring none of these to mind if one never has read scripture. The revelation pole in the amateur theologian's consciousness must be high enough to attract some attention. On the other hand, the experiential pole grows higher when we can add data of revelation.

In a bad personal relationship, the data might be labeled "sin," "creaturehood," or "redemptive suffering." We can reach for security when these hurt us, and be tempted never to risk love again. Wrapped like a porcupine, we would make ourselves a tight little ball. When the pain goes down, though, faith suggests that we reconsider the life of a porcupine. You don't see much when your head is tucked under your tail. You don't feel much when your skin is all sharp quills.

So, how did Jesus bear himself toward the world? How did he respond to misunderstanding, deception, and betrayal? Even if Jesus' example seems beyond us, the honesty to face it is a spiritual healing. In time, we may be able to imitate Jesus' large-heartedness. And, the logic of such imitation is intriguing. Those who imitate Jesus wager that they will gain light and peace. For instance, the saints wagered that they would find the center of things, the still point of the turning world. Winning, they said they learned more by trying to stand toward human beings as Jesus did than by either withdrawing or joining the tepid mainstream. Ultimately, of course, the saints did not trouble themselves much with logic. Ultimately they simply fell in love with Christ. But along the way Christ intrigued them. There is no good reason why he cannot intrigue us similarly.

Personal or amateur theology, then, is simply reflective Christian living. It goes to scripture, tradition, or current theologians simply to sharpen its perceptions of faith. The faith is primary, the reflection secondary. Living in face of mystery, amateur theologians use whatever helps them understand it more. The medievals were convinced that theology could disclose an objective order. The amateur theologian shares this conviction, for he reflects the hope to understand. The moderns sensed that much "reality" stems from our own interpretations. The amateur theologian shares this sense, too, for she wants faith to show her what interpretations yield the most light. When she hears faith answer, "The interpretations that are most loving," the Spirit plucks at her heartstrings. Amateur theology is but love's interpretation of time, but an intelligent effort to treat our neighbors as ourselves.

A SHORT FORMULA OF CHRISTIAN FAITH

Our description of personal or amateur theologizing assumes that reflection can find profit in both good experiences and bad. Most of us have to struggle to believe that all the times of our lives come from God, especially the destructive ones. What "profit" can parents find in the death of a tiny infant? What "growth" justifies a destructive divorce? To say times of war come from God is to risk obscenity. Surely a mature faith must be more critical.

Indeed it must, but at the end of all criticism the mystery still remains. In short form, Christian faith is a loving response to mystery, based on the story of Jesus Christ. Since mystery embraces our whole lives, it entails sin and evil, as well as grace. The loving response of faith does not demand closing our eyes to sin and evil. It does not demand denying the anger, hurt, or diminution they bring. Half the world suffers real diminution, real loss, through poverty and its aftereffects. All the world experiences things that should not be, things that rightly cause anger. Christian faith should take these realities seriously. In fidelity to conscience, it cannot whiten black deeds. In fidelity to history, it cannot forget that Jesus suffered evil unto death. The deepest liberation is from evil and death. There would be no absolute savior were there no mortal sin.

Despite this unblinking realism, Christian faith still finds life's mystery good. Where sin abounded grace abounds the more. Where evil twisted the spirit into knots, good remained what the spirit was made for. If there is a mystery of evil, so is there a mystery of good. If it is a puzzle that an aged person should have to die, it is more a puzzle that a child should be born. Because of Jesus, Christian faith makes all these equations unbalanced. It says, better to have lived than never to have been born. Better to have loved and been hurt than never to have loved at all. Better even to have done evil than not to have been free. Joining its contemplation of Jesus to its contemplation of experience, Christian faith struggles to live out such confessions.

An articulate theology can aid confession immensely, but confession finally is a choice we each face at heart. Rahner's theory of anonymous Christianity reminds us that Jesus clarifies a universal condition. All people live amidst mystery. All come to know both evil and good. So all have to choose, to interpret their time. Even if they affirm an established tradition, their affirmation is a matter of personal choice. We cannot abdicate responsibility for our time's deepest issue. We cannot transfer to others our yes or no to God. At the quietest hour, we can only follow Jesus or hold back, only commend our spirits trustingly or refuse to go gentle into the dark night.

The advantage of short formulas is their condensation of endless implications.[3] If Christian faith is saying yes to mystery in virtue of Jesus Christ, a thousand collateral issues fall into the shade. To be sure, the "yes" must be active, practical. It must be the deed of our life, the synthesis of our love. Not those who say "Lord, Lord," but those who do his will, please God. Not those who talk about the twofold commandment, but those who really pray and serve, fulfill the law and the prophets. Still, Jesus makes the task blessedly plain. We are given time in order to learn our lives' gravity. Theologically, that gravity is an image of the

Trinity. Our weightiest product, our fullest humanity, reflects the fathomless Father, the expressive Son, and the gathering Spirit of love.

Philosophically, our reflection of God engages a reality with four primary zones. Nature, society, self, and divinity are the four irreducible factors of a human being's world. Therefore, the Christian's response to mystery relates her to all these factors. To deny nature or society is almost as distorting as denying God. Even to undervalue one of the four factors is to warp one's response to mystery. For instance, our bodies give us a basis in matter which faith denies at its peril. From sacraments to relaxation, nature impresses itself.

So too with society. A church is as inevitable as a tribe. There are no independent human beings. All of us have mothers, fathers, and collaborators. There are no Christians who have not received from the Church and do not owe recompense. When they try to pay it, they learn what the relation between society and self ought to be. Society ought to enhance the individuality of its members. Conversely, the members ought to find their fullest selves in social relationships. When a given local society does not know this, and so crushes individuality, the individual can rightly stay away. But even staying away shows her what ideally would obtain. The Church is emptier than it ought to be, and many individual lives lack an important luster.

Thus, the underlying themes of the main commitment involved in Christian faith unfold soberly. Though grace abounds more than sin, sin is by no means meager. Though peace is inseparable from the Spirit of grace, peace may only be found at rock bottom. Christian faith does not promise us a sinless life, nor a life where peace is unthreatened. It has nothing to do with financial success, and little to do with social status. It has everything to do with the self's definition, its absolute relation to God. Is God a mystery worth loving? Does time suggest parental concern? Believers say yes to these questions—true believers on the basis of experience.

For Karl Rahner's mature theology, mystery, grace, and Jesus are the Christian nub. The common, foundational reality is mystery. The goodness faith finds comes from grace, God's love. The sign and manifestation of God's love is Jesus. If one begins with the deepest common denominator, the theological word is "mystery." To be human is to have a reflective consciousness that plunges one into life's fullness. Hindu, Hottentot, or Hamite, the human being is the animal that asks why. Asking why is responding to mystery. At core we *are* responses to mystery, embodied questionings. A child is born and we ask why love becomes so wrinkled and wiggly. A government collapses and we ask why human beings still haven't learned to cooperate. We turn a page and a biblical image transposes such asking. Creatures should not expect full understanding. Full understanding depends on full responsibility, full initiation. No creature has full responsibility, so no creature has full understanding. For there to be full understanding there must be a Creator. If there is not a Creator, creation is casual. Both our minds and creation repudiate that. A casual, senseless creation gives our minds no reason to be. It does not square with scientists learning to make nuclear fission, psychiatrists learning to heal sick spirits. Mystery, then, is a fullness, not a void. It is more than we can handle, not less.

That is an argument of common sense, raised slightly by Christian philosophy. Ultimately, it comes from a second naivete: Tulips spring from bulbs, tides from wind and moon. If something is "there," there is a cause. If something changes, there is a reason. We may not be able to grasp this reason fully, but a single experience of understanding proves it must exist. Grace buttresses this reasoning. Shoring the mind, it tips the scale against absurdity. Though the mind is limited, discovery after discovery proves it can investigate the world successfully. The mind has to be patient, come to know its limitations, but its limitations do not make the world an idiot's tale. When Heisenberg formulated indeterminacy, he helped set physicists' limitations. Obviously, though, he did not say that physicists cannot know, waste their time. His own theory claimed to be a knowing. Its validity says he used his time well.

Similarly, grace shores the heart. The senselessness that really unravels human beings is moral evil. Physical evil—earthquakes and cancers—is as logical as statistical probability. Moral evil makes no sense, violates constitutional laws. We are the species who can violate our own constitutional law. We can see the good and not do it, specify the evil and take it home. Partly from finitude, which makes us fallible, and partly from disorder, which has no intelligible cause, we can frustrate our inmost calling. Such frustration writes a tragicomedy. Our inhumanity tells heaven it did bad work. The irony of knowing and not doing makes us blush and then smile. Grace urges the blush and blesses the smile. Against God's invitation, mystery's largess, we are ingrates who do well to blush often. But when we accept the humiliating truth, it becomes a liberating humility. Graciously, God forgives our sin. With her there are new beginnings. So our pretense to sufficiency becomes funny, our drones and struts vaudevillian.

Most societies have understood tragedy, and many have glimpsed irony. Deep comedy, though, is a child of grace. For grace finally is divinization, humanity's complete success. Taken into God's own life, our time ends discretely. Death is a leap, a final saltus, beyond the happiest extrapolation. That leap makes human time a *divina commedia,* a play or puppetry. Too subtly for our sensing, God makes creation *elevation.* The mystery we move in is an amniotic fluid. From death a new, glorified existence is born. The delivery room is so oxygenated that "heavenly" life is humanity at its most intense and most fulfilling. It is humanity living like the resurrected Christ.

Jesus, then, anchors all Christian talk about mystery and grace. Without his Resurrection, there would be no comedy. Similarly, there would be no shoring against life's evil. And, historically, there would be no Christianity. Christianity depends on the resurrection of Jesus. It is the memory of God's eschatological act, the burgeoning of time's core relevation. Because of the resurrection Jesus' followers preserved the story of his painful death, remembered his wonderful teaching. Because of the resurrection, they created liturgies. Many theologians were kids enthralled by liturgies. In long treatises, they have spun out the liturgies' wisdom. In short formulas, they have condensed grace's power. The power and wisdom is Christ.

DISTINCTIVELY CATHOLIC FAITH

In a general book on Christian faith, we have tried to indicate some of the special gifts that the three great families of churches (Protestant, Catholic, and Orthodox) now offer the ecumenical Church.[4] As catchwords, we have spoken of Protestant prophecy, Catholic wisdom, and Orthodox worship. This is not to deny that Catholics have been prophetic and worshipful, Protestants have been wise and worshipful, or Orthodox have been prophetic and wise. It is merely to make a first, somewhat impressionistic separation of the three families in terms of their most salient, and perhaps profound, characteristics. In this section, let us elaborate on Catholic "wisdom."

By wisdom we mean the capacity to see things in a whole or orderly fashion. The wise person or tradition does a remarkably good job at giving each element in a complex mosaic its due, neglecting none of the vital forces. This, in turn, leads to an appearance of sophistication (in a good sense), of being patient with the diversity and richness of human experience. Characteristically, then, Catholicism, in our view, has been an interpretation of Christian faith that has striven mightily for balance, synthesis, and inclusiveness. As the name *(kata holos)* suggests, it has wanted to embrace and honor what the *whole* of the faith, the Church, the revelation of God has entailed. So the Catholic tradition has tended to say "both/and," rather than "either/or." It has generated a rhetorical style of "on the one hand—but on the other hand."

At the end of his fine two-volume work on Catholicism, Richard P. McBrien comes home to a similar summation: "Catholicism is characterized, therefore, by a *both/and* rather than an *either/or*. It is not nature *or* grace, but graced nature; not reason *or* faith, but reasom illumined by faith; not law *or* Gospel, but law inspired by the Gospel; not Scripture *or* tradition, but normative tradition within Scripture; not faith *or* works, but faith issuing in works and works as expressions of faith; not authority *or* freedom, but authority in the service of freedom; not the past versus the present, but the present in continuity with the past; not stability *or* change, but change in fidelity to stable principle, and principle fashioned and refined in response to change; not unity *or* diversity, but unity in diversity, and diversity which prevents uniformity, the antithesis of unity."[5]

In our own work, we briefly developed four examples of this Catholic balance. First, we dealt with scripture and tradition. For Catholic Christianity, they go together like partners to a marriage. In the beginning was scripture, because Jesus and the first Christians lived within the world of the Hebrew Bible, had their language and faith thoroughly spiced by the Law, the Prophets, and the Writings. In the beginning, however, there also was tradition. The Hebrew Bible but collected the traditions of Israel. The traditions about Jesus were the raw materials for the New Testament. The determination of the New Testament canon and the interpretation of writings such as Paul's letters depended upon custom or tradition.

In the beginning, however, (again), there was Christian scripture, because from the time of the apostles, the writings of Paul and the evangelists became privileged templates or models, interpretations of faith that achieved classical, normative status. And so, throughout subsequent history, scripture and tradition have jockeyed back and forth, always reaching out to one another for foundation, complement, and correction. We could not understand the New Testament without the traditions that Christians have developed through centuries of living with the New Testament. We would have no privileged traditional materials, no interpretations of Jesus that stand as first among equals, were there no Christian scripture. The whole realm of the data, therefore, writes a demand for both scripture and tradition.

Similarly, the Catholic instinct is that faith and reason are not so much adversaries as partners, helpers, dance mates. Reason is our God-given ability as human beings to seek out meaning, grasp sense, and thereby raise our minds to the Creator who has left traces everywhere. If reason were utterly incompetent in matters of faith, faith would be utterly irrational, and so suspect of being utterly immoral. On the other hand, unless reason is in the grasp of a wholehearted faith, a trust in the divine mystery, an openness to the God who has acted so dramatically in Christ, reason will not achieve its full stature. The love of God that comes to the person open in faith gives reason a new orientation. Guided by reasons of the heart, as Pascal called them, the mind is able to come to deeper, finer, more holistic truths than ever it could gain all alone. So, faith and reason need one another. In Catholic interpretation, they are not enemies but friends, even lovers.

A third instance of Catholic balance or wisdom is the complementarity of clergy (or religious) and lay people. As it works out, this complementarity provides for both immersion in the world and withdrawal to the desert, both the passionate use of sex and the celibate consecration, both spiritual and physical parenting, generativity, and taking care. As they crisscross in living faith, clergy and laity constrain and fill out one another. They honor one another's special competencies, call upon one another's special experiences. The clericalization of the Catholic church in many historical periods has muted the harmony in which these vocations should have sung, but in principle Catholicism honors both of them to its core, confessing that the Church will be less than God wills so long as any set of gifts is not flourishing.

The last example of balance that we bring forward is the Catholic promotion of both prayer and work. Neither work alone, nor prayer alone, fulfills the Catholic ideal. If we are to praise and serve God with all our minds, hearts, souls, and strength, what we do with our hands and minds at work is as important as what we do when we pray in the quiet of our hearts. The collaborative ventures we undertake with other people pour into the pot as surely as the communal prayers we send up at the Sunday liturgy. The God of Catholic faith is not sacral, in the sense of concerned only with a special, fenced-off realm. The God of Catholic faith says that anything we work with, or pray about, is matter fit to be transformed by the Spirit of grace.

THE POPE AND THE PEOPLE

The man presiding over the Catholic tradition of wisdom and balance is the pope, John Paul II as we write. By his travels and use of the contemporary communications media, John Paul II has made himself seen by, somewhat known to, more people than any of his predecessors. His strong stand on social justice, his defense of labor, and his opposition to nuclear war have won him considerable support worldwide. His positions on such internal church matters as doctrinal development, sexual morality, and governance have brought him considerable criticism. So he is a controversial figure, charismatic but opposed in many quarters. In the resolution of his currently knotted relations with the Catholic people will lie to a great extent of the future of Catholic Christianity.

In his interesting book *The Catholic Heritage,* Lawrence Cunningham treats Pope John Paul II as a humanist. After describing the pope's rich background (philosopher, poet, working person, sufferer under the Nazis and Communists), Cunningham summarizes John Paul II's understanding of the human condition: "The papal analysis of the human condition is preparatory in the sense that to understand humanity is a necessity prior to an understanding of what the Gospel adds to, or contributes toward, the needs of humanity. In the papal view the Gospel does not free-float like some set of abstract mathematical formulas; it is a revelation, eternally true, that is addressed to human history. The individual is precious because he or she is made 'in the image and likeness of God'; persons are to be honored and freed from exploitation because of the redemption of Christ; the physical world is not to be abused because we are given stewardship over it by God; we must avoid a materialist view of history because we have a transcendental end; and so on. In what sense is this a religious humanism? Or, to use a language more congenial to the papal usage, a Christian personalism? It is a humanism in the sense that Pope John Paul sees Christian revelation not as an alien force superadded to humanity but as a gift which completes and perfects an already good humanity. At the core of the pope's philosophy is the unique, unrepeatable individual, already redeemed by Christ and at least potentially aware of that redemption."[6]

In Cunningham's digest, one can see very clearly the balance that we have been associating with the Catholic tradition. Reason and faith, nature and grace, hinge quite nicely. Nonetheless, as Cunningham goes on to point out, progressives within the Church tend to criticize John Paul II's traditional theology. His basic analysis of human nature is fine, and his championing of social justice is admirable, but many find his resistance to freer (ironically, more personalist and communitarian) interpretations of Christian faith and Church life a major roadblock to Catholic Christianity's flourishing. For instance, although most European churches now suffer a dreadful shortage of priests, the pope will not seriously consider changing the Church's celibacy law. Although women increasingly feel marginalized by an all-male power structure, he will not seriously consider opening orders to women. Although bishops from Third World countries have made it plain that faith needs to be adapted if it is to grow well in their cultural soil, a European stamp continues to press for uniformity. The result is more disappointment within the Church than among John Paul II's outside observers. Indeed, those who most want a free, personalist style that would produce lively critical communities have become the pope's strongest critics.

Representative of those who desire these critical communities are the Dutch poet Huub Oosterhuis and the Belgian theologian Edward Schillebeeckx. The following exchange between them epitomizes much of what John Paul II will have to deal with, if his church is not to continue to lose a great many of its best and brightest:

O. "This book containing our conversations may perhaps be bought by people who no longer feel at home in the Church and who have no possibility of criticizing or accusing that power that you have mentioned. The only way they may have of protesting is just to stay away—the silent 'lapsing' that has taken place during the past thirty years in the Netherlands and elsewhere. And hardly anyone comes forward now as a candidate for the priesthood! But the bishops still ask us to pray for new vocations. What do you think ought to be done about this?

S. "On the one hand, our bishops are making it impossible for people to come forward as priests, but on the other hand we are asked to pray for priests. That is a falsification—a falsification of what prayer really is as well. . . . The centralization of the Church's power in the Roman structures began in the eleventh century. Luther's and Calvin's criticism of the Church—and the criticism of the whole Reformation—didn't just come down from heaven! The Church had identified itself so completely with a Christ it had made into an absolute ruler—a misrepresentation of Christ, in other words—that it had in fact become a power structure, an institution that was removed from the criticism of the gospel. Those encyclicals written during the nineteenth century, for example, transferring the power of Christ directly and almost unreflectingly to the pope—they were terribly mistaken. And the same thing is happening again under the present pope!'"[7]

Thus the question looming before Pope John Paul II and his people is, "How shall we understand the power of Christ?" Will future Catholic church power be the influence of love, the challenge of poverty, the self-spending of service? Or will it continue to be orders from rulers at the top to underlings at the bottom, the dictates of a bureaucracy greatly intent on its own preservation? We frankly hope that John Paul II will be converted from his present ways, and the present ways of the Roman **curia**, to something less legalistic and fear-ridden, something freer, more loving, more reminiscent of Pope John XXIII, whose gift it was to inspire warmth and commitment rather than try to command them.

A WORLDLY HORIZON

Oosterhuis and Schillebeeckx are written off in many quarters because they insist that Christian faith is authentic only to the degree that it duplicates the love of Jesus for those who suffered most among his contemporaries. In many quarters, this insistence sounds too secular, too like the political programs of Marxists or Socialists. Still, the declining church attendance that Oosterhuis and Schillebeeckx mention is real, and appealing to nineteenth-century views of authority and revelation is unlikely to reverse it. Is there then a futuristic form of incarnational Christian faith that might renew the gospel, once again let the power of Christ's Kingdom break forth without seeming to make that power just another political program? Among the Catholic Christian writers who have impressed us in recent years, Rosemary Haughton stands out for precisely such a worldly, yet more than political, perspective. To bring our exposition of contemporary Catholic theology back to its starting point in the debate about the Church's future, let us borrow from Haughton's recent book *The Passionate God.*

To get her argument in gear, Haughton relates her convictions to the invitation of the wisdom of God: "It is an invitation to experience Heaven and Hell, life and death, to know them in facts of nuclear power and food co-ops and police methods, of attitudes to babies and the poor and the handicapped and what we put in the soil. So it has to do with God, and with bread, and with sex, because there is a God-bread-sex continuum as there is a matter-energy continuum, and in exactly the same way. Wisdom is simply the apprehension of God in human experience through its whole extent."[8]

In search of wisdom, Haughton's Catholic instinct is that wisdom must be something worldly, concrete, holistic. Unless it throws light on the matters that shape our real selves—what we eat, how we get our energy, how we love and reproduce—it does not do the job we ask the Spirit to accomplish.

To many minds, traditional Christian faith today is not doing the job we ask the Spirit to accomplish: "We live in a world which in east and west and north and south makes all its really crucial choices—political, economic, social, sexual—in relation to values which do not contradict so much as ignore the Gospel description of the nature of humankind. But worse than this is the fact that the Church generally behaves the same way, without even noticing the concealed premises underlying its adaptation to the world. Only in a narrow band of specifically 'Christian' concerns do 'official' churches normally display moral indignation or act in ways which offer any contrast (let alone challenge) to the usual patterns of social adjustment. Having lived alongside such a Church for a long time most people (people, that is, whose lives are not bound to that 'Christian' area by emotional need and religio-social pressure) have ceased to be interested in what Christians say or do. They do not even, like old-fashioned humanists, get worked up about Christianity; it is merely irrelevant and smells a bit fusty, though as folklore and folk custom it has a certain interest."[9]

This is the voice of such continental critics as Oosterhuis and Schillebeeckx, translated into British irony. A Church that spends most of its energy on institutional politics, or that mainly serves as a prop of the bourgeois status quo, has nothing to offer people who want a better world, a place of freedom and justice. Unless the Church—we Christian people—distinguishes itself as passionate for the passionate God, alive to razor-edge intensity for a Kingdom that would throw the rascals out and put loving servants in their places, it has nothing to offer the world. Because it is neither hot nor cold, many hungry for good fare now vomit the Church out of their mouths. If it is to continue the work of its master, the Church must regain words of eternal life, the power to heal and make all things new.

For Rosemary Haughton, the best analogies to the doings of God in our world come from passionate, life-questing love. God passionately, almost unreasonably, loves the world and race he has created. The power of the divine life that God would communicate is gentle and unobtrusive, yes, but if need be it will press through rock, grow violent and ruthless. For God would do a new thing, make a new reign of grace. Until we see the breadth and depth of this new thing, God's presence in the birth-throes of history, we will continue to minimize the Resurrection, continue to miss the influx of God's heaven: "Like spring, this breakthrough of newness is violent. We are sentimental about spring. We concentrate on fluffy birds, the chubby pinkness of apple-blossom, the reassuring soft green of new grass. But spring is not gentle or cosy. It is an eruption of life so strong it can push bricks apart and make houses fall down. It thrusts through, and because of, layers of rotten past. The diamond brilliance of the cuckoo's note is the result of many fledglings shouldered out of the nest to their deaths, as all new life thrusts aside whatever impedes it. Even in the sheer perfection of each growing thing there is an integrity which is painful in its accuracy. The scent of lilacs in the dawn cuts through the fuzziness of disordered desire, the etched whiteness of lily of the valley against dark leaves sears the imagination. These are not soft things; they have a tenderness ascetically fined down to an essential longing. This is the violence of absolute love, which takes the Kingdom of Heaven by storm in a silence of total concentration on the one thing necessary."[10]

The one thing necessary is the love of God so great that God gave his only-begotten Son to save the world. Most essentially, we are the objects, the intended, of that love. Faith in an incarnate God is as staggeringly concrete and physical as that. Here, now, for you, for me, the divine passion forms up its ranks for the assault. Catholic Christianity believes that the members of Christ should aid this assault, be its vanguard and demonstration centers. The critical communities of the Haughtons and Schillebeeckxs keep this gamble alive for the twenty-first century. Protèstors and mystics opening themselves to God's newness, they try to let the Resurrection take hold. Even when it wrenches their limbs, sears their hearts, takes their breath away, they try to believe that Christ is both fully human and fully divine.

SUMMARY

Our conclusion begins with personal theologizing and a short formula of Christian faith. Collecting the emphases developed in the preceding pages, we try to apply them to average Christians' situations, so as to make theology part of their vocation. This means broadening or democratizing the traditional notion that theology is "faith seeking understanding." Essentially, it creates an "amateur" theology: reviewing daily experience with an eye of faith. Daily experience asks faith for cogent interpretation. Conversely, faith asks daily experience for examples and instances. Karl Rahner has pioneered the use of "short formulas" that put the Catholic substance of such instances in a nutshell. Having exposed how "everyman" can be an amateur theologian, we suggest the core content with which amateur theology deals.

Among the specifically Catholic overtones that even an amateur review will come upon stands wisdom: the instinct for wholeness. The distinctively Catholic dictum is "both/and" rather than "either/or." Applied to the presently somewhat complicated relationship between the pope and the Catholic people, this dictum might say, "Both the fine stress on social justice and a new freedom and love within the church." Were this new balance to be struck, the Church might come alive with the power of the passionate God, the Creator who made us a world we should keep fit to live in.

STUDY QUESTIONS

1. In what modest but realistic way does a mature Christian faith produce amateur theologians?
2. Compose two short formulas that sum up traditional Christian faith: the first centered on death and the second centered on Jesus.
3. What are the assets and liabilities of the traditional Catholic inclination toward balance and wholeness?
4. What are the implications of Schillebeeckx's assertion that "our bishops are making it impossible for people to come forward as priests"?
5. What does Rosemary Haughton mean by saying "there is a God-bread-sex continuum as there is a matter-energy continuum"?
6. What is "the violence of absolute love"?

NOTES

1. See Gerald O'Collins, *What Are They Saying About Jesus?* (New York: Paulist, 1977).
2. See Bernard Lonergan, *Method in Theology* (New York: Herder and Herder, 1972).
3. See Karl Rahner, *Foundations of Christian Faith* (New York: Seabury, 1978), pp. 448–60.
4. See John Carmody, *The Heart of the Christian Matter* (Nashville: Abingdon, 1983).
5. Richard P. McBrien, *Catholicism*, vol. 2 (Minneapolis: Winston, 1980), p. 1174.
6. Lawrence S. Cunningham, *The Catholic Heritage* (New York: Crossroad, 1983), p. 160.
7. Edward Schillebeeckx, *God Is New Each Moment* (New York: Seabury, 1983), pp. 80–81.
8. Rosemary Haughton, *The Passionate God* (New York: Paulist, 1981), p. 4.
9. Ibid., p. 243.
10. Ibid., p. 17.

Appendix:
A Brief History of Catholic Theology

SCRIPTURE AND THE FATHERS
MEDIEVAL THEOLOGY
THE COUNTER-REFORMATION
MODERNITY
SUMMARY
STUDY QUESTIONS
NOTES

SCRIPTURE AND THE FATHERS

Catholic theology begins in the Hebrew Bible. There was no inevitable connection between Abraham and a Church centered in Rome, but after the fact one can trace definite lines. For Jesus and the first Christians, "scripture" was the Hebrew Bible, above all the Pentateuch. Reading scripture they found a transcendent God. Unlike the Canaanite baals, Yahweh stood beyond nature. He was the Lord, the source of all creation. Human beings could commune with him, but their sin made communion difficult. Were God to judge harshly, none would survive. Still, God had chosen Israel as his people. The covenant pledged his presence, and the Hebrew Bible witnesses to Israel's search. The focus of the search was history. Unlike an Eastern Absolute, Yahweh participated in human time. As a result, Jewish religion was singularly concrete. It was what you did, how you lived, whether you fulfilled the Law that determined your righteousness. It was how you treated your neighbor. What you thought was secondary.[1]

Jesus worked several transformations on these themes. First, he turned Lord into Father. Second, without denying sin he spoke more of God's love. If one would repent and believe the gospel, God's love would make one whole. Third, Jesus told God's people they were in crisis. He brought the hour of judgment and opportunity. The great image Jesus used to drive the crisis home was the Kingdom. Momentarily, God would oust Satan, and establish a new eon of justice. The way to enter the Kingdom was through faith. Accepting the gospel, one had only to keep its twofold commandment. Ever since Jesus' preaching, Catholic theology has made love of God and love of neighbor the crux of authenticity.

The writers of the New Testament shifted faith from the Kingdom to Jesus. Thus, the proclaimer became the proclaimed. As early as Paul, the New Testament separated Jesus from ordinary humanity. In virtue of his cross and resurrection, Jesus became the saving Lord. When they first sought to describe Jesus' status, the New Testament authors seized upon Jewish notions. First, they tried "Messiah" on for size. Jesus was the anointed deliverer Judaism had long sought, though his deliverance was not political but spiritual. Second they considered Son and Word. Word, like Spirit, was an aspect of Yahweh that Jesus seemed to manifest. Thus, Jesus was like a son who expresses a father, like a divine Word become flesh. By the end of the first century, when Johannine theology had matured, Jesus had a solid pre-existence. When God made the world, the Logos was with him. By faith, followers of Jesus could join the Logos' "body." Thereby, the Incarnation continued in the Church. The Church expressed divine life in word and sacrament. Its missionaries continued Jesus' proclamation of the gospel.[2]

The early apologists of the generations after the New Testament writers had a twofold task. When Christians became numerous enough to attract attention, the apologists began a "political" defense of their Christian faith. Primarily, they tried to show that Christianity was neither immoral nor subversive. Jews had won a grudging respect in the Roman Empire for their high morality, and Christians argued that they deserved the same. Far from being subversive, they were Caesar's most solid subjects, so long as he did not ask them to call him Lord. The second task was more philosophical. Educated Christians lived in a Hellenistic milieu. Hellenism lay great stress on philosophy. Though the schools that dominated the early Christian years were inferior to those of Plato and Aristotle, the love of wisdom remained a high ideal. With the mystery religions come from the East, it focused a great longing for a truth that could save. The apologists therefore translated Christianity as a philosophy— a saving truth, God's own wisdom. Jesus not only fulfilled Jewish prophecy, he fulfilled Plato and Aristotle. His church had a knowledge *(gnosis)* more saving than the mystery religions'.

Justin Martyr (ca. 100–165) related all human illumination to the divine Logos. Clement of Alexandria (ca. 150–215) expanded Justin's approach, trying to show how Christian revelation and sacramental life were a rich humanism. Origen (ca. 185–254) made Clement's efforts flower, writing voluminous scriptural commentaries remarkable for their allegorical interpretation. These commentaries and other Alexandrine efforts showed that Christians could be intellectuals. Without denying the need for practical charity, they developed Christian *theoria* (contemplation). For classical philosophy *theoria* was the highest human activity, the best reflection of God. Though Origen came under a cloud for seeming to subordinate the Son to the Father, his brilliant use of Platonic philosophy gave Christian theology its first great speculative consolidation.

This consolidation was important because Arianism, the most potent early heresy, relied on hard reasoning. Arius (ca. 250–336) tried to solve the mystery of the Trinity and concluded that the Logos was not substantially the same as the Father. Many Church leaders instinctively rejected this conclusion, but only those competent philosophically could meet Arius's challenge head-on. It was not sufficient to repeat biblical descriptions, because the Bible did not focus on the question of substance. So when Athanasius (ca. 296–373), leader of the "orthodox" party, considered meeting Arius on his own grounds, the foundational issue was whether Christian doctrine could develop beyond biblical categories. Backing Athanasius's decision that it could, the bishops at Nicaea (325) proclaimed that the Son *is* of the same substance as the Father. Thereby, they backed the implicit proposition that the Church is competent to apply scriptural faith to new situations in new language. Later theology has shown that the problems of focusing such competence and determining whether a given development is indeed faithful to the New Testament can be very weighty. Nonetheless, by its conciliar responses to such early challenges as Arius's, the Church endorsed theological reasoning and doctrinal development.[3]

The other challenges of the early centuries helped round out a theological core. In christological controversies, bishop-theologians developed the orthodox view that Jesus was truly human and truly divine, one person in two natures. The ultimate mystery of Jesus' identity lay beyond human grasp, but he was both like us in all things save sin and the eternal Word. An important notion that this Christology sanctioned was the *theotokos*. To concretize its belief that the Word took flesh from Mary, orthodoxy labeled her the "God-bearer." Not only did this label summarize the mystery of the Incarnation, it also established Mary's singular place in Christian salvation. Indeed, all her other titles derive from her dignity as the Mother of God. Eastern Christianity has greatly reverenced the *theotokos*, and greatly contemplated the Incarnation. Its later controversy about icons probably would not have arisen except for the *theotokos*, for the most influential icons showed God as a small child with a lovely human mother. When the Emperor Leo III (717–740) attacked icons, calling them an impediment to the conversion of Jews and Muslims (who thought their use idolatrous), those who defended icons pointed not only to the consonance of icons with the Incarnation, but also to the centuries through which the faithful had prayed before images of Jesus and his Mother.

The Western fathers were not so influential in conciliar decisions as the Eastern, but they produced significant theological reflections. Indeed, Augustine (354–430) finally became the greatest figure of the patristic age. He used Platonic philosophy to speculate on the Trinity, and took the Roman Empire's decay as an occasion to ponder the theology of history. In his *Confessions* Augustine sounded like a modern—autobiographic, personal, existential. In his controversies with Pelagius, who seemed to deny salvation's gratuity, Augustine ventured into the deep waters of predestination. Principally, he sought to establish God's utter priority in human salvation. But the complexity of the question, and his less than complete lucidity, sowed seeds for the tedious discussions of grace and freedom that distressed theologians in the sixteenth and seventeenth centuries. Another Westerner, Pope Leo I, made the fifth century the time when Rome consolidated its influence. When his "Tome" was accepted by the Council of Chalcedon (451) as a standard of christological orthodoxy, Rome's magisterial primacy was set.

Other great theologians of the patristic age include the Cappadocians and Jerome. The Eastern Cappadocians—Basil, Gregory of Nyssa, and Gregory Nazianzen—dominated the Council of Constantinople (381), which dealt Arianism more doctrinal blows. These three bishops combined speculative acumen with great concern for the spiritual life—so much so that Basil gave Eastern monasticism its primary rule. Jerome (ca. 342–420) was a Westerner who lived a monk's life at Bethlehem and made his greatest impact through scriptural translation and commentary. His Latin Vulgate version of the Bible became the common text in the West, and his choleric observations of the contemporary scene make him a vivid stop on the patristic tour. With Athanasius, who was intrigued by Antony's desert experiences, and Basil, Jerome pushed monasticism to the Christian fore.

From the patristic age, then, Christian theology received a considerable clarification of the original, New Testament faith. This age reverenced scripture, but its experience of Church life showed the need for greater precision in both doctrine and morality. The fathers mainly used Greek categories in their systematic speculations, and they struggled, not always successfully, for a balanced view of the flesh in their moral theology. Overall, their theology had the vitality of intelligent pastors trying to explain on all fronts. It may strike us as time-bound and antifemale, but it was wonderfully alive.[4]

MEDIEVAL THEOLOGY

The East never lost the patristic conception of theology. Until the capture of Constantinople by the Turks in 1453, Eastern Christianity continued to enjoy the cultural unity of the old empire. This supported a strong bias against innovation. What one found in scripture, the seven ecumenical councils (II Nicaea in 787 is the last on the Eastern list), and the fathers constituted *paradosis:* "tradition." The East was loathe to change tradition. The bad aspect of this was a tendency to stagnation. The good aspect was a sense of unity with past ages. Nonetheless, Eastern interests shifted significantly. Kallistos Ware has noted four major changes. From 325 to 381 doctrinal discussion centered on the Trinity. From 431 to 681 it focused on Christology. The iconoclast controversy dominated the years 726–843. The years 858–1453 featured polemics against the West and a strong interest in mystical theology. John Damascene (ca. 675–749), St. Symeon the New Theologian (949–1022), and St. Gregory Palamas (1296–1359) were the luminaries of later Eastern theology who provided it originality and systematization without departing from its fusion of thought and life.

Catholic theology ought to consider Eastern developments part of its own store, for before the division of 1054 there was one church, however strained, and after 1054 theological differences remained relatively minor. Still, Roman Catholicism developed its distinctive character in the West, above all in medieval scholasticism. Where the Eastern mind tended to be speculative, Roman law impressed the Western mind deeply. As early as Tertullian (ca. 160–220) moral questions dominated the West, for sin and salvation were its chief theological interests. To be sure, Augustine was a great speculative power, and he remained the scholastics' chief tutor, but even Augustine worried about sin and salvation considerably.

During their slowly widening estrangement, the Eastern and Western Church zones shared several controversies. The monothelite controversy about Christ's wills and the iconoclast controversy are primary examples. Popes involved themselves in these originally Eastern issues, but not always to the benefit of Church unity. In the *filioque* controversy the West ran afoul of the East's traditionalism, for the Western proposition that the Spirit proceeds from the Son as well as the Father was not explicit in the Nicene Creed. The filioque was the major doctrinal divergence between East and West, but several disciplinary divergences also developed. Thus, the East protested some of the privileges the popes had assumed, the rise of compulsory celibacy for the clergy, the West's denying priests the power to administer confirmation, the Western doctrine of purgatory, and other relatively minor issues. The main fault in them all was their innovation.

In the ninth century, Western theologians debated the nature of the eucharist, and also aspects of predestination. Charlemagne had brought some unity to the Western tribes, and monastic schools began laying the foundations of a new theological intellectualism. Anselm (1033–1109) sprang from this foundation, and he clarified the importance of reason.

For example, his notion that theology is faith in search of *understanding* spotlighted reason, as did his inquiries about the rationale of the Incarnation and the proof of God's existence. With Peter Abelard (1079–1142) dialectical argument took center stage. By laying out reasons for and against a theological proposition, Abelard contributed to the scholastic *questio:* the interrogation of evidential grounds and supposedly probative reasonings.

Bernard Clairvaux (1090–1153) was Abelard's polar opposite, his mystical bent running directly counter to Abelard's rationalism. In fact, Abelard and Bernard symbolize the two poles medieval theology struggled to reconcile. Peter Lombard (1100–1160) did later medievals the favor of collecting traditional opinions on various doctrinal points, and many later giants commented on his *Sentences.*

In the background of the theology of the Middle Ages stand the medieval university and the papacy. Theology was queen of the sciences, but by no means the only intellectual interest. The medieval university assumed Christian culture, but under that umbrella considerable secular study went on. The West had received Aristotle, largely through Arabic interpreters, and with him came a new power of argument. For both philosophy and natural science, Aristotle became the starting point. The medieval papacy had ongoing struggles with various imperial centers, as Church and state battled for supremacy. This battle stimulated canon law, which tried to detail Church powers. Some Church powers concerned sanctification, so from the twelfth century there was considerable interest in the sacraments. Penance and matrimony slowly entered the sacramental ranks, and by 1439 they were on the list of seven sacraments proposed to the Greeks in ecumenical discussion as part of Catholic faith.

The two schools that fought for theological primacy in the thirteenth century were the Franciscan and the Dominican. Both orders had arisen as innovations on traditional Benedictine monasticism, to give greater mobility. The early Franciscans stressed poverty, the early Dominicans preaching. In the university they tended to stress love and understanding, respectively. Bonaventure, the most prominent Franciscan, continued the Augustinian emphasis on love, will, and mystical union. The roots of this Augustinianism were in Plato, for whom knowledge was the soul's vision.

Aquinas, the most influential Dominican, opted for Aristotle's more realistic epistemology, which made understanding an active cooperation of senses and intellect. With this in hand, he had the tool to probe faith's intelligibility more lucidly than any of his predecessors had. Indeed, Aquinas's great achievement was to integrate reason with revelation and construct a full overview, a "summa." Because of its balance, he later came to represent "official" Catholic theology.

Aquinas did not merely apply Aristotle to Christian faith. Though he admired much in the "Philosopher," Aquinas changed Aristotle's meta-physics. Aristotle had stressed individual beings, noting that their intelligibility derived from their form and considering form their essential act. Aquinas stressed existence, the act of being, from which he could show God to be the inmost reality of all that is. The difference in these two metaphysics stems from Aquinas's Christian view of creation. If God makes all beings from nothing, the "is" of each is a divine gift. Further, Aquinas moved beyond Aristotle's anthropology, conceiving human destiny as the beatific vision of the trinitarian God. Beyond "nature," then, Aquinas saw a new order wholly dependent on God's gratuity. He clarified what nature could know and do by itself, but he knew that in the concrete, human beings are fallen into sin and solicited by grace.

Indeed, Aquinas read scripture to say that human sin provoked the Incarnation. The Word took flesh to redeem a fallen race. Therefore, Adam's transgression was a "happy fault." Nothing showed God's goodness more than the cure worked through Jesus. On the cross, Jesus redeemed us by his love and obedience. That the Father would give up the Son for our sakes shows how great is the Father's love for us. We now struggle to outgrow our selfishness and respond with obedient love.

Overall, the mark of Aquinas's theology is its balance. Reason and revelation, nature and grace, interlock carefully. Scripture plays an important part, as does tradition, but reasoning too receives respect. Faith enables reason to understand more of the divine mysteries than it would alone, but even without faith reason can perceive vestiges of God. The world is God's creation, so all of it speaks of the divine truth. We may miss many overtones, but in itself the divine work is a fullness of intelligence. Thus, even in heaven reason will remain active. The vision of God that beatifies is a sublime act of understanding. It does not remove God's mystery, but it does give limited intellects all the happiness they can bear.

Shortly after his death Aquinas came under suspicion because of his Aristotelianism and rationality. Advocates of Augustine and the Fathers branded the Thomist synthesis insufficiently "Christian." They had support from mystical theologians, whose philosophical inspiration often was neo-Platonic. Aquinas seemed too dry, too logical, compared to the concrete imagery of scripture, the vivid rhetoric of Augustine. In fact, Aquinas never intended to supplant either. He knew scripture inside out, and he reverenced Augustine as his great teacher. But he was convinced that theology serves a useful purpose when it concentrates on understanding. To be sure, theoretical theology is not the theology to preach popularly. Equally, it is not the language for prayer. But it answers a need as legitimate as the needs of preaching or prayer: the mind's need to understand. Aquinas himself likely was a mystic, and he wrote hymns for the liturgy. Before him, the theologians called the Victorines had joined contemplation with theology, and after him the Rhineland mystics did.

Thus, medieval theology was far from divorcing the mystical and the intellectual. In Aquinas, though, the intellectual gained its greatest medieval depth.

The problem modernity has with the high medievals is not their lack of piety or depth. In their own way, the medievals resemble the fathers, for they seldom forget that the God of their discourse demands whole-hearted love. But from the end of the thirteenth century scholasticism declined. The logic that had served three centuries well now had no giants to call master, so it became master itself. The result was that theology became arid, deductive, lifeless. Diversely, the forerunners of the Lutheran Reformation, such as Wycliffe in England, Hus in Bohemia, and Groote in the Netherlands, made the fourteenth century a search for new vitality. That century suffered both the Black Plague and the greatest Church disarray—the "Babylonian Captivity" of the popes in Avignon. Thus, the spirit aborning was a search for personal meaning and ecclesiastical reform. It generated controversies about the eucharist and the nature of the Church, and received back heavy-handed persecution by Church authorities. Regrettably, the thirteenth-century scholastic synthesis was tarred by this faithlessness. It could have helped the classical Protestant Reformers of the sixteenth century keep faith and reason together.[5]

THE COUNTER-REFORMATION

The fifteenth century witnessed a Renaissance in Italy that soon spread to the rest of Europe. This movement entailed both a rediscovery of classical Greek and Roman culture and a new personalist mood. Educated Europeans like Erasmus (1469–1536), who led the Renaissance in Northern Europe, found the Church failing their humanistic ideals. Far from being a mother and teacher, it was a grievous burden. Erasmus's scholarship helped Christendom recover the New Testament and opened theology to historical research. There was little impressive scholasticism to renovate the fifteenth century, so when the sixteenth-century Reformation dawned the times were ripe for upheaveal. Politically, culturally, and religiously, the going Roman system seemed to be rotten. Martin Luther was the prophetic figure who put the axe to the roots.

Luther observed the roots firsthand during a visit to Rome in 1510. Returned home and assigned to teach biblical studies, he discovered a new message. Personally, Luther had for some time suffered scruples about his religious observance and found it hard to gain peace of soul. When he grasped Paul's teaching that justification comes through faith rather than works, it seemed a personal message. Though he could never be sure his own observance pleased God, Paul told him God justifies us apart from human merit. This was hardly a novel doctrine, for commentators on Paul, including Augustine and Aquinas, had exposed this meaning plainly. Indeed, the Council of Orange (529) had defined the gratuity of salvation unmistakably, using Augustinian language. Thus, it was Luther's personal investment, and the works orientation of his time, rather than a gap in the tradition, that set the torch of the Reformation burning.

The personal investment donned scriptural garb. Luther had found his key Christian doctrine in the Epistle to the Romans. The New Testament was the only place where Christ, that doctrine's cause, could be found unalloyed. Therefore, to *sola fide* (by faith alone) one had to add *sola scriptura* (by scripture alone). Scripture alone deserved the total allegiance due God's Word. Tradition, at least as interpreted by prevailing Church leaders, was not trustworthy. Unless scripture ruled the Church, the Church was not God's household. Thus, faithful interpretation of scripture became a matter of private conscience. Luther joined the emerging personalism to his scriptural findings and pushed forward the concrete "I." A person must stand behind his commitments. No one can say yes or no for him. Before God, faith is a matter of individual responsibility. Social convention, including Church law, is something secondary. It testifies to Luther's influence that a majority of Americans now take these tenets for granted.

Luther's theses—both the 95 of 1517 and those he developed later— set the agenda for Reformation times. Other reformers developed his notions of faith, scripture, grace, and the Church, while the Catholic opposition had to meet his terms. In John Calvin (1509–1564) the Reformation gained a first-rate exegete and dogmatician, who put its main tenets into systematic form. However, Calvin discoursed more deeply on human depravity, the sovereignty of God, and predestination than Luther had. The Catholic counter-reformers thought both Luther and Calvin had lost a traditional balance. On the relation of sin and grace, they found the Reformers too pessimistic. Granted that Adam's sin separated humanity from God, it did not vitiate human nature. In this the Catholics could claim Aquinas, who made grace nature's healing and perfecting, not its substitute.

On the relation between scripture and tradition, the counter-reformers again tried to redress what they considered an imbalance. Granted the importance of scripture, it was historical fact that scripture had always been interpreted by the Church. The canon that determined what books belonged in "scripture," and the explanation of its faith, had fallen to the magisterium. Indeed, what was the function of bishops and councils, if not to determine scriptural revelation's true sense?

The counter-reformers continued this balancing act on the question of faith and merit. It was true that salvation is gratuitous, a gift of God's bounty in Christ. Thus, no fulfillment of the law forced heaven to open. Nonetheless, God wanted good morality (which Luther did not deny), and faith not issuing good morality was suspect. Whether such "morality" or "works" was identical with keeping Church laws was secondary.

The counter-reformers could agree there had been abuses in the "system" of masses and indulgences. Too many Christians did think that mere attendance at Mass, or crass almsgiving, gained them heaven. But this was something to clean up, not cause for tearing down.

Moreover, there was scriptural evidence (Hebrews) for the Mass's sacrificial character which Luther, in his insistence on its merely memorial character, underplayed. There also was good reason behind indulgences, for Christians formed a communion, an organic whole, such that the good deeds of one redounded to the benefit of all. As the saints served common Christians good example, so common Christians could share in the saints' merits. Not that saints could save other Christians by themselves, apart from Christ. They ought never be more prominent than Jesus. But one Christian reached out to all, even those in purgatory and heaven. Few later writers have judged this Catholic defense of indulgences satisfactory, but at least it shows that the doctrine of indulgences had roots other than simple greed.

The official, conciliar form of the Catholic response was the twenty-five sessions of the Council of Trent (1545–1563). Beset by political troubles, the Council was frequently in recess, but slowly it hammered out doctrinal and disciplinary reforms. Benjamin Drewery has summarized the doctrinal topics under three heads: Scripture and Tradition, Justification, and the Sacraments.

The Council's hallmark was a reassertion of Church authority. Pointedly, it made the Catholic church the sole legitimate interpreter of scripture. While this position had hermeneutical merits, since all texts stand in a history of interpretation and none springs from heaven directly, it neglected the unique character of the New Testament, which was the Church's own founding book. On justification the Council disputed the Reformers' notion that righteousness is merely imputed to believers because of Christ. Rather, original sin really is removed, though after baptism concupiscence or the "tinder of sin" *(fomes peccati)* remains. Justification leads on to sanctification or inner renewal, for the grace that makes one righteous presses further to make one holy. Finally, the Council denied the teaching of some Protestants that true believers know their own salvation with certainty, and it insisted on the validity of works and merit.

Concerning the sacraments, the seventh session (1547) first stressed their necessity: "All true righteousness either begins or is increased or is restored through the sacraments." Jesus instituted all seven sacraments, and they confer grace objectively *(ex opere operato)*, not merely through the recipient's faith. The eucharist is the preeminent sacrament, in which Christ really is present, body and soul, humanity and divinity. The Mass represents the sacrifice of Calvary and is efficacious for the remission of sin. The traditional requirement that mortal sins be confessed to a priest is to continue.

Thus, the doctrines of Trent served to distinguish Catholicism from Protestantism. By Trent's end reconciliation with Protestants seemed impossible, so its decrees, with their corresponding anathemas, became a sort of boundary line. Summarily, the Council repudiated the Reformers' main charge that the Roman church had become discontinuous with early Christian faith. Rather, it justified the main lines of Christian evolution, often reading sixteenth-century structures back into New Testament times.

After Trent, polemics became the order of the day. The prince of Catholic polemicists was Robert Bellarmine (1542–1621), a Jesuit cardinal. Jesuits had served as theologians at the Council of Trent, and throughout the counter-reformation they were the papacy's main arm. Bellarmine, though, was moderate in his interpretations of Trent, and in his temporal claims for the papacy. He realized through the Galileo controversy (early seventh century) that the Roman church would have to accommodate to new scientific knowledge. On the central issue of justification, Bellarmine stressed God's cooperating grace, which allowed the believer to become responsible for her good deeds and so merit heavenly rewards.

Grace also was the key issue in the Jansenist controversy, an infra-Catholic affair of the mid-seventeenth century. In brief the Jansenists thought human nature so weak its only hope for salvation lay in Christ's grace. This seemed to endanger human freedom and merit, so papal theologians succeeded in getting Jansenism condemned in the 1650s and 1660s. The great Jansenist propagandist was Blaise Pascal (1623–1662), whose *Provincial Letters* satirized the Jesuits and popularized the notion that they defended human freedom excessively. Behind the Jesuits' stance was the theory of Luis Molina, hammered out in the "De Auxiliis" controversy (ca. 1597–1607) between Jesuits and Dominicans, that God bestows grace in light of his foreknowing who will freely cooperate with it.

The seventeenth century also witnessed a controversy about Quietism, the view that one does well to abandon human freedom and depend totally on God. This position originated with Miguel Molinos (ca. 1640–1697) and was condemned by Pope Innocent XI in 1687 because it seemed to make God the author of sinful acts. A leader in the fight to condemn Quietism was Bishop Jacques Bossuet (1627–1704), a great preacher of the day. Bossuet defended the Roman church as the true guardian of Christian tradition, but he opposed the ramifications of papal power.

In a nutshell, the Counter-Reformation settled few of Protestants' grievances and determined many subsequent Catholic characteristics. Rome became the guardian of tradition, and the Roman system became something to be defended tooth and nail. Rome stressed the outward things of Church life—hierarchy, magisterium, works, sacramental rituals

—because Protestants emphasized inward personal experience and faith. Scripture took on "Protestant" overtones, as did any stress on the lay vocation.

Further, the Reformation controversies hardened the perennial Western tendency to concentrate on the moral aspects of Christian life and neglect the ontological. The debates about justification entailed ontology, for they had to take up how divinity and humanity interacted, but they were at least one step removed from the Greek view of grace, which was divinization. With divinization went a clear focus on the Trinity, the source and substance of "uncreated" grace, and a contemplative attitude toward the sacraments. Thus, the justification controversies advanced Western legalism and distanced both Catholics and Protestants still further from Eastern Orthodoxy.[6]

MODERNITY

The last four centuries have been a time of increasingly rapid cultural change. By 1800 contact with non-European cultures, Newtonian science, new philosophies, the divisions of the Western church, and a repugance induced by religious wars had left traditional theology beseiged. In the nineteenth century Darwin and Marx changed social thought, while in the twentieth century Freud and Einstein overthrew accepted views of the psyche and the universe. The dominant influences on modern Catholic theology, then, have been the massive changes in Western culture to which it has had to react.

First, changes in philosophy and physical science severely challenged traditional belief. From Descartes to Hegel, Catholicism's old balance of faith and reason came under fierce philosophical attack. Hume, Locke, Kant, and Hegel, who fired the most powerful salvos, agreed "revelation" was a dubious proposition. They had appropriated a new subjectivity that made revelation seem wooden, extrinsic. How could a heavenly knowledge come into human senses and brains? Catholic theology has struggled with modernity's stress on the personal subject since Luther, first bitterly attacking it and lately trying to appropriate its manifest truths. Except for Cardinal Newman (1801–1890), successful appropriations date only from the last sixty years or so.

The scientific theories of Galileo, Copernicus, and Newton overthrew the geocentric universe. For many believers, this entailed a traumatic ousting from a privileged place in the heavens. Insofar as the new astronomy and physics conflicted with biblical accounts, "revelation" again came into question. Those who accepted the new science but wanted to remain religious tended to water faith down to Deism—a clock-maker God who merely got the universe ticking. Although Stanley Jaki, a historian of science with traditional Catholic commitments, has argued passionately that modern science in fact has relied upon a realistic epistemology quite compatible with Christian faith, most eminent modern scientists have not expressed themselves in traditional theological terms. Publicly, then, the appearance was that science and religion collided. As with its philosophical collisions, Catholic theology has only responded positively in the past few generations.

Second, the past three centuries have produced massive social changes, history both speeding up and expanding. The American and French revolutions dramatically altered European consciousness, but Catholic thought tended more to fear their anarchic possibilities than to support their outreach for justice and freedom. Marxist theory made such progress after the Russian Revolution of 1917 that the Catholic fears of socialism developed in the nineteenth century seemed well warranted. We noted the Catholic response after Leo XIII, which lately has become a full counter-program for social justice, but until John XXIII that response seemed rather hedged and unapplied.

The expansion of consciousness that foreign discoveries entailed altered world history itself. For instance, when one laid the traditional historical scheme developed by Augustine, and retained to Bossuet, beside Voltaire's new general account (1756), "sacred history" seemed provincial indeed. New information about China, India, and other nations made laughable the notion that salvation runs only through Jerusalem and Rome.

The most eminent figure of eighteenth-century Catholic theology was Alphonsus Liguori (1696–1787), who concentrated on morality. His work moved in the wake of the earlier debates about human freedom, seeking a middle ground between laxity and rigor. The result was an influential "equiprobabilism": An opinion or proposed course of action is licit if it is as probably correct as the alternatives.

During the nineteenth century Roman authority hardened and largely turned its back on modernity. The First Vatican Council (1869–1870) capped a consolidation of papal power with its decree on infallibility, but already in 1864 Pius IX had condemned eighty propositions that represented "errors" of mid-century Europe. The last proposition that he condemned supported progress, liberalism, and civilization as then understood. Collectively, these notions amounted to what we might call "secularism." Pius was especially aggrieved that traditional Italian politics were encroaching on Catholic education, and that Europe in general was trying to make Christian religion just another ingredient in a pluralistic culture based on tolerance.

The Catholic theologian of the nineteenth century most praised today is Newman, whose conversion from Anglicanism forced him to contend with his times' most pressing problems. Above all, Newman had to contend with historical consciousness, which was making deep impacts on Protestant biblical and doctrinal theology. As critical history revealed the time-conditioned quality of both scripture and past formulas of faith, it easily led to *historicism*—the relativistic view that all times change; nothing past is sacred. This was anathema to a church championing "tradition," which it understood in terms of Vincent of Lerins' (ca. 425) "everywhere, always, and by all." Newman's achievement was to show how doctrines could develop, not so much changing their original thrust as unfolding their implications under the impact of later times.

Such development was central to "modernist" efforts to update Catholic faith, but Pius X's antimodernist decree *Lamentabili* (1907) specifically condemned Loisy's version, seeming to enforce a uniform faith untouched by history. Similarly, Pius's oath against modernism (1910) rejected "the false invention of the evolution of dogmas." This denial of history was bound to founder, but it kept the "manual" scholasticism of the nineteenth century in the driver's seat for another forty years.

The philosophical and theological manuals prescribed for Catholic seminaries were a model of abstract precision. They lined up biblical proof texts, gave "adversaries' " positions in a sentence or two, and then pounded out syllogistic arguments for the thesis in question. Completely lost were the history of the question, its relation to living faith, and its intellectual complexity. Yves Congar and Gerald McCool have shown that manual scholasticism was not the only theological force of the nineteenth and early twentieth centuries, but it did disastrously narrow traditional theological understanding.[7]

Pius XII's *Humani Generis* (1950) was the last great gasp of Roman conservatism. From the early years of the twentieth century, Catholic studies in the history of faith and doctrine had implied that the manualists' aridity was a sorry aberration. In works on liturgical practice, patristic thought, medieval scholasticism, and biblical criticism, Europeans unearthed a past richness the manualists little suspected. The liturgical movement finally broke through with reforms of the Easter liturgy and holy week in the 1950s; the biblical movement got a charter for scholarship in Pius XII's *Divino Afflante Spiritu* (1943); and under the leadership of Henri de Lubac and Jean Danielou patristic studies flowered in France after World War II.

Dogmatic theology was under a tighter rein, but the efforts of philosophers (for instance, Pierre Scheuer, Joseph Maréchal, Max Scheler, Maurice Blondel, Jacques Maritain, and Etienne Gilson) to reconcile Aquinas and modern thought began to bear fruit after the war. Rahner and Lonergan are probably their most eminent yield, but Schillebeeckx, Küng, and others also have their roots there.

Were one to try to epitomize the recent burst of creativity in Catholic thought, most of it sanctioned by Vatican II, key words would be "history" and "pluralism." Finally appropriating modernity, Catholic theology has entered the battles over interpretation that modernity entails. Because we human beings are temporal and subject to change, none of our institutions is static. Equally, none of our understandings is static, for we always understand "from where we are." The first postulate from these verities is sophistication: One has to know the circumstances of the text she is studying, and also the circumstances of her own study. When history forms a scholar's critical consciousness, it forces hermeneutical obligations.[8]

Because of the complexity that historical sensitivity finds in Catholic theology of the past, many theologians are willing to accept pluralism in the present. Factually, Catholicism never has been monolithic. It has always varied in worship and belief, from place to place and time to time. The several Catholic liturgies, many schools of spirituality, and many theological schools all testify to a past multiplicity. As new regional areas, such as Latin America, Asia, and Africa, enter the theological scene, we should expect more multiplicity in the future. Indeed, we should welcome it, for different regional experiences, like different philosophical outlooks, help display the fullness of Christ.

To be sure, multiplicity can become chaotic, if theologians fail to find a common center. But few Catholic theologians deny the centrality of Jesus, and in a world-historical horizon that gives them great commonality. Making Jesus the decisive interpretation of human reality separates Christians from atheists, Buddhists, Muslims, agnostics, and the like. It makes Christians' sense of life different, because the horizon in which one sets experiences shapes their meaning. For instance, suffering is different if one sets it against Christ's cross rather than the Buddha's first noble truth ("All life is suffering"). To choose Christ, then, is to choose a bànd of brothers and sisters who have chosen similarly. Their unity is far more important than their differences.

We believe this unity should be the fulcrum of future ecumenical theology, and a prime hermeneutic in infra-Catholic discussions of orthodoxy. If a theologian confesses Christ's decisiveness, her basic plank is solid. Sophisticated existentialists, such as Rahner, have shown how such decisiveness implicitly entails Christ's divinity. Sophisticated methodologists such as Lonergan have distinguished the various horizons—mythic, commonsensical, theoretic, and so forth—which vary a statement's significance. They show the benefits of modernity's having forced philosophers to study consciousness intricately.

In Catholic theology, "intentionality analysis" now tries to make such studies bear on the religious self's different levels and moods. The end of intentionality analysis is not yet in sight, so the present is no time for heavy-handed determinations of what a traditional proposition *must* mean. Such determinations will only cause future embarrassment. The mystery at the core of human being has myriad forms of expression. As Aquinas noted, "It is not the property of the wise person to care about names." The wise person cares about realities. Fortunately, current Catholic theology cares passionately about the reality of a truly divine, incomprehensible God and the reality of the social justice Jesus demanded. That is good ground for forecasting its future with hope.

SUMMARY

Our treatment has four subdivisions. The formative period of Catholic theology was the first five centuries or so, when scripture and the fathers predominated. Against the background of contemporary Judaism, Jesus introduced several striking innovations. Reflecting on Jesus, the apostolic age produced the New Testament. Joined to the Hebrew Bible, it is Catholic theology's charter. The early apologists began the task of translating this charter into Hellenistic categories. As heresies arose, bishop-theologians and episcopal councils developed Catholic doctrine by reaction.

Greek theologians dominated the formative period, but Latins dominated the medieval. By the time of Peter Abelard (1079–1142), the West had Aristotelian categories, and theological reasoning had gained greater precision. Aristotelianism found its great Christian interpreter in Thomas Aquinas, with whom scholasticism reached full flower. Unfortunately, by Luther's time scholasticism had greatly wilted. Put off by nominalism (word games), Luther went back to the Bible. Responding to the Reformers, Catholic theology regrouped at the Council of Trent. The doctrines and disciplines hammered out there shaped Catholic faith to the twentieth century. From the seventeenth century, however, Catholic theology was in decline. Slow to accept modern science, and bitterly opposed to modern philsophy, its luminaries were few. At the turn of this century, though, the giant awakened. After World War II it began moving, and there seems no stopping it now.

STUDY QUESTIONS

1. How did Jesus develop the theology of the Hebrew Bible?
2. Summarize the key dogmatic definitions of Nicaea and Chalcedon.
3. What use did Aquinas make of Aristotle?
4. What were Luther's key theological themes?
5. Summarize briefly the position of the Council of Trent on justification.
6. How has physical science shaped the agenda of modern Christian theology?
7. What does it mean to say that contemporary Catholic theology is pluralistic?

NOTES

1. See J. B. Bauer, ed., *Encyclopedia of Biblical Theology* (New York: Crossroad, 1981).
2. See Xavier Léon-Dufour, *Dictionary of the New Testament* (San Francisco: Harper & Row, 1980).
3. See Bernard Lonergan, *The Way to Nicaea* (Philadelphia: Westminster, 1976).
4. See Jaroslav Pelikan, *The Christian Tradition*, vols. 1 and 2 (Chicago: University of Chicago Press, 1971, 1974).

5. See Jaroslav Pelikan, *The Christian Tradition*, vol. 3 (Chicago: University of Chicago Press, 1978).
6. See Hubert Cunliffe-Jones, ed., *A History of Christian Doctrine* (Philadelphia: Fortress, 1978).
7. See Yves Congar, *A History of Theology* (Garden City, N.Y.: Doubleday, 1968); Gerald McCool, *Catholic Theology in the Nineteenth Century* (New York: Seabury, 1977).
8. See Mark Schoof, *Breakthrough: Beginnings of the New Catholic Theology* (Dublin: Gill and Macmillan, 1970).

Glossary

Albigensianism: A medieval heresy that erred by condemning the flesh and rejecting the human imperfections of the Church.

androgynous: Male-femaleness; the complementary joining of both sets of sexual characteristics.

anthropocentric: Pivoted on human beings; their interests and concerns.

apostolic: Concerning the original witnesses or missionaries of Jesus, or the ongoing work of missioning.

Arianism: The heresy, originating in the fourth century C.E., that denied the Son's equality with the Father.

asceticism: Self-denial, discipline, and training.

atheism: The speculative or practical denial of God.

Babylonian exile: The deportation of the Southern Kingdom (Judah) to Babylon in the sixth century B.C.E.

baptism: The Christian sacrament of initiation into the Church and divine life by ritual washing, abjuring of sin, blessing, and profession of faith.

baptism of desire: The implicit wish for Church membership that all good, moral living contains.

beatific vision: The "view" of God that will be at the heart of the Christian fulfillment called "heaven."

biosphere: The realm or zone of life; animate reality.

canon: A rule, law, or official list (e.g., of the authoritative books of the Old or New Testament).

Christology: The study of the Messiahship of Jesus, in both its human and divine aspects.

civil religion: The ultimate rights and beliefs of a people as ingredient in and inseparable from their tribal or national culture.

community: People so joining that their whole is more than the sum of their parts.

confessional: Having to do with one's profession of faith; the place where one enacts the sacrament of penance.

contemplative prayer: Communication with God that is largely quiet and nonverbal.

contingency: Non-necessity; not having to exist.

corporate personality: Adam, Israel, or Christ as a more than individual or communal sort of conscious reality.

covenant: A (divine) compact or contract that binds God and a people.

cult: (a) Worship of God; (b) an idiosyncratic sect.

curia: The administrative or bureaucratic apparatus of the Catholic church in Rome.

discernment of spirits: The traditional art of distinguishing helpful, godly inspirations from harmful or diabolic ones.

discursive: The step-by-step process of ordinary human reasoning.

divinization: The process by which God communicates trinitarian life.

doctrine: Teaching; faith in its intellectually communicable aspect.

dogma: Doctrine officially promulgated by the magisterium.

ecclesiology: The study of the Church.

ecumenical: Referring to the world-wide church, all Christians

elevation: God's raising human beings up into a share in the divine life.

emanation: A waving forth or overflow.

encyclical: A papal teaching letter addressed to the whole Church.

Enlightenment: The eighteenth-century European movement that stressed the autonomy of human conscience (in contrast to divine revelation).

epistemological: Concerning the study of how we know.

eschatology: The study of the final things—death, judgment, heaven, hell—or the consummating dimension of history.

eucharist: The sacrament of the Lord's Supper

evangelical: Pertaining to the gospel *(euaggellion).*

exegesis: Reading out the meaning of something; interpreting texts.

Exile: The sixth century B.C.E. Jewish sojourn in Babylon.

existential: Having to do with one's concrete, here and now, personal being.

faith: The submission of mind and heart to God or something else that is more than the individual.

fideism: The over-reliance on faith, especially in its willful aspects, and the neglect of critical reasoning.

filioque: The Doctrine that the Spirit proceeds from the Father *and from the Son.*

Gentile: Non-Israelite or non-Jewish.

Gnosticism: A system that speaks of a special, secret knowledge—usually one claiming to point the way to salvation.

gospel: The glad tidings or good news of Jesus.

grace: The favor of God that climaxes in the grant of forgiveness and divine life.

Hellenism: The Greek cultural ideals, originating with Alexander the Great, that dominated the eastern Mediterranean in the centuries before and after Christ.

hermeneutics: The study of interpretation, especially that of written texts.

holistic: Concerning wholeness, completeness, or adequacy; giving all relevant factors (for example, both mind and body) their due.

hope: The theological virtue or power given by God to anticipate good things from the future.

hypostatic union: The unique, mysterious connection between the divine and human natures of Christ.

idealism: The view that mind and notions are the major (or sole) reality.

ideology: Views that select and shape our experience into largely uncriticized perceptual and evaluative patterns.

Incarnation: (a) The enfleshment of the Divine Word; (b) any embodiment.

Inquisition: The authoritative pursuit, trial, and punishment of heretics that was a fact of Church life from the thirteenth century to the nineteenth century (especially in Spain).

intellectualism: A viewpoint that lays great stress on the mind.

justification: The process of becoming right, on good terms, with God.

Law: The Jewish conception of God's prescriptions for holy living.

liberation: Freedom, release from bondage or oppression.

limbo: A place of natural happiness for those who neither merit hell nor have received heavenly grace.

magic: The effort to constrain the Divine to do the will of human beings.

magisterium: The formal teaching office of the Church, located most ultimately in the bishops.

mammon: Money and material prosperity.

Marxism: The views of the world that acknowledge a founding debt to Karl Marx (for their stress on economic and class analyses).

Messiah: The anointed king to whom Jews have traditionally looked for deliverance and a golden age of prosperity.

metaphysics: The study of reality in its most basic principles (sometimes to the neglect of the personal consciousness of the student).

methodological: Having to do with orderly, disciplined, and fruitful ways of proceeding.

miracles: Events that seem to exceed the ordinary happenings of nature and so raise the question of religious faith.

misanthropy: Hatred of either: (a) things human, or (b) things masculine.

misogynistic: Hatred of things feminine.

mission: A sending forth (to spread the gospel).

moral theologian: One concerned with the ethical implications of faith.

mysticism: Direct experience of the divine.

mythological: Having to do with a storied mode of presentation that often exceeds the ordinary constraints of space, time, and human limitations.

natural law: The regularity of the physical and human worlds, often insofar as it seems to be a directive or legislation of God.

nature: The whatness or essence of something.

necessity: The quality of having to be; the opposite of contingency.

neo-Thomist: Referring to the revived theories of Thomas Aquinas.

novitiate: The first, trial period of religious life.

office: Position among those who hold formal Church power and leadership.

ontology: The study of being, existence.

pantheism: Seeing the Divine everywhere or calling everything a god.

papal infallibility: The notion that, under certain quite restricted conditions, God assures that the formal declarations of the Vicar of Christ do not fail the truth.

parousia: The return of the Messiah in power to complete history.

participation: The Platonic view that things below partake of the being and form of archetypes above.

patriarchal: Having to do with a social structure in which male heads of households hold the major power.

penance: Asceticism or prayer undertaken as a means of trying to make reparation for sin and express a sincere purpose of amending one's life.

person: The possessor of a unique act of existence; a center of reflective consciousness.

personalism: An outlook or philosophy that places a central, orienting value on human consciousness—knowing, loving, imaging God.

pluralistic: Admitting a variety of viewpoints or approaches.

praxis: Doing, especially insofar as it ought to correct and guide thinking.

prophet: One who calls present times to account, usually because of a vocation from God and sometimes with predictions about the future.

propositional: That which is expressed in (inevitably partial) statements or notions.

religious: (1) Concerning ultimate reality or divine mystery; (2) those who consecrate themselves to God by public vows of poverty, chastity, and obedience.

rabbi: A Jewish teacher of Torah.

rationalistic: An excessive evaluation of reason, to the neglect of love and emotion.

revelation: The disclosure or self-communication of God. For Christians, the prime instance is the Christ event.

sacramentality: The intrinsically symbolic or metaphoric character of the sacredness of Christ and the Church.

salvation: Healing from sin, saving from meaninglessness and ruin.

scholastic: Having the quality of a school's or tradition's careful and sustained study; applied especially to medieval theology.

scientific theology: Faith seeking disciplined, critical, academic understanding.

secular: Pertaining to this world of space and time.

soteriology: The study of salvation.

spirituality: Concerning personal, existential religious values and practices.

"supernatural existential": Karl Rahner's notion that God is active in all places offering grace.

synagogue: The Jewish place and event of coming together to hear Torah and pray.

synoptic gospels: Matthew, Mark, and Luke, so called because the similarity of their materials allows one to lay them out in parallel columns and take all three in at a single glance.

systematic: That which takes into account the connections and dependencies among things or ideas that make them into something integral or holistic.

Torah: Israelite revealed guidance, law, or teaching, as epitomized in the first five books (Pentateuch) of the Hebrew Bible.

transcendental: Having to do with the forces or qualities that go beyond space-time limitations and reach out to ultimate reality.

Trinity: God as Father-Son-Spirit.

Vatican: The official headquarters of the Catholic Church in Rome.

Vatican II: The Second Ecumenical Council that met at the Vatican 1962–65.

wish-fulfillment: Something that we call real or valuable not because of a critical judgment but because we so much want it to exist and be good.

worship: Formal praise, thanksgiving, petition, and adoration of God.

Yahweh: The God of biblical Israel

Select Annotated Bibliography

Bauer, J. B., ed. *Encyclopedia of Biblical Theology.* New York: Crossroad, 1981. A fine
    one-volume wordbook.
Bokenkotter, Thomas. *A Concise History of the Catholic Church.* rev. ed. Garden City,
    N.Y.: Doubleday Anchor, 1979. A good one-volume overview.
Brown, Raymond E. *The Community of the Beloved Disciple.* New York: Paulist, 1979.
    A fascinating recreation of the conflicts behind the Johannine literature,
    by a leading Catholic New Testament scholar.
Brown, Raymond E., and Meier, John P. *Antioch and Rome.* Ramsey, N.J.: Paulist,
    1982. Good studies of two key churches in their formative periods.
Carmody, Denise Lardner. *Seizing the Apple: Feminist Spirituality as Personal Growth.*
    New York: Crossroad, 1984. Rahner and Lonergan set in dialogue with
    contemporary feminist insights into caring and freedom.
Carmody, Denise Lardner and Carmody, John Tully. *Becoming One Flesh.* Nash-
    ville: The Upper Room, 1984. A holistic view of growth in Christian
    marriage.
Carmody, John. *Ecology and Religion.* Ramsey, N.J.: Paulist, 1983. The dialogue
    between ecologists and religionists today, and a sketch of the new Chris-
    tian theology of nature it seems to demand.
Carmody, John. *Holistic Spirituality.* Ramsey, N.J.: Paulist, 1983. An overview of
    the major zones of personal Christian life, integrated in terms of the
    twofold commandment.
Carmody, John. *Reexamining Conscience.* New York: Seabury, 1982. The matter and
    form of a contemporary Christian spirituality pivoted on the examina-
    tion of conscience.
Coleman, John A. *An American Strategic Theology.* Ramsey, N.J.: Paulist, 1982. Good
    action-oriented theology in an American sociopolitical context.
Cooke, Bernard. *Ministry to Word and Sacraments.* Philadelphia: Fortress, 1976. A
    masterful study of the history and theology of Christian ministry.
Cunningham, Lawrence S. *The Catholic Heritage.* New York: Crossroad, 1983. A
    study of the major "types"—humanist, activist, outsider, and so on—
    through which Catholic Christians have lived out their faith.
Durkin, Mary G. *Feast of Love: Pope John Paul II on Human Intimacy.* Chicago: Loyola
    University Press, 1983. A good summary of John Paul II's allocutions on
    marriage.
Egan, Harvey. *What Are They Saying About Mysticism?* Ramsey, N.J.: Paulist, 1982.

A good recent survey showing the rightful place of mysticism in the ordinary Christian's life.

Fitzmeyer, Joseph A. *A Christological Catechism*. New York: Paulist, 1981. A good question and answer presentation of what current New Testament scholarship says about Jesus.

Gremillion, Joseph. *The Gospel of Peace and Justice*. Maryknoll, N.Y.: Orbis, 1976. Basic papal documents on this theme from John XXIII to Paul VI.

Groome, Thomas H. *Christian Religious Education*. San Francisco: Harper & Row, 1980. A solid foundation for contemporary Catholic catechists.

Haring, Bernard. *Free and Faithful in Christ*. 3 vols. New York: Crossroad, 1978. Probably the best comprehensive Catholic moral theology now available.

Haughton, Rosemary. *The Passionate God*. New York: Paulist, 1981. A brilliant interpretation of the life of the Church today.

Hellwig, Monica. *Jesus: The Compassion of God*. Wilmington, Del.: Michael Glazier, 1983. A good, readable overview of the currently most pressing Christological problems.

Hennesey, James. *American Catholics*. New York: Oxford University Press, 1981. A readable history of the Catholic church in the United States.

Keller, Ralph. *Blessed and Broken*. Wilmington, Del.: Michael Glazier, 1982. A good, brief introduction to contemporary eucharistic theology.

Lawrence, Fred, ed. *Lonergan Workshop*. Chico, Calif.: Scholars Press, 1978. An ongoing volume series of studies by the leading disciples of Bernard Lonergan.

Lonergan, Bernard. *Method in Theology*. New York: Herder and Herder, 1972. The key work behind the whole Lonergan school, stressing the division of the theological enterprise into functional specialties.

McBrien, Richard. *Catholicism*. 2 vols. Minneapolis: Winston, 1980. A thorough overview of all the major doctrinal issues.

McGinnis, Kathleen and McGinnes, James. *Parenting for Peace and Justice*. Maryknoll, N.Y.: Orbis, 1981. A good blend of practical and theoretical approaches to training children for peace and justice in the home.

McGovern, Arthur F. *Marxism: An American Christian Perspective*. Maryknoll, N.Y.: Orbis, 1980. Probably the best North American Catholic work on this subject.

McKenzie, John L. *The New Testament without Illusion*. Chicago: Thomas More, 1980. Trenchant essays on New Testament topics by a good biblical scholar with little patience for hypocrisy.

Miranda, José. *Being and the Messiah*. Maryknoll, N.Y.: Orbis, 1977. Stimulating studies of the Johannine writings from the perspective of liberation theology.

Miranda, José. *Marx and the Bible*. Maryknoll, N.Y.: Orbis, 1974. A thorough study of the affinities between Marx and the prophetic views of the Bible.

Mitchell, Nathan. *Mission and Ministry*. Wilmington, Del.: William Glazier, 1982. A good introductory history and theology of the sacrament of orders.

Novak, Michael. *Confession of a Catholic*. San Francisco: Harper & Row, 1983. A provocative view of post-Vatican II Catholic faith by a leading conservative thinker.

O'Donovan, Leo, ed. *A World of Grace.* New York: Seabury, 1980. The best general introduction to Rahner's theology.

Pannikar, Raimundo. *The Unknown Christ of Hinduism.* 2d ed. Maryknoll, N.Y.: Orbis, 1981. A challenging concretion of Rahner's notion of the supernatural existential.

Rahner, Karl. *Foundations of Christian Faith.* New York: Seabury, 1978. The best one-volume presentation of Rahner's views.

Rahner, Karl. *The Practice of Faith.* New York: Crossroad, 1983. A good collection of Rahner's thoughts on Christian spirituality, under the headings of faith, hope, and love.

Rahner, Karl and Vorgrimler, Herbert. *Dictionary of Theology.* 2d ed. New York: Crossroad, 1981. A comprehensive overview of Catholic Christian faith through brief articles on most of the main topics.

Ruether, Rosemary Radford. *Sexism and God-Talk.* Boston: Beacon, 1983. A good reformation of traditional Christian theology in light of current feminist insights and sensibilities.

Schillebeeckx, Edward. *God Is New Each Moment.* New York: Seabury, 1983. Conversations with Huub Oosterhuis in which Schillebeeckx gives his views on today's most pressing questions about faith.

Schillebeeckx, Edward. *Interim Report on the Books Jesus and Christ.* New York: Crossroad, 1981. Responses to critics of the first two volumes of Schillebeeckx's massive project in Christology.

Schillebeeckx, Edward. *Ministry.* New York: Crossroad, 1981. A stimulating study of the historical development of office in the Church and the major reforms needed today.

Schüssler-Fiorenza, Elisabeth. *In Memory of Her.* New York: Crossroad, 1983. A major work on the roles and status of women in the New Testament church.

Sobrino, Jon, *Christology at the Crossroads.* Maryknoll, NY: Orbis, 1978. A major liberationist interpretation of Jesus' teaching and work.

Stoeckle, Bernard, ed. *The Concise Dictionary of Christian Ethics.* New York: Seabury, 1979. A useful wordbook covering the major concepts.

Thomas, David M. *Christian Marriage.* Wilmington, Del.: Michael Glazier, 1983. A good, brief look at the major historical issues and the main ingredients of a contemporary marital spirituality.

Tracy, David. *The Analogical Imagination.* New York: Crossroad, 1981. A difficult but rewarding speculative work by a leading American Catholic foundational and systematic theologian.

Wojtyla, Karol (Pope John Paul II). *Sources of Renewal: The Implementation of Vatican II.* San Francisco: Harper & Row, 1980. The views of the former Cardinal of Krakow on the main themes of the conciliar documents.

Index